The Arbutus / Madrone Files

READING THE PACIFIC NORTHWEST

The Arbutus / Madrone Files
READING THE PACIFIC NORTHWEST

LAURIE RICOU

Oregon State University Press
Corvallis

The paper in this book meets the guidelines for permanence and durability of the Committee on Production Guidelines for Book Longevity of the Council on Library Resources and the minimum requirements of the American National Standard for Permanence of Paper for Printed Library Materials Z39.48-1984.

Every reasonable effort has been made to acquire permission for copyright material used in this book, and to acknowledge such indebtedness accurately. Any errors and omissions called to the publisher's attention will be corrected in future editions.

Library of Congress Cataloging-in-Publication Data
Ricou, Laurence.
   The Arbutus/Madrone files : reading the Pacific Northwest / Laurie Ricou.— 1st ed.
      p. cm.
ISBN 0-87071-543-7 (alk. paper)
1. American literature—Northwest, Pacific—History and criticism. 2. Canadian literature—Northwest, Canadian—History and criticism. 3. American literature—Alaska—History and criticism. 4. Northwest, Canadian—Intellectual life. 5. Northwest, Pacific—Intellectual life. 6. Northwest, Canadian—In literature. 7. Northwest, Pacific—In literature. 8. Alaska—Intellectual life. 9. Alaska—In literature. I. Title.
   PS282 .R43 2002
   810.9'9795—dc21

                              2002001209

Cover photo: W.H. New

First published in Canada by
NeWest Publishers Ltd, Edmonton, Alberta
www.newestpress.com

First published in the United States by
Oregon State University Press
101 Waldo Hall
Corvallis OR 97331-6407
541-737-3166 o fax 541-737-3170
http://oregonstate.edu/dept/press

OREGON STATE
UNIVERSITY

PRINTED AND BOUND IN CANADA

for my students,
because they have been my teachers

Home is alive, like a tree. . . . Home is the whole earth, everywhere and nowhere, but it always wears the masks of particular places, no matter how often it changes or moves.

Robert Bringhurst
"Fast Drumming Ground"

Contents

Illustrations

Acknowledgements

My primary debt is to the writers and artists whose words these files celebrate. I am especially grateful to those writers (only some of whom appear in these pages) who have encouraged me by showing various kinds of enthusiasm for what I have tried: Robert Kroetsch, Ron Smith, Robert Bringhurst, Florence McNeil, David Wagoner, Bill New, Theresa Kishkan, Smaro Kamboureli, and Kim Stafford.

Libraries have been my other region. I am grateful to those which have made me feel at home: Special Collections at Washington University in St. Louis; the University of Washington (especially the Special Collections Division), where one reads surrounded by *Raven Brings Light to this House of Stories*, a collaborative art work—a cedar table by Ron Hilbert Coy, poems by J.T. Stewart, broadsides printed by Mare Blocker, rugs designed by Carl Chew, and a gathering of ravens made by all the artists—spread throughout the building (a project of the Washington State Arts Commission and the University); Special Collections at the University of Oregon in Eugene; the Oregon Historical Society in Portland; and the British Columbia Archives in Victoria. I have always felt that the staff at the University of British Columbia (UBC) was exceptionally helpful and dedicated to service; I am particularly grateful to the staff in Special Collections, especially George Brandak, Anne Yandle, and Brenda Peterson, not only for assistance with this project, but also for hosting the various graduate seminars in archiving northwest writing that gave impetus to this book.

The Western Literature Association (WLA) has been my home in Sacramento and Albuquerque and Estes Park and Salt Lake City, and its members have listened to me try out some of these ideas in those versions of West, and many others. Among scores of good friends, and good teacher-students in that organization, I must especially thank Cheryll Glotfelty, Dick Etulain, Dick Harrison, Fran Kaye, Linda Ross, Bob Thacker, Ludwig Deringer, Anne Kaufman, and Michael Peterman. Stalwarts of the WLA, Glen and Rhoda Love, have in many cases *created* Northwest Studies by always paying steady attention to ways across the border; for their generous gifts of time and advice, I thank them. I also thank the many people unnamed who have kindly answered my personal, post, and e-mail queries. Work on this book has often been made easier and more enjoyable by some superbly supportive people in the office of the Faculty of Graduate Studies (particularly Dale Yamaura, Angel Lam, Sandra Shi, Rayleen Nash, Grace Lee, Lucy Negris, and Katriona MacDonald) and in the Department of English (particularly Pat Lackie, Dominique Yupangco, Niroshi Sureweere, Debbie Simpson, Laurel Wickberg, Eileen Conning, Tim Conklin, Carol Wong, and Margaret Tom-Wing). Lynda Miller did many hours of keyboarding in the project's opening stages. Yashmin Kassam performed electronic miracles when all the files had to be combined, on short notice, into one. I especially salute the good-humoured patience of Rosemary Leach, with whom I worked closely in the 1980s and who, as this book neared publication, again became an indispensable collaborator.

I am fortunate to be surrounded by colleagues who have been willing to read and comment on my drafts: Jane Flick, Anne Rayner, Joel Martineau, and editor extraordinaire Bill New. Many other colleagues at UBC and at Simon Fraser University have helped along the way: Jean Barman, Carole Gerson, Cole Harris, John Grace, David Stouck, Bob McDonald, Dianne Newell, Shel Cherry, Diana Brydon, George Bowering, Roy Miki, Peter Buitenhuis, Olav Slaymaker, Charles Menzies, Janet Giltrow, Robin Ridington, Lil Rodman, Shirley Sterling, Richard Ericson, Dave Randall, Julie Cruikshank, Dale Kinkade, Jo-Ann Archibald, Jay Powell, Ethel Gardner, and Vickie Jensen. Add to these, my more immediate departmental colleagues in Canadian and American Studies: Eva-Marie Kröller, Richard Cavell,

Peter Quartermain, Margery Fee, Kieran Kealy, Peter Taylor, and especially Sherrill Grace, who tried to give me space from other duties to finish this book—long after it should have been finished.

Several fine research assistants have helped shape this book: Kathleen Scherf, Jessica Mathers, and Alanna Fero in early stages of the project, Carol (McIvor) McConnell, Marian Gracias, and Laurie McNeill in the later stages. Thanks also to Diane Farris and Nick O'Connell.

This book quotes from some of my students and, no doubt without proper acknowledgement, indirectly from many others. I cannot list them all, but by mentioning here some of the names that kept reappearing as I was writing, I try to pay several hundred students my biggest tribute, and largest thanks. They were in courses numbered English 438, 441, 492, and 545. Many UBC graduate students have shared and continue to share their research and insights with me: Anne Rayner on the Gulf Islands, Joel Martineau on ecotourism in Haida Gwaii, Nancy Pagh on border-crossing women on the water, Charles Dawson on river writing, Gudrun Dreher on Haida poetry, and Richard Lane on Bertrand Sinclair, Jack Shadbolt, Malcolm Lowry, and the idea of British Columbia. They, along with Christy Collis, Hilda McKenzie, Noel Currie, Yael Katz, Glen Thielman, Julie Walchli, Julia Denholm, Kathy Chung, Theresa Scott, Lauren Carter, Shirley Mahood, Carlene Dingwall, Erin Wheeler, Rishma Dunlop, Derk Zimmer, Shari Urban, Jane Slemon, Robyn Chadwick, Anna Ziegler, Gary Lewis, and Angela Waldie, have taught me the hybrid configurations of local invention and regional loyalties. A supplementary "file," created by the students of English 545 (Spring 1998) is the Trail 3 website at www.english.ubc.ca/projects/trail3/. Lis Hewalo, Tessa MacKinnon, Jenny Stam, Jessica Folk-Farber, Thomas Wong, Michelle Hignell, Deborah Schamuhn, Susie Lindsay, and Michelle Hollington created one of my favourite regional texts, the Pacific Northwest literary dumpster.

The Social Sciences and Humanities Research Council of Canada provided a grant to support the research and writing of this book. A special grant from the office of the Vice-President (Research) at the University of British Columbia made it possible to include the illustrations.

Smaro Kamboureli helped me to imagine the book, and then edited the manuscript with attentive generosity. I am grateful for all those many places where her enthusiasm and her gentle skepticism intersected. Ruth Linka and Erin Creasey at the Press have been both quietly professional and encouragingly supportive.

I think there is no better way to learn to love rain than to stand in it for hours watching soccer. In the Pacific Northwest it is also a reasonably effective form of stress relief, for you can walk the sidelines twelve months of the year. For their creating space in the (as yet unwritten) Soccer File, I thank the players and parents of the Kerrisdale Express, the Kerrisdale Hotshots, UBC Alumni, the Vancouver Kickers, the Vancouver Magic, and the Vancouver Wave.

First and finally, my loving thanks to those closest to home: Marc, Liane, Stephen, and Treva—and my Mom.

I am grateful to the following sources for permission to reprint, in revised form, or to adapt material from the earlier publications:

"Dumb Talk: Echoes of the Indigenous Voice in the Literature of British Columbia" *BC Studies*, 65 (Spring 1985): 34-47.

"No Writing At All Here: Review Notes on Writing Native," *Canadian Literature*, 124-25 (Spring-Summer 1990): 294-301. Rpt. in *Native Writers and Canadian Writing*, ed. W.H. New (Vancouver: U British Columbia P 1990): 294-301.

"Children of a Common Mother: Of Boundary Markers and Open Gates," *Zeitschrift der Gesellschaft für Kanada-Studien: Kanada-USA/USA-Kanada* 19/20(1991): 151-62.

"The Writing of British Columbia Writing," *BC Studies* (Winter 1993-94): 106-120.

"Crossing Borders in the Literature of the Pacific Northwest," *Borderlands: Essays in Canadian-American Relations* (Toronto: ECW Press 1991): 286-308.

"Articulating Ectopia," *To See Ourselves/To Save Ourselves: Ecology and Culture in Canada*, Canadian Issues Vol. 13 (Montreal: Association for Canadian Studies 1991): 51-62.

"Two Nations Own These Islands: Border and Region in Pacific-Northwest Writing," *Context North America: Canadian/US Literary Relations*, Camille R. La Bossière ed. (Ottawa: U of Ottawa P 1994): 49-62.

"The Pacific Northwest as a Cross-Border Region," "David Wagoner," in The Western Literature Association, *Updating the Literary West* (Fort Worth: Texas Christian UP 1997): 262-67, 289-94.

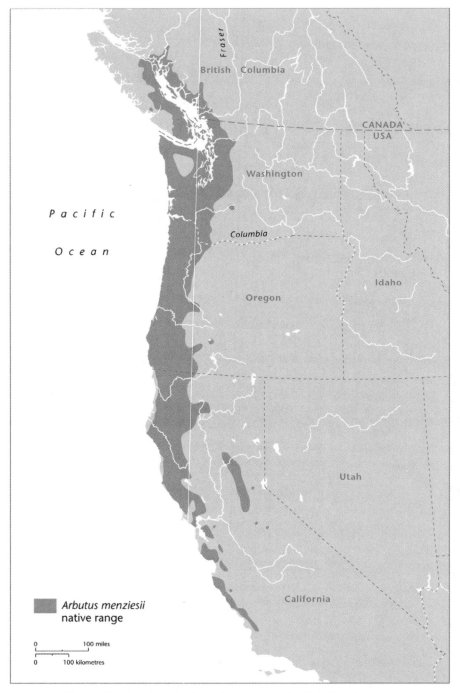

Fig. I: *Mapping arbutus/madrone*, Cartography by Eric Leinberger.
Adapted from "The native range of Pacific Madrone,"
a map in the online publication *Silvics of North America*
(US Department of Agriculture Forest Service. www.na.fs.fed.us/spfo/)

The arbutus tree (*Arbutus menziesii*), a native broad-leaved evergreen, often serves as a regional symbol; the boundaries of its distribution offer one way of mapping the Pacific Northwest. Readily identifiable, even to someone who can't tell a Douglas Fir from a Western Red Cedar, the arbutus keeps its leaves but is always losing its papery bark to reveal a burnished, well-oiled salmon-coloured wood. It doesn't transplant well and is notoriously difficult to cultivate. It's useless—commercially. And it's messy—to a gardener. Arbutus is a strange tree, untree-like you might say. An eccentric, organic sculpture growing in the rock, hanging over salt water (PLATE 1).

What I name *Arbutus*—and my home in Vancouver, British Columbia, is just three blocks from Arbutus Street, and the Arbutus Shopping Centre—is in Bellingham, Eugene, and Vancouver, Washington, called *Madrone*. One species, one shared regional marker, with two names: one Canadian and one American.

I hope my title suggests some of my aspirations for the book, and a sense of its form and possibilities. The slash separating and joining Arbutus and Madrone figures the artificial/real border that contributes to the region's doubleness and fluidity. It allows for either/or, and for a *both* that is a uniquely interdependent fusion. This book is about the Arbutus/Madrone region, a region sharing a biogeoclimatic zone, and flora and fauna, and icons of place, yet bisected by an international boundary, and, hence, sometimes subtly, sometimes blatantly, by differing histories, differing needs and aspirations, and differing "languages." And it is especially about writing and reading a region. It focusses on some of the writing I attach to the region called the Pacific Northwest. It offers readings of that writing, and reflects upon these readings.

I have assembled the book as a group of "files." Chapters would be the conventional designation, but I wanted to signal a slightly less than precise organization and editorial discipline, although my dictionary thinks the noun "file" has a great deal to do with *order* and *convenience*. Dividing my reading notes into files implies *collecting* rather than systematic linear argument: stories and words and discoveries clustered according to some shifting set of associations. The sorting process that intends to respect a careful system soon comes up with a document that could readily settle in any of three or four files. A quick and arbitrary assignment is often essential to getting the filing done. And then there's the item that will obviously not fit in any file: to avoid creating still more categories, I sometimes place this article and that note randomly, in hopes that, when next encountered, it will surprise me, and the reader, into some as yet undetected connection.

The word "file" comes to us from the Latin *filum*, meaning thread or string, which, in turn, gave the Old French *filer*, "to wind or spin thread," or, in Middle French, "to string documents on a thread or wire." So, think of these files as winding and stringing: spin the salmon thread, pull the logging thread until it touches the raven thread. Sometimes the documents follow one another plausibly; sometimes bizarrely. Interruptions, apertures, within the primary text suggest, within the limits of bound serial pages, the disparate forms that often crowd into our files. In a landscape, they would be passages—or, text might be peeling back to reveal another colour or texture.

At the end of these twelve "files," I have gathered a set of *After*files. These sections began as bibliographical essays. In suggesting they might be called Afterfiles, Bill New gave me the notion that they might also be a supplement—complementary certainly, but also, in their relation to the Files, alternate, resistant, approximate. *After* is inherently paradoxical as a prefix: it could imply an imitation or copy, a second try, but also a consequence. Afterfile describes a form answering to my subtitle—*reading* the Northwest—by being at once cause and effect, a

reciprocally continuous process. Afterfile, I hope, will
as analogous to aftermath—after*math*, after "a mowing" co
growth of grass. Home is alive: it changes and moves and grow
new greening.

The title also hints at spy thrillers. *The Ipcress File* or, on television,
the science fiction thriller *The X-Files*. So I hope something slightly
clandestine adheres to these files—in part, because I am discussing
often unknown texts (in one national community or the other) and, in
part, because some readers will undoubtedly see here an advance agent
for annexation, an inference my own sense of national self-confidence
and Canadian modesty finds preposterous.

I have not attempted here a survey or history of Northwest writing,
either of *high* literature—which might, with sufficient controls, be almost
manageable—or of writing in general, which would clearly be unman-
ageable for any single human (or lifetime). I have selected texts partly
because others have said they are worth reading, or because I wanted to
recognize some out-of-the-way, sometimes wacky, books, or because
amidst a rainforest of mellow, entrepreneurial, extractive, often highly
oral series of cultures, I wanted to include some material that was not
merely bookish. And in some cases I had a mission. David Wagoner, for
example, is a poet who, in my view, has not received nearly the regional
recognition his guide-book poetics deserve—a conviction reinforced
when I had an opportunity to read his early manuscripts and papers.
Other writers' archives revealed extra dimensions of their regional passions—Ethel Wilson, Malcolm Lowry, Ken Kesey.

I have tried to recognize writers from various cultural backgrounds, to honour the stories of many different places, to engage with
different styles, forms, and techniques, but in none of these categories
do I pretend to be inclusive. I have tried to ask how various writers write
their versions of the Pacific Northwest region: in particular to ask what
words they choose to describe setting, community, work, speech patterns. But, of course, no one with this aim can be unaware of how
much assumption, often unconscious, one brings to reading the world.
Do I have a file on salmon because a lot of people write about salmon,

ecause I was taught from childhood to associate salmon with the

t Coast? Clearly the answer is both.

In the *Arbutus/Madrone Files*, I take some books which I admire (and

niration, for me, often incorporates puzzlement), quote them, let

em have their say, and respond to them, either by interpreting, trying

get at how they have extended my own sense of place, or often by writ-

ıg obliquely and tenaciously off on a tangent suggested by them. I allow

myself to shift focus, sometimes to a non-literary topic, in order to
unsettle some of the regionalist's inclination to homogeneity. Shifts to
apertures and illustrations will, I hope, do the same. At the same time,
the files, evidently, also select and impose; they reinforce, and concoct,
tropes of the Pacific Northwest. Yet, in making twelve files I mean to
suggest variety and overlap and the unventured file names that would
inevitably occur to other readers. Similarly, I try to discuss novel, poem,
essay, and editorial together, in part to resist neat generic distinctions,
and I have tried, less confidently, to make negotiating cultural crossover
part of the process of reading the Pacific Northwest.

Several of the books which extended and deepened my first impressions of the Pacific Northwest contend in my mind as models for this
project. William Bevis's *Ten Tough Trips: Montana Writers and the West* (1990) is
one such book because it allows books and their authors to shape its
arguments, and because it is well researched yet enthusiastically
addressed to an audience beyond the professional reader. I also admire
the genre David James Duncan labels "river teeth," in his book of that
title, the brief not-quite-narratives that remain still resistantly untold
after the long and careful telling of an autobiography. And, for Duncan,
autobiography also means imagining the life story of the fish and bird
and sword fern. Several other possible models will be evident in the files
that follow. The most tempting guide, however imperfect the fit with my
talents or range of topics, is Ivan Doig's *Winter Brothers* (1980). In that
blend of personal essay and natural history, Doig defines his region in
an extended dialogue with James Swan, ethnographer and inadvertent
historian of the northern Olympic peninsula. The reciprocal writing of
diary and letter ambles and loops: Doig muses on Swan's words, and

considers how, in another context, and another time, they resonate while taking on new resonances. He lets Swan have his own say in extended quotations, all textured with the words of other artists, with short passages from other documents, and with his own imaginative telling of himself into place. Doig permits himself to drift a bit with his subject. In the same spirit, I hope the pages that follow will celebrate the fine phrasing of many writers, will prod and ponder and interpret, will slide in and out of more personal anecdote, and will occasionally bounce sideways to other, at first glance unrelated, documents, and surprise them into unexpected meaning.

For all that it urges a close-up knowledge of salal and salmon, for all that it honours the hand-logger's gruelling twelve-hour-a-day fight with sodden undergrowth, this remains a bookish book. It seeks to appreciate, and maybe unwittingly appropriates, and to mull over, the ways some writers have articulated the Pacific Northwest. I engage Northwest writers from a vantage point that is coastal, urban, cultural, and Canadian. Definitions of the Pacific Northwest region vary, shrinking and expanding as source and context alter. This book folds together many of these shifting, overlapping, and disappearing maps: it is not my aim to tie down a definition, but to layer possible configurations through the accumulated interleaving of these files. But, contemplated primarily from Vancouver, British Columbia, my Pacific Northwest undoubtedly whispers more Pacific, more rain, more mist, and more arbutus than does Harold Rhenisch's *Okanagan*, or, for that matter, if I consider all his books, than does Ivan Doig's *Big West*. Although at various junctures I argue that the Northwest conceals an interdependence—economic, climatic, and cultural—of desert and rainforest, I am implicated, inescapably, in some form of Lower Mainland imperialism. Even this term for the greater Vancouver area declares a presumption of what is "main" and what is "secondary" (although "lower" may supply a balancing connotation). I live in Vancouver, and have studied in archives in Bellingham, Seattle, Eugene, Portland and even Sequim—but in Vernon and Ellensburg, Prince George and Wallowa, Nelson, Lewiston, or Vancouver,

Washington, I can claim no more than a tourist's veiled understanding.

My profession is books: reading and re-reading books, teaching about and through them, and sometimes writing them, is what I do. Where I fancy an inside and first-hand knowledge of cedar and ravens, of seine-fishing and orcharding, the familiarity originates mainly at the desk and in the library. When I am outdoors for any length of time in this mythically outdoorsy world, it is most often to jog through Kerrisdale, to ski at Whistler-Blackcomb, to coach youth soccer, or to picnic at Spanish Banks—activities and places that also suggest the class and generational bias and limitation from which the book emerges.

I first thought to write a book defining writing in British Columbia, to analyze a neglected literary region within a national culture where regionalism has been an ideological conundrum and a political force since well before Canada formally became a country. But a year into contemplating the possibility of British Columbia as a coherent "region," I realized that the focus had to be on the region figured by ocean currents and species distribution. Of course, I was influenced, largely unawares, by cultural and economic forces which have emerged, over the time I have been writing, as a "Cascadia initiative."

A place is a story happening many times.

~Kim Stafford *Places & Stories*

TO INTRODUCE THIS BOOK ABOUT PLACE AND story, I try to conjure some account, not quite a story, of my own introduction to the north Pacific coast. Treva and I moved to Vancouver in 1978 with our children Liane and Marc (then aged six and eight). In the mid-1960s, Treva had studied at the University of British Columbia—library science (and sailing)—and always knew she wanted to return to Vancouver. I looked forward to teaching and studying at the same university, an institution that had made a mission of teaching and studying my home country's literature. Marc and Liane, then hesitant, in 2001 show every sign of wanting to make the West Coast their lifetime home. This attempt to write a book about the Pacific Northwest, less than two decades after arriving, also presumes the role of a "local" and an "insider": taking such a liberty itself says something of the upstart indigenousness that has permeated the urbanization of the Pacific Northwest over the past two centuries.

I grew up in Brandon, Manitoba. Family and friends made a small prairie city a precious home, but when I graduated from Brandon College with a Bachelors degree, adult in all the official senses, I would have been hard-pressed to tell you much about where I lived— at least about southern Manitoba's geography or plant life, or history, or (especially) of its pre-history. Robert Kroetsch's long poem *Seed Catalogue*, with its wry litany of the "absences" that unshape the traditional story of growing up, came along in 1977, just as I was deciding to move. It articulates the ignorance of home that was the odd consequence of a small-town prairie culture and education in the 1950s and 1960s. When I left Brandon in 1965 to study for two graduate degrees at the University of Toronto, I probably spent less of my time discovering Toronto than in trying to decide to remember where I had come from. Toronto— oddly enough, for all I have reiterated its mythology of self-absorption—allowed me to go home: first, courses in Canadian literature encouraged me to read shelves of books by Canadian writers, and then, alerted to the possibilities, I wrote a thesis, and a book, about how Canadian prairie writers had taught us to

infinitely elusive of ~~sence was one of their~~ ~~igs~~. Eight years of teach- ~~y~~ of Lethbridge wore a ~~gh~~ my assumptions about prairie, and blew a chinook or two through my mind, but I had, more or less, defined prairie to my satisfaction (then, not now), and had turned a delayed search for home into a profession or an avocation, had become a "specialist," in some sense, on Canadian prairie regionalism and prairie writing.

When I moved to Vancouver—before 1978, I had been on the West Coast only once, for a three-day visit—high-gloss foliage (in January), saltwater tides, arbutus trees, and decidedly unhorizontal landforms riddled my sense of place. I soon realized that I was not confined to one home, that, although I would carry my prairie home with me (*prairie crude*, as one friend summarizes its continued presence in my vocabulary and intonation), I also felt almost immediately at home with evergreen mountains, and even mist. I set out to read my way into that place and climate. This book is a record of that continuing encounter.

⁓

Of Boundary Markers and Open Gates

> The boundary is like a mighty heart, in systolic and diastolic pulse, nourishing one community of two parts, separate but organically interdependent.
>
> Bruce Hutchison *The Struggle for the Border*

Just a few kilometres from my home lies Peace Arch Park, between the communities of White Rock, British Columbia, and Blaine, Washington. Here the international boundary at the 49th parallel of latitude is marked by a plain obelisk, which I assume is standard Boundary Commission issue, and a whitewashed angular arch perhaps fifteen metres high. Within the portal of the arch, built in 1921 to commemorate 100 years of peace between Canada and the United States (1814-1914), are two iron gates fastened open, and the inscription "May These Gates Never Be Closed."

Along the top of the arch run two inscriptions: on the Canadian side, "Brethren Dwelling Together In Unity" (Psalm 133.1), and on the American side, "Children Of a Common Mother" (source unknown). (FIGS. 2, 3).

Since the Douglas-Blaine crossing is among the busiest on the Canada-US boundary, a cross-border traveller often has a good deal of time to ponder these inscriptions. Somewhat improbably, given the supposed openness of the gates, thirty-minute waits are routine, and one-and-a-half-hour waits not unusual. Some Vancouver radio stations

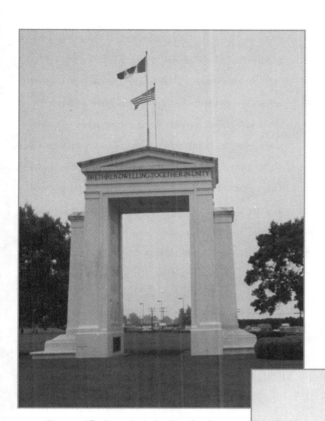

Figs 2: *The Peace Arch: Looking South*
Photos by Marian Gracias.
PRINTED WITH THE PERMISSION OF THE PHOTOGRAPHER

Figs 3: *The Peace Arch: Looking North*
PRINTED WITH THE PERMISSION OF THE PHOTOGRAPHER

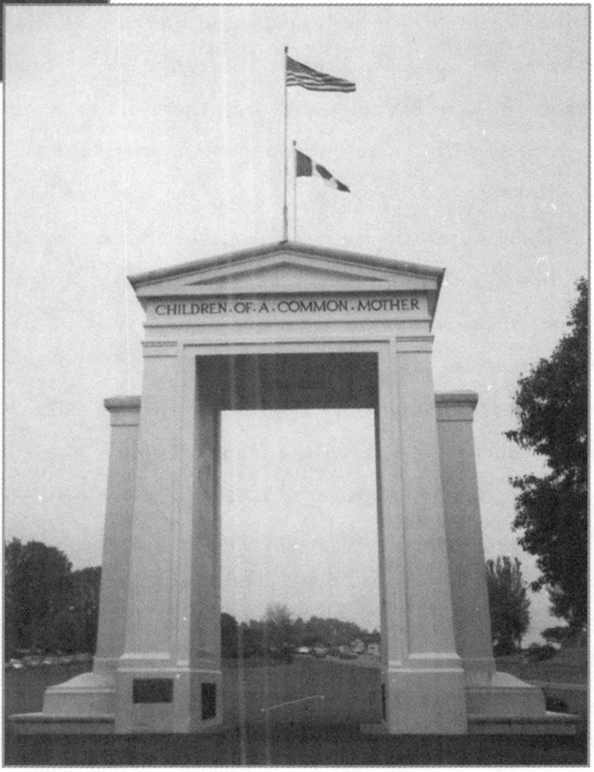

broadcast the border-crossing wait almost as frequently as the time and temperature. Sitting, at once eager and apprehensive, on an imaginary, invisible boundary line, I contemplate the boundary markers and open gates that complicate the regional culture.

Children of a common mother. These four trochaic feet run on, fall off, somehow unfinished. The author (authors?) no doubt thought of them as finished, the meaning unmistakable: two countries were both "born" of Great Britain. When the one-time British colonies grew into nation states, they still supported—militarily and economically—the motherland. Samuel J. Hill, the American road-builder who donated much of the money for the Peace Arch project, would have assumed countries uniformly white, Anglo-Saxon and largely Protestant—and, therefore, children with a common *mother tongue* (Bellinger).

But I wonder if he recognized the motto implies they would always be children, by turns gangly and awkward and rebellious and rambunctious. Did he see the "children" forever filled with a sense of awed innocence, or still tentative, hesitant, dependent, endlessly awaiting the rites of passage? If Britain is the mother country and belongs equally to both Canada and the United States, the most rebellious children might act as if *common* also implies mediocre, or inferior, notorious, and even vulgar. But in its root sense *vulgar* means *belonging to the people.* And this mother's virtue may be her low ordinariness: the common mother of the common people.

Slogans are, by nature, short-lived and must be constantly replaced. This one surely shifted fundamentally in the late 1960s, about the time I began to teach Canadian literature. In those years, when Canada was living through an intense post-centennial nationalism (the most significant wave of nationalism since the Canada First Movement), 125,000 US draft-resisters arrived. We can date a new reading of the slogan to 1977 when President Jimmy Carter granted amnesty to the "draft dodgers," and allowed them to go home—and they didn't. They saw themselves as children of a common mother.

The sense of Canada as another American home, safe and familiar, has always been a source of great unease for Canadians. Significantly, "children of a common mother" is the slogan that faces south on the Peace Arch, the one Americans see as they drive north, approaching Canada. It speaks with conviction of an undoubted similarity. A Canadian hears a trace of the rhetoric of imperialism. A Canadian approaching the United States reads the hope of peaceful coexistence: "Brethren dwelling together in unity." Even at this site, two subtly different attitudes are articulated in two different directions of travel.

Canadians pay attention to the United States—necessarily. Americans have ignored Canada—self-confidently. Until quite recently (the growth of an Association for Canadian Studies in the United States is one sign) most

comparisons of Canadian and American literature have come from the Canadian side of the
boundary. These views have been shaped by
curiosity, sometimes envy, and especially by the
ideology of difference and self-preservation,
self-defence. "Peace, order, and good government" is a constitutional ideal different from
(and preferable to?) "life, liberty, and the
pursuit of happiness." Before the late 1970s,
Edmund Wilson was the most prominent literary critic to look the other way, but in *O Canada*
(1965), although he draws some cultural contrasts (Canada is "less hurried and more
polite"[41]), he offers few comparisons
between the two literatures.

Seymour Lipset (as an American, an
exception to my rule) has defined the differences more succinctly and more extensively
(many would say, more simplistically) than any
other writer:

> My central argument is that the two countries differ in
> their basic organizing principles. Canada has been and is
> a more class-aware, elitist, stateist, collectivity orient-
> ed, and particularistic (group-oriented) society than
> the United States. (1990a)

Margaret Atwood reduced these propositions to the more portable: "If the national
mental illness of the United States is megalo-
mania, that of Canada is paranoid schizo-
phrenia" (62). It might be thought that
cross-border comparisons are inevitable,
although through most of their very different
histories Canadian and American literature

have been read, and studied, as if they could
be confined to a single nation state.

I found my own prompt to a cross-border
approach when I attended "Crossing
Frontiers," the conference held in Banff in
1978 (see Harrison, 1979). This conference
marked the passing of the most recent period
of strong cultural nationalism in Canada and
in Canadian studies. In the 1980s, international associations of Canadian studies multiplied and numerous cross-border literary
studies appeared. But the general national
bias persisted. Stanley Fogel's *A Tale of Two
Countries* argues, for example, that

> cathetic America is a country that has, in the minds and
> works of most of its pre-eminent writers of fiction, rei-
> fied and rigidified many of the attitudes, values, and
> symbols that have coalesced as the American identity;
> anorectic Canada is a country which has not yet, in the
> minds and works of its most pre-eminent writers of fic-
> tion (as well as most of its government officials and cit-
> izens), formed and sustained those same entities, both
> concrete and abstract, that give a country its definitive
> and distinctive character. (9)

Commenting on various concepts of Canada
in American literature, James Doyle depends
on this analogous, if less pathological, differentiation:

> The nineteenth-century United States was creating an
> indigenous body of legend involving Pilgrim fathers,
> revolutionary heroes, and frontier adventurers, who
> were all being molded into the representation of an
> aggressive and individualistic notion of liberty. The
> Canadian chronicle, however, presented a confusing

panorama of French colonial despots, aristocratic societies, French and English conflict, and finally a rather placid and unheroic chronicle of migration and settlement, emphasizing communal rather than individual activity. The setting for these events, furthermore, was not always consistent with American imaginative conceptions of the New World. Instead of being located on the edge of an infinitely expanding and readily accessible frontier, Canadian settlements usually gave onto a cold and hostile wilderness where survival, let alone subjugation of nature, seemed scarcely possible. (1983 5)

Where American critics (usually with some family or personal ties to Canada) contemplated Canadian and American literature, they were more likely to see similarities and connections. The dominant difference in ideology is neatly distilled in two works on prairie/plains fiction. Canadian critic Dick Harrison argued for a

central distinction between typical American and Canadian fictions of the West. They present the relationship between man and nature differently because the Frontier and Garden myths embody two contrasting visions of human order. (1979 76)

In contrast, Robert Thacker, American-born but with a Canadian doctorate, pushed a view of the inescapable similarity: "The boundary does not, however, alter the landscape's effect on the writing, nor does it preclude consideration of all prairie fiction as something of a closed system, one defined by landscape" (216).

As arguable as these propositions are (and both studies are more alert to differences than these single sentences imply), they define the paradoxical positions that confound the binational region. Thacker's book was published in 1989, when issues of gender, for example, raised a much stronger challenge than in 1977 to defining any body of literature primarily by national borders. Strategies of deconstruction questioned the neat binaries that had so often shaped Canadian-American literary comparison: near any pair of contrasts hovers a third element ready to redefine. Among the third elements reconfiguring the US/Canada binary were not only the United Kingdom but also China, and Japan, and Poland, and Egypt, and Jamaica, and Chile, and Pakistan, and Vietnam. The element *in common* was no longer a single country to which all citizens could trace their ancestry (quite obviously always an ethnocentric illusion and prop), but a commingling of national, religious, and ethnic backgrounds and languages. But manifestly multicultural, polyglot societies are only one of the powerful forces disrupting our habits of comparison.

Indeed, reading the Pacific Northwest is necessarily to find assumptions about national difference (which Canadians feel so strongly at the US border because the externals are so often undifferentiated) confused by moveable regional boundaries of shared landforms, climates, and watersheds based in geography. To return to the motto: the children come from a mother "common" because she has had so many partners, and in a positive sense, because she is so many women with a *common universal experience as woman.*

In worrying the phrase on the Peace Arch, I have obviously considered an interpretation that is demeaning to women: I include it, uneasily, for the shock it gives to facile assumptions about racial purity. But we must now also read this motto, if we give any validity to it at all, as children of a common *mother earth.*

So this version of the region is written from Canada, by a once-and-future fiercely proud patriot, who believes he has a great deal to learn about home from Kim Stafford and Ursula Le Guin—and believes they (and their

separate and mutual feel for place.

Feel for place. As these first few pages have already made clear, I believe a book about region and home will have to admit to nostalgia while it strives to resist it. Home equals feeling and emotion. I will not try to write of region in a way that hides all sentiment: perhaps the best I can do to appease the gods of objectivity is to shape and texture it. I take sentimentality to be part of a regionalist's make-up and motive: where I exaggerate mist or mountain or a myth of the Salmon People, I justify the magnification, when I'm aware of it, as a part of my method, as a reflection of the tropes of excess which are themselves a staple of the Northwest (as in British Columbia's favourite tourist slogan: "Super Natural BC"). It makes sense to me that Richard Hugo matured into a regional poet in the cul-

> the world is disappearing
> underneath us all the time, and more than just hospitals:
> look, the lava the salmon carry to melt the shore is going
> sure as the moment it takes to add the rain up on the sill
> is going and your own heart's life, so near to you and quaking
> all the time with tremors and waves and fire, is quickly going.
> Tim Bowling
> "To Vancouver, with Love"
> *Dying Scarlet* (1997) 30

readers in the United States) have a great deal to enjoy in the pages of Jack Hodgins and Daphne Marlatt. Certainly, cultures are continually border-crossing in the Northwest. The July/August 1996 issue of Vancouver's *City Food Magazine*, for example, featured the wines made near Yakima and in the Willamette Valley, and the restaurants of Seattle. In April 1990, the Seattle Chamber of Commerce held its annual meeting in Vancouver, British Columbia. But trading in poems and novels may be less frequent, if more crucial, to our

ture of public passion and extrovert emotion he found in Italy during visits in 1963 and 1967. I am both following and revising William Bevis's comments when I suggest that Hugo's Italian experience somehow "opened" him to his own Northwest place(s), gave him permission, as it were, to acknowledge them through *feeling*, and to acknowledge his own vulnerability (Bevis 1990 145).

Regionalists announce—usually quietly and deferentially—WE MATTER.

This book is an argument for paying

attention to Salish dog-wool blankets, bald eagle habitat and the Meadowland Dairy wagon in Portland's Annual Rose Festival (Duncan 1995 11-14). It lingers over writers whose work presents an alternative, just by virtue of their reading details of the local. At one level, I suppose I have chosen to discuss the writers' confirmation of self: their books say to me, "See, you're important: your world is there in a book." But not easily. George Bowering's *Kerrisdale Elegies* (1984) could have made for a bulging file because, in reimagining Rainer Maria Rilke's *Duino Elegies*, he constantly complicates and unsettles any sense of being comfortable in place; Kerrisdale has as much Trieste, Italy, as Vancouver in it. When I touch home base in this book, I both tempt nostalgia (Bowering makes poems to surround the sights and place names of daily life in my neighbourhood), and disturb complacency.

The Pacific Northwest these writers have shown me lives in the shadow of volcanoes, and over the unpredictable movements of the Pacific, Juan de Fuca, and North American plates. I have felt my whole house shiver at 6.4 on the Richter scale, and gulped at the tectonic violence that underlies the mythology of the pacific Pacific and a laid-back lifestyle. The region does not have a visible surface fault like the San Andreas, but we might find faulting on the seabed if we could drain the ocean. Imponderable fault lines, in human art as in primordial deep structures, intensify a growing intimacy with place just by keeping conclusions unstable and geological process (the great invisible of the landscape) in mind: "the earth always poises over us, grumbles under us/cocking its thunderous guns" (Trower 1978b 74-75).

～

Amity Harbor

I suspect, from its long stay on bestseller lists on both sides of the border, that David Guterson's *Snow Falling on Cedars* (1995) is the most widely read Pacific Northwest novel of all time. Beneath the placidity signalled in the fictional place name—Amity Harbor—run the nervous fault lines of workplace animosity and interracial erotics. Rain, predictably enough, is "the spirit of the place" (6): its inevitability in regional consciousness drips from the "shamanic rain that feeds the imagination" in

Tom Robbins's *Still Life with Woodpecker* (69), as it does from the proud bumper sticker extolling "The Pacific North Wet," and the commonplace gesture of resignation, "At least you don't have to shovel it."

Of course, I do not need to read another poem or short story to convince me that rain is the most persistent cliché of regional identity. But when I read Guterson, I woke myself into a new attention: "[Amity Harbor's] long, steep inclines lay broad and desolate; its high-curbed gutters swarmed, most winter nights, with traveling rain" (6). On first reading, I didn't pause to consider the buzz that might issue from rain in "swarming" gutters, but I was surprised by that adjective "traveling." The term undercut any sense of speed or destructiveness: Amity's rain, even on steep inclines, runs, however purposefully, in a meandering, un-frantic way. One thing we can be sure of: whatever its association with desolation—very slight, apparently—it will soon move on.

When Guterson describes rain as "traveling," he is certainly not mimetic; indeed, the phrase has almost no sensory dimension. It connotes no sense of smell or taste; some motion is hinted, but it can scarcely be visualized. Sentiment notwithstanding, I do not value the phrase for its localizing detail: San Piedro Island is an invented name for a fictional setting (although it closely resembles Bainbridge Island, with possible attachments from San Juan Island). More germane is that mobile sense of the process of place. The Pacific Northwest surveyed by "traveling rain" is not neatly boundaried; its limits evidently shift from one winter rain to another. Its exten. and possibilities enable and in turn promo. the love of place that comes from appreciating how things connect in the land.

~

From the Heath Family *(Ericaceae), Arbutus menziesii* fits my purpose in several ways. Its Latin name, as does so much else in West Coast topography, remembers Captain Vancouver's mapping, and the botanical (secondary) focus of his expedition's questions. As the "only native broad-leaved evergreen tree in Canada" (Straley 102), it marks a regional difference. It is easily identified, even by people who don't know their trees, as Archibald Menzies recognized: "[I]ts large clusters of whitish flowers and evergreen leaves, . . . its peculiar smooth bark of a reddish brown colour will at all times attract the Notice of the most superficial observer" (Kruckeberg 1982, 60). The difficulty in transplanting them will also suggest the spontaneous localness and magic of a tree which thrives on rocky, dry slopes.

Despite the unusual snow falling on David Guterson's cedars, his novel emphasizes a pattern of connections appreciated by most of the region's writers. San Piedro's culture rests on "[t]he fear of the sea that was always there, simmering beneath the surface of their island lives" (16). The novel's central narrative follows the mystery of a death at sea. And that mystery is linked to the fish story which speaks so insistently in the Northwest: "San Piedro lived and breathed by the salmon, and the cryptic places where they ran at night were the subject of perpetual conversation" (13). To speak of the mysterious migrating homes (and guises) of the salmon is to breathe Northwestern. Guterson twice uses the ancient phrase "spirit of place." Once, it honours the rain. Next, it serves to encapsulate Ishmael Chambers's adolescent attraction to Hatsue Miyamoto: "Hatsue was the spirit of the place" (99). She is, therefore, a companion to the

atsue, in her fourteen-year-
nes herself as a dwelling con-
vater, stones, and forest. She
d in tranquil composure—"to
as a leaf on a great tree" (83).
She finds in the hollow of a cedar tree "'a place to think'" (111). The certain fusion of woman and landscape is crucial to her role in the central trial narrative as the prescient wife of the accused murderer. As the spirit of the place, Hatsue also embodies a history of Japanese American presence (extending back to 1883) (75-76), and the brooding memory, carefully unmentioned in much of the novel, of the internment and evacuation during World War II—of the racism which shaped it and lingers still. Guterson intently observes the work of the Japanese immigrants and their families, the work of the "Canadian Indians" (77), and of the Germans, the loggers who had cleared the island, and of "the silent-toiling, autonomous gill-netter" (38). He pays homage to the importance of even his minor characters by acknowledging the work that they do (for example, the jurors [4] are identified by their jobs)—a link to the strong tradition of labour consciousness on the West Coast.

If I pause to retrace the *genius loci* in these last three paragraphs, I live and read a place whose living connects rain to sea to salmon to Japan to cedar to racist exclusion. The linearity of both English syntax and typesetting does not do justice to the complex ecology—the home process—upon which Guterson's story depends. But such a chain of associations may, when linked in turn to the grey-white palette, to the "sweet but insipid" (Underhill 7) fruit of the thimbleberry, and the grey-white shell of the giant Geoduck, signal the network of colour, work, and breathing that defines the "extra West" (Doig 183).

Snow Falling on Cedars embraces the key stories that have been told and retold to make the Northwest: the Gold Rush (and all the connected tales of extraction), the dream of utopia and ecotopia, a tale of travelling the Pacific, which is also the salmon narrative, and the story of Raven stealing the light. The only element that still does not quite fit my own expectation is the prominence of the economy and culture of growing strawberries. I could—maybe should—ignore it. That is what we often do to construct a place. But I would rather mention it, because my Pacific Northwest prefers to keep a few oddities in place.

⁓

Storied Mist

I never studied color, but I have good eyes, and color is one of the
charms of the coast region. Not brilliant, primary colors so much
as partial shades. . . . Morning and evening there is every shade

from light pearl to deep purple, changing as the sun shifts, like a *delicately tinted mist* that finally clears to a deep, woodsy green, fir-and-cedar green. Sometimes I find it restful just to stand and stare at that. I don't know why.

Bertrand Sinclair to Bertha Bodger, 9 February 1925

Looking south-southeast from La Pointe restaurant in the Wickanninish Inn, about 5:30 on a mid-February afternoon, just minutes after sunset, we study the colour that is no colour. Sea, waves, beach, trees, sky, islands, all—in light rain and lighter fog—shades of monochrome. An entire landscape seems to be printing in greyscale. And throughout the hotel the black-and-white matte photographs (by Edmonton photographer Peter Ramos) seem to answer back. In this greyscape you remember that Edmund Burke considered indistinctness, unknowability, the source of the sublime. And you are surprised at the unanticipated analogies in Rodney Hall's *A Dream More Luminous than Love: The Yandilli Trilogy* (1994): that near-sightedness which might also blur the shapes and distances, "goes along with being bookish" (6), that it might sharpen a compensating sense of hearing and smell (25), that it would necessitate knowing through direct contact with the ground (43).

Books have also taught me the restfulness of grey, just to stand and stare at the missed and misted. Brenda Peterson, in *Living by Water: Essays on Life, Land and Spirit* (1990), decides that "in the misty San Juan Islands, in the gray, rain-swept cityscapes of Seattle, in the high, snowed-in hollows of the Olympics, and the cloud-shadowed deserts of Eastern Washington, there is so much hidden about the land, the lives. Here, what you see is not what you get" (2-3). What you get, according to many Northwest artists (and marketers), is something beyond the sensibility of the mystic, as in this publisher's blurb for Carol Windley's *Visible Light* (1993): "lit with the grey lucency of BC's west coast, where often the line between sky and water is nearly imperceptible, where memory and the eye are sometimes deluded into seeing just outside the range of ordinary light."

So with the paintings hung in the "Early Modern Art of the Northwest" room in the Seattle Art Museum when I visited in January 1994. The leitmotif of Northwest art, if this exhibition were allowed to stand as representative (although it does change frequently), would be mysticism. The curators cite an article by Dorothy Seiberling in *Life Magazine* (1953) identifying "Mystic Painters of the Northwest":

All your best pictures are in black and white, and need a careful eye to call their shades of gray by name and know the ones to love, to see, in all the shadows, one called home.

R.P. Jones
"Duwamish: Remembering Richard Hugo"
Left Bank No. 1 (Winter 1991): 46

Kenneth Callahan, Guy Anderson, Mark Tobey, Morris Graves. Tobey's lines form a "whirling mass," yet they are never purely abstract, never quite detached from the world (connected, in a sense, through his long adherence to the Ba'Hai faith). And within the whirl, transformation of, or to, animal forms is always potential: in Morris Graves's "Bird Experiencing Light," for example, which Graves himself called whimsical. Throughout the small gallery, sponsored, ironically perhaps, by Weyerhaeuser, the traceries of subdued light constantly promise emergence into a different consciousness (PLATES 5, 6, 14).

In *Land Sliding: Imagining Space, Presence and Power in Canadian Writing* (1997), W.H. New remarks about Daryl Hine's poem "Point Grey" that the place name for the western extremity of Vancouver, where the University of British Columbia, and my office, sit, is itself an expression of the *somehow* and *not exactly* of mist. This version of my home, the west-coast edge, is a paradox of point (absolute, definite) and grey (obscure, indeterminate) (174-75), (PLATE 2). On the late April morning that I first read New's shrewd linking of palette and the destabilizing of imperial naming, the world outside my window agreed. It was a dull day, high cloud and intermittent fine rain, enough to make the sidewalks and concrete buildings harmonize in their damper shade of pale. And yet, against this essential ground, the audacious, "unnatural" colour of the asters, more magenta perhaps than the artificialest Estée Lauder lip paint. In the grey, a point of colour: everything blossoms.

⁓

Reading Northwest

Brandon, Manitoba, is within 100 kilometres of the border (and another International Peace Park—no arch). I was nineteen before I first ventured further south than that borderline. Then we drove nervously to Midge's Bar, about two kilometres south of the line. As Clark Blaise suggests, the remotest US outpost may function as a cherished destination for a Canadian eager to try on new identities (1990, 31). I wrote a PhD thesis about the Canadian prairies and I had a poster on my office wall in the early 1970s that waved a flag and urged READ CANADIAN. In the 1990s I compiled a small book entirely devoted to an American poet (David Wagoner) and to a bit of American land (Dungeness Spit). And here I am writing a book which combines US and Canadian writers in one regional study. What happened? Where did my border go?

I once traded one-word summaries of the West Coast with a student of mine. Shannon Timmers suggested the whole culture might be summarized as "slugspace."

It's a term that serves very well, for it

describes a pace of living, a sticky transforming, and—to add the concept of the slug in typesetting—a world beyond expressing in language. The best I could counter was "mistory," a coinage I imagined placed the filter of mist and mysticism into the formula and intrigue of mystery. But my made-up word could also be pronounced *my* story. In that variation, as I wondered at the beginning of this file, the coincidence of moving to Vancouver and the conference "Crossing Frontiers" helped to tell where the borders went. Vancouver is a Canadian city that can be American—George Faludy described it as a "relaxed, unpretentious" San Francisco (1)—because it is far enough from Ottawa and Toronto to be comfortably pacific and Northwestern without having to give up being Canadian. Of course, European economic union, the growth of instant circumglobal communication, and the cross-disciplinary, cross-cultural urgings of that catch-all movement, postmodernism, shaped my shifting interests too.

Not that I have given up on Canadian literature. And I am still enough of a nationalist to cherish the constructions of our national differences. "In front of a department store," Faludy also observes,

> I found a Tibetan monk begging with great dignity in his saffron robes. Almost any place else in the Western world he would be, I imagine, a local sight. In Vancouver (which an American poet once described to me as being "as laid back as a duck's ass") he was just a Tibetan monk in front of a department store. Canadian reserve, I decided long ago, is a more impressive quality than New York sophistication (1-2).

Exactly, I decide, and quickly scribble this down as identifying a difference to be cited—even promoted. But a moment later I am uneasy with the neat distinction. I would rather test it, refine it, recognize its limitations, reading along the edges of a cross-border region.

Doonesbury

BY GARRY TRUDEAU

Fig. 4: *The ideal region according to Doonesbury.*

Pig War

The children of a common mother could build a monument to 100 years of peace only by ignoring the ringing memory of the Pig War. It's a memory that surfaces in *Snow Falling on Cedars*. For decades after European contact, what we now think of as the Pacific Northwest was a single administrative region "ruled" by the Hudson's Bay Company. "Oregon Territory" included most of present-day British Columbia, and what is now Portland, Oregon, was in the Diocese of Quebec. When the treaty defining the boundary west of the Rocky Mountains was signed on 15 June 1846, it neglected to specify where the line ran among the islands between Vancouver Island and the Washington Territory mainland. Was San Juan Island American or British?

This question became crucial when Lyman Cutler, a no doubt dastardly American living on the island, shot a pig belonging to the Hudson's Bay Company. This was an extremely valuable pig. To protect British pigs, Governor Douglas dispatched to the island a hastily appointed Justice of the Peace; the British even threatened to put Cutler on trial. On the same day that the Justice landed, so did a force of sixty American troops sent to defend American interests. Governor Douglas responded by sending a "powerful vessel of war" to prevent further American landings. Volleys of insults and counter-propositions ensued, and diplo-

mats scrambled vehemently. Meanwhile, Americans and near-Canadians secretly mingled amicably on San Juan Island, no doubt over dinners of pork chops and bacon. Finally, in 1871, the boundary question was referred to international arbitration—to no less a presence than the German Emperor. With that momentous struggle in mind, I have come to judge carefully the fine distinctions between Canada and the United States.

Kaiser Wilhelm, incidentally, decided in favour of the claim of the United States. But this Canadian takes some comfort from the summary of the historian who told me this story:

It is easy to see the conflict in both nations between those who felt keenly that they could not take the responsibility of relinquishing the slightest part of the national heritage entrusted to their care, and those who took broader and saner views of the national interest.

It was not very realistic to insist on interpreting strictly the words of a treaty which had obviously not been based on as close a survey of the topography as its interpreters had at their command, and to rely on the treaty as if it had been carefully drafted to deal with islands which it had not, at the time, been thought worthwhile to mention in it. (Howay 226-27)

~

Island File

*I*n my best dream I have crossed the border
and my coins are wrong. . . .

. . . .

Maps are hard to read. Two nations own
these islands. The shade of green on one
could be Canadian, but firs and grebes
are mine. The latest run of Springs
are far too international to claim.
Yet they use our rivers for their graves.

~Richard Hugo "The Anacortes-Sydney Run"

FLYING OVER THE SAN JUAN/GULF ISLANDS in October 1992, I am amazed at the map below, at its complicated asymmetry (the ordered disorder of fractals, I wonder). An aerial Rorschach test, I decide, requiring deep thought, and much guesswork, to determine the minds of the gods who made it this way. I thought the geology lay on a northwest axis, but no island seems to point parallel to another. Some are perfect ovals; some have lakes in them; fjords seem to split others almost into sub-islands. From this vantage point, the mobile juxtapositions of totem poles and Jack Shadbolt paintings make a jarring kind of sense (PLATE 4). At the edge of the continent, the land looks to be breaking into pieces. Its map is a confusion of islands.

Midway through the "infernal rigmarole" (143) of Oregon homesteading stories in H.

L. Davis's *Honey in the Horn* (1935), the gawky hero, Clay Calvert, arrives unexpectedly at the limit of the land—and at a limit of understanding, where islands are more cultural than geographical:

Here, he thought, was the very last land on the continent, place so rank and wild that even the United States hadn't been able to spare enough people to cultivate it and live in it. Beyond was the Pacific Ocean, seven thousand miles of it, and then China, where people were so abundant that they worked for ten cents a month and killed their children to get rid of them. (245)

Clay Calvert's fitful beach thoughts—he is exhausted but cannot sleep—anticipate for me the restless musings of Earle Birney's more orotund "November Walk Near False Creek Mouth" (1963), a poem in which the speaker shivers his aimless way along English Bay and the Stanley Park seawall in Vancouver, British Columbia:

> *and I on the path at the high-tide edge*
> *wandering under the leafless maples*
> *between the lost salt home*
> *and the asphalt ledge where carhorns call*
> *call in the clotting air by a shore*
> *where shamans never again will sound*
> *with moon-snail conch the ritual plea*
> *to brother salmon or vanished seal.* (90)

Birney's slightly apocalyptic incantation exaggerates the most nervous moments of Davis's bulging novel but, at least in their pondering the line where North America meets Pacific Ocean, these two imaginations run in parallel. In each a meditative loner teeters precariously in a setting that is neither wholly land nor wholly sea, at once fascinated by lushly tangled wilderness and drawn toward the remote proximity of Asia's perplexing cultures. (Birney, in not-quite-articulated memories of Hiroshima and Nagasaki, hints at prejudices that could dispose of an entire people, not just of selected children.) These motifs of kooky eccentric (and lost shaman) rainforest jungle, and Pacific Rim community seem to attach themselves to almost any definition of Pacific Northwest. In Davis's case, the widely accepted proposition that his Pulitzer Prize-winning novel is the *first* Northwest novel reinforces its stature as defining regional text.

That other alluring imagining of Pacific edge, Ivan Doig's *Winter Brothers* (1980), probes the multiple meanings of "the very last land on the continent." The subtitle of Doig's double "diarying"—*A Season at the Edge of America*—evokes the same region of the mind as do Davis and Birney. In one of his unconcluding conclusions, Doig writes of the land-sea border, rewriting regional commonplace into a unique syntax of place:

> *Swan . . . too stands to me now as something of a template, an outlining human gauge: but of western possibilities rather than western past. Swan literally is a being of our continental edge, rimwalking its landscape and native cultures. If I could put questions to Swan across time I think they would try to reach toward invisible inward lines, those riggings of curiosity and gameness-for-damn-near-anything, hung deeper in him than anyone else I have encountered. Difficult to phrase, not say answer, but: what is the tidal pull of an earlier way of life, of the timescape of* first people *such as the Makahs and the vanished Haida villagers? What instruction does their West offer any of ours?* (221-22)

Doig's compound question (he almost always writes in questions) reaches toward another version of Pacific edge, one more refined and augmented by the inward lines, however imperfectly perceived, of its Aboriginal cultures. "The timescape of the first people" pulls more persistently in the culture of the Pacific Northwest, and more prominently in almost every book, than in Canadian and American literature generally (where, from Walt Whitman to Rudy Wiebe, it is already a potent force). *Winter Brothers* is pulled toward the first peoples as Doig realizes how indigenous culture might shape his form (despite his mistaken description of the Haida as "vanished"): in dating his diary, he rimwalks the winter ceremonies, the season for the collective performing of stories among the Northwest's First Peoples; the linearity of diary blends with layered re-tellings as Doig exchanges masks with Swan. Doig comes to recognize that, as he is creating Swan in words, Swan is (and the Makah *were* and *are*) creating him. Most Northwest storytellers try some version of that reciprocal instruction.

In the Pacific Northwest, some borders run east-west: the 42nd parallel separating California and Oregon, the more sinuous (both east-west and north-south) Columbia River forming the Oregon-Washington border, and especially the 49th parallel defining two countries. But many formative borders run mainly north-south: the Rocky Mountains, the Cascade Range, the Coast Mountains, and especially the edge separating sea and land, "this nothing's place" as Emily Carr called it (1941 10). Rimwalking the edge between Canada and the United States also requires negotiating those other precarious borders where definitions seem sharpest and then suddenly elusive, where the questions are "difficult to phrase, not say answer, but" (222). Doig's syntactically tortured phrase expresses my own ambivalence, particularly at the US-Canada boundary. I find myself intensely annoyed, for example, at how easily (and how uncharacteristically dogmatically) Ivan Doig figures Swan as a frontier hero who is constantly searching for a new territory to conquer. But I am just as annoyed that few Canadians living almost on the British Columbia-Washington border know *Winter Brothers*, this diary that makes contemporary their cultural history.

I have already noted that the temptation to write of Canada and the United States in neat binaries is irresistible. When I first tried a cross-border comparison of Canadian and American novels in the late 1970s, I wrote:

Whatever its serious points, we are sure that Even Cowgirls Get the Blues *[by Tom Robbins] is a lark.* . . . *Whatever its humor, we are sure of the seriousness of Robert Kroetsch's* Badlands. . . . *A nation raised on hoards of old field notes is very different from a civilization built on the adventure of hitchhiking. (1982 123)*

In the late 1990s, living in Vancouver, Canada, where an unwaveringly linear and visible border dissolves into a meandering hypothesis traced in water, and subject to all the undecideability that calls itself postmodern, I find the map harder to read. Islands are everywhere, but which belongs (in whatever way we might understand that verb) to whom, and how? A regional literature and culture might be discovered where the boundary becomes indeterminate—perhaps it must be discovered in a shared ecology far too international to claim.

In Richard Hugo's poem, which serves as

the epigraph to this File, a passenger on a ferry in transit through the San Juan and Gulf Islands will not be able to tell at any given moment whether she is in "Canadian" or "American" waters and, unless assiduously studying the marine chart framed near the head of the stairs to the car deck, whether the land masses in view are in Canada or the United States, are islands or part of the mainland, or of the nation-sized Vancouver Island. Moving, somewhat unlocated, between two countries, configures the Pacific Northwest as "the latest run of springs"; the region, the place, is an event, as Kim Stafford's poem urges (1987 11). When we try to own islands, or read them, the association with isolation and stasis dissolves in some interdependence of island, river, and moving ocean. Region emerges in a layering of stories, stories of lives in nature, fish stories, island stories. Hugo senses a mystery: the run is not only international in that it extends across the United States-Canada boundary, but also perhaps *inter*-national in that it links peoples and cultural backgrounds: Duwamish, Vietnamese, Bella Coola, Salmon People, Finnish, Tillamook, and Chinese. The weaving of their stories and dreams, the confusion of

their coinage, makes it absurd to think to *lay claim*. And in fortunate, if inadvertent, muddle, Hugo points up the problem in his misspelling of Sidney (the ferry terminus, on Vancouver Island, in British Columbia) as "Sydney," thus sending his dreamy ferry across the Pacific and into the Southern Hemisphere, to Australia (or to Nova Scotia).

At home, such globalling can intensify a sense of provincial inadequacy:

I do not think the Northwest will produce a form— whether in painting, sculpture, poetry, or fiction—that is peculiarly identifiable as its own. . . . A regional culture results only from a long period of isolation and insulation. . . . The Northwest, not much more than a century old in settlement, hasn't much of a culture to look back upon. (Griffith 93)

Perhaps literature in the Pacific Northwest has islanded indifference, blissful self-satisfaction, or distraction. Those attitudes may describe the very nature of region itself, a response to being distanced from industrial, economic, and political centres. On the Pacific slope, massive geographical barriers have exaggerated the response.

Yet the idea of a Pacific Northwest transborder region (however diverse the constituent

It seems, indeed, somewhat strange that in a British country the Fourth of July should be a gala day, and it might be taken abroad as an illustration of the political sympathies and characteristic of the population, but it is no such thing. . . . Our American cousins are among the best of our population. . . . The principles embodied in the cause which led to the origin of Independence Day are essentially British.

Cariboo Sentinel
Barkerville 7 July 1869
Watters *British Columbia: A Centennial Anthology* 52

communities) has a considerable history, perhaps more so than in any of the other regions which look at one another—and, therefore, at themselves—across the Canada-US boundary. Aboriginal peoples in what is now British Columbia, Washington, and Oregon shared and share language groups, art forms, and economic and political cultures. Captain George Vancouver's enthusiasm for honouring crew members, friends, and prominent English associates in the late eighteenth century rewrote (or, more correctly, wrote what was once wholly spoken) the toponymy of the region on both sides of the eventual boundary. When Theodore Roethke turned in his later work to his adopted region (centred in his teaching at the University of Washington), one of his most effective poems, "Meditation at Oyster River" (1975), wondered at the shapes and layers of a river on the east coast of Vancouver Island. Malcolm Lowry's bravest boat, in the story with that title, set out from Fearnought Bay, five miles south of Cape Flattery on the Olympic peninsula, and ended in Vancouver's Stanley Park (Lowry 1961 13 27).

The history of the establishment of the international boundary in the Pacific Northwest also records several configurations of a single region eventually divided by an arbitrary political line. Whereas the 49th parallel defined the Prairie provinces and Midwestern states on 20 October 1818, it was

not legally established between what bec. British Columbia and Washington State until 1846, and then only on the continental mainland. In the intervening crucially formative years, the principle of a "free and open" (64) territory was in force: the idea of a free trade zone and movements for a Pacific Republic, according to American historian Herman J. Deutsch, sustain the notion of "international curiosities which just could have worked in the Pacific Northwest (69)." Yet Deutsch's conclusion that "awareness of the existence of a political cleavage wrought by a boundary should pervade every study of the various facets of the region's history" (79) rests on the exuberant sentiment that the "unusual, the unfamiliar, the unorthodox, . . . the freakish, the cockeyed, and the screwy have at times appeared to be the norm in the Pacific Northwest" (77 n 91).

Gary Geddes apparently found that "Northwest" applied to British Columbia, and so titled his regional anthology *Skookum Wawa: Writings of the Canadian Northwest* (1975). His scope in that collection extends to the Yukon, which borders on the *Northwest Territories,* the name of a political entity which 150 years earlier designated what is now Manitoba, Saskatchewan, and Alberta (and still designates a university, Northwestern, in Chicago). In the United States, the Northwest frequently includes Alaska, as well as Idaho and western Montana.

-crossing short story notes
: political boundary destabilizes
..dn't they found, whenever they
..ie border driving north, that the
shell o.. .. et sky over the Pacific Northwest suddenly cracked and left them pinched into the southwest corner of something else?" (de Barros 8). One region. Two nation-states. Multiple nations interacting. Not surprisingly, the shifting usefulness of the term Pacific Northwest to describe a cross-border region is part of the complexity of comparison. I, for one, am not eager to settle the claim: it's just this triangulation that makes writing in and of the Pacific Northwest such a lumpy and flowering subject.

When writers write explicitly about a region labelled Pacific Northwest, or when they articulate interdependencies of communities of people, animals, plants, and land-forms in places I recognize as being in Oregon, Washington, or British Columbia, I pay attention. I know that I am selecting, manipulating, imagining, proclaiming some entity that does not actually exist. It's cautionary and exciting to acknowledge that every map I see, or guess at from words, has different limits and shifting centres.

For Gary Snyder, the "natural" definition of place suggestively discovered in native place

names is the "Ish nation . . . the drainage of all Puget sound and the Straits of Georgia." This concept, he insists, provides

> *a starter in learning where you are. For example, it's a great help in realizing where you are to know that the border between Canada and the United States is illusory; there's nothing to stop you from going over there and feeling as at home as you feel here, and vice versa. It comes down to the nitty-gritty when you get into water quality control, air pollution control questions, or salmon runs. The salmon don't give a fuck which border it is, nor does the air pollution or the water pollution. So we're talking about administering things for human affairs in consonance with their natural regions so that human affairs may be non-harming to natural affairs. (317-18)*

Other terms, other mappings, and their implicit concepts have become attached to the idea of Pacific Northwest, adding to its useful polyvalence (FIGS. 1, 10, 14). Snyder's description by watershed (with its paradoxical grammar of "there" and "here") emerges in a more explicitly political version as Cascadia, "an imaginary country . . . that eschews national and state boundaries but respects that natural integrity and socio-cultural history that have united the region for centuries" (Quigley 3).

The Cascadia "project," or "initiative," primarily a trade and marketing alliance, uses

~

The Northwest region is broadly taken to include southern British Columbia and the territory south through Washington and Oregon to the northern counties of California; its eastern boundaries are the northern Rocky Mountains and the Great Basin.

Kruckeberg 1982 3

Cascadia

Yukutat Bay

MT CUSHING

HAIDA GWAII

MT ROBSON

Queen Charlotte Sound

LOGAN PASS

Juan de Fuca Strait

Columbia

Yellowstone

MEADE PEAK

MT SHASTA

Cape Mendocino

Fig. 5: *Mapping a Watershed*, cartography by David D. McCloskey (1990).

y have found preferable to
n Artibise, a professor of
regional planning, draws a
vs of Cascadia," that illus-
_____tions among the Pacific
Northwest Economic Region (extending to
Idaho, Montana, Alberta, Yukon, and
Alaska), Cascadia (Oregon, Washington, and
British Columbia), and "Main Street"
Cascadia (the Vancouver, BC, to Eugene,
Oregon, corridor) (FIG. 10).

Kim Stafford's "Naming the Northwest,"
the Introduction to his collection of essay-
stories *Having Everything Right*,
suggests why such overlapping and "confusion" make
sense. In this prose version
of "There Are No Names But Stories,"
Stafford senses that Franz Boas's transliteration of Kwakiutl (Kwakwa̲ka'wakw) place names
on Vancouver Island marks a distinctive and
crucial epistemology of place.

> For [the Kwakiutl], a name was a story. We say
> "Vancouver," naming an island for a captain; we say
> "Victoria," naming a village for a queen. For them, a
> place-name would not be something that is, but some-
> thing that happens. They called one patch of ocean
> "Where Salmon Gather." They called one bend in the
> river "Insufficient Canoe." . . . If the Kwakiutl habits of
> naming were childlike, naive, they were also utterly
> mature. Their language shows connections where we
> have made separations. (1986, 3-5)

Stafford does not set out to write a cross-border

comparison, but, as with Snyder's concept of
the Ish nation, he recognizes that knowing his
place obliges re-reading the political boundary and approaching the deep structure of
Aboriginal languages. Like both James Swan
and Ivan Doig (the reciprocal diarists of
Doig's *Winter Brothers*), he has to *read north* in
order to write about Washington and Oregon
landscapes and folkways.

One other imaginary map romances the
place I'm trying to get at. No writer has so
extensively developed the idea of North
America's cross-border regions as has Joel

~

Near this rose, in this grove of sun-parched, wind-warped madronas,
Among the half-dead trees, I came upon the true ease of myself.
                    Theodore Roethke "The Rose" 199

Garreau. He names the "nation" on the Pacific
slope Ecotopia. For Garreau, it runs from
Point Conception, north of Los Angeles, to
Homer, Alaska, in a coastal strip defined by the
mountain ranges which cause the plentiful rain:

> The name Ecotopia for the nation of the Pacific
> Northwest comes from the title of a melodramatic, but
> nonetheless brilliant, 1975 novel by Ernest Callenbach.
> . . . Taken back to its Greek roots, Ecotopia means home
> place, but the more obvious meaning lies in the contrac-
> tion of Ecological Utopia, which, in the novel, is pre-
> cisely what the Northwesterners proceed to build, after
> sealing off their borders to the insidious influences of the
> rest of the continent. (250)

This weaving of concern for ecological health
and dreaming of utopia (intensified by the

emotional and imaginative barriers of rock—mountain ranges running north-south) tantalizes Northwest writers. Alan Artibise wryly summarizes the popular commitment to environmental "concern": "For Cascadians, environmentalism has become a sort of secular religion. Residents might not always do the right thing, but they do know when they or someone else has sinned" (12).

To imagine an Ish nation, a Cascadia, or an Ecotopia, is to animate a political force. Responses to the Cascadia project have been particularly political in the sense that they have been provoked by considerations of how to get and keep power. Apparently, the British Columbian government in place in 1997 shunned any official use of the term Cascadia. Even within literary politics, notions of a Northwest writing will provoke reactions to prevailing privilege. If such a distinction is tenable, I would like to think of this book as putting the emphasis of regional study on the politics of appreciating difference, rather than on the politics of control:

> The truly regional voice is one that declares an internal political alternative: in possession of the immediate and local, representing the voice of the polis, the people, it makes of the vernacular, the local attitude and the spatial allusion not simply a descriptive posture but a political gesture. . . . Our sensitivity to region may at one level make us aware of place and landscape, but a sensitivity to regional nuance—that is, to the literary structures and metaphors of region—will make us aware of the link between language and political attitude. (New 1984 17)

I incline to that strain of regionalism which Wendell Berry said "could be defined simply as *local life aware of itself*" (67). The politics are more personal, more concerned with some imaginative power, rather than physical or regulatory or jurisdictional power; in short, "a particular knowledge of the life of the *place* one lives in and intends to *continue* to live in. It pertains to living as much as to writing, and it pertains to living *before* it pertains to writing. The motive of such regionalism is the awareness that local life is intricately dependent, for its quality but also for its continuance, upon local knowledge" (Wendell Berry 67).

Regionalists of this mode—inordinately, if still somewhat casually intent on local detail, and with the objective of learning how to live empathetically in place—will still come in many guises. I like the differentness of American novelist John Keeble and Canadian poet Daphne Marlatt, two dissimilar writers who share the awareness of local life I would describe as "good teaching." Keeble's suspense thriller *Yellowfish* (1980) and Marlatt's long poem *Steveston* (1974) differ in genre, in style, and even in attitude toward language, but both carefully record a set of connections between language and place. They read their local topographies through earlier texts; that is, each book layers the writing of place by overtly citing and incorporating earlier writing about its place. In their re-reading, the authors have established their books as essential re-reading for those interested in the culture of the region.

The road map on the cover of the Perennial Library edition of *Yellowfish* extends from North Vancouver to Port Townsend, from Victoria to Mount Baker, while the map in the frontispiece, based on a 1797 gazetteer, encompasses most of North America, south of roughly the 51st parallel. The map in the frontispiece of *Steveston* encompasses only about ten square kilometres. Keeble's scope is the "big" Northwest and Marlatt's the "little." But they soon seem to trickle and run into one another. Their maps are stories happening many times.

The scaled grids of maps imply truth, accuracy, and objectivity in representation. Daphne Marlatt, for all the self-reflexive method of her poem, keeps warning herself of the obligation to represent the observed local objects: "the physical matter of/the place (what matters) meaning, don't get theoretical now, the cannery" (19). She is cautioned by the physical world that dictates the daily work of the people of Steveston. How do these two writers take the words we usually find on maps and assemble them in their texts? Consider two passages, the first from Keeble, the second from Marlatt:

> The Port Mann Bridge, spanning the Fraser River, came into view. At the same time Mount Baker slipped behind more nearby mountains. The bridge stood out at a distance because of its paint—the arch orange, the railings and undergirdings yellow, the colors bizarre against the pale-green bottom land of the river valley and the darker green of the hillsides. It was a margin, the bridge. When one crossed it one was out of Vancouver for certain. After that came the ascent and the high country, the towns spotted every thirty or forty or fifty or even more than a hundred miles apart like rolled-up porcupines in a wilderness of wolves, their names Scotch and British and Native and descriptive of what was found, what was made and by whom and of what had always been there: Langley, Chilliwack, Cheam View, Laidlaw, Hope, Mile 55, Princeton, Hedley, Keremeos, Cawston, Chopaka, Osoyoos, Bridesville, Rock Creek, Midway, Greenwood, Eholt, Grand Forks, Christina Lake, Paulson, Kinnaird, Trail, Fruitvale, Erie, Salmo, Creston. Erks checked the rearview mirror once, and the Lincoln was there, then again, and it was gone, then anxiously, again and again, and the Lincoln stayed gone. (93)

Pour, pour

> from its bank) this river is rivering urgency, roar
> (goku, goku) thru any hole, like boats race tide a millrace, as,
> the possible entry of this channel for, invisible under their hulls
> & flying heels, the fish re-enter time, racing north of Roberts Bank
> past Albion Dyke, then Woodward Reach opposite Woodward Landing
> (where the ferry ran) by Woodward Slough, then Gravesend Reach &
> City Reach the river proper lies, past any tidal reach (renew) fish
> seek their source, which is, their proper place to die. . . .
>
> (15; author's ellipses)

Keeble lists twenty-six place names (a full alphabet?); implicitly, this list defines "the high country" and perhaps, in their breathless accumulation, "the ascent." Each name is set off by a comma; no connecting words appear— Keeble imitating in print the towns "spotted" in isolation through the mountains. The names appear in the exact sequence in which they would be encountered driving west-to-east on British Columbia's highways 1 and 3.

This at first unremarkable fact gains in significance because of Keeble's fondness for trick fictional geographies:

> In Crab Canon . . . *the opening description of the farm in Saskatchewan is geometrically rendered. A close examination of that description would reveal that the farm is impossibly laid out, or that in fact the farm can't exist. Similarly, the protagonist of that novel grows up in the Bay area, and a close examination of the description of his place there would show that the house is in the Pacific Ocean, that the place where he lives can't exist either . . . In the case of* Crab Canon *the meticulous descriptions of places that can't possibly exist are attempts to get at the inaccessible.* (Newberry 11)

As Keeble goes on to suggest in this interview, the meticulous serial listing of place names is the register of Wes Erks's peculiar sensibility. In this passage he is reciting the future as if to calm himself and make his thinking linear. Surrounded by uncommunicating people, and on an unexplained dangerous mission, Erks declines "to get at the inaccessible." Instead, his mind recites a structure of certainty—a list of place names. Erks is comforted that these places exist in the external world and that his security is defined by successfully passing by or through them one after the other. Furthermore, as someone "fixed on West coast history . . . practically a scholar" (14), he knows that a more complex security may be discovered in place names—a social,

economic, and geological history. Erks's mind will often detour into such information, as it does when he arrives in Osoyoos, so that the listing provides not only an outline of the route that the road novel will follow (up to page 147) but a promise of further information to come (16).

Keeble instructs his reader to read closely the significances in place names. Marlatt's *Steveston* differs in that the reader shares immediately in the process of writer (as reader) writing: for example, the three "Reach"-es on the map of *Steveston* prompt her to think of the word "reach" as spoken and its connection (in the sense, perhaps, of influencing, extending) with "(renew)." Keeble is more essayistic; Erks adopts a didactic discourse, as if he is instructing himself in encyclopedia-entry taxonomy. Or is he? The comparison with Marlatt points up the central problem of Keeble's novel: the outlaw caught by the law of language.

By citing so many names without interruption, Keeble accelerates the narrative. Erks—both literally and metaphorically—has to cover a lot of road in a short time, without pause to contemplate. I suspect a lot of readers don't actually *read* such a list—the eye-mind skips it. Readers will skip it precisely because they anticipate getting to something like the last sentence of the paragraph, where in a series of short phrases the possible pursuer is glimpsed, and the mind-style shifts to the rough ungrammaticalities of mechanic or underworld: "the Lincoln *stayed gone*" (93; my emphasis). *Yellowfish* refuses to be the chase novel it at first appears to be. As it inclines toward "the physical matter of/the place" (90), it resists its own ideology in favour of topographical documentary.

Marlatt's discourse of mapping—that is her poetic use of a series of place names—accelerates the movement of the passage as it does in *Yellowfish*. The close proximity of seven place names in this passage reinforces the "urgency" and the "racing" of tide-spawning salmon. As in Keeble, the place names follow a careful west-to-east sequence on the map of the mouth of the Fraser River (*Fraser River*). In a distinct difference from the sample verbal map in Keeble, Marlatt maps in "time" and space. In the prepositions and conjunctions which connect the series—"north of . . . past . . . then . . . opposite . . . by . . . then . . . &"—spatial and temporal mingle and blur. For all its interest in history, Keeble's maps (or Erks's need for them) are out of time; Marlatt's are in time, formed, by and through language, as she writes them.

We could hardly say Marlatt is uninterested in the public history inherent in place names. But we are not likely to ask first who Woodward was, what ethnic group he belonged to. The reader is more likely to discover that the salmon migrating up the Fraser are moving "wood-ward" (that is, toward the woods) to "graves" and "end." For Marlatt, place names have equal status with all other words, provok-

ing the interlingual play essential to learning.

Steveston uses few place names familiar outside a restricted circle of locals. Keeble uses the place names available on generally accessible maps, read on road signs on public highways. Marlatt uses place names found, if at all, only on very specialized maps; even the historical maps reproduced in *Steveston* and *Steveston Recollected* do not show the names that appear in the poem. (With the exception of Roberts Bank, none of these place names would be generally recognized by today's resident of Vancouver, or even, I suspect, of Steveston.) These particular place names are, however, essential to people making their living on board boats navigating in the mouth of the Fraser. What we have here might be called oral mapping. Much of the poem derives from the interviews conducted by Maya Koizumi, which Marlatt edited for an oral history project and published in *Steveston Recollected*. The place names in Marlatt's poem are truly vernacular: they are names spoken by people engaged in the same work, rather than names recorded in public documents. The parenthetic definition of Woodward Landing, "(where the ferry ran)," confirms this oral local history.

For Marlatt, the place names are important because they are spoken in a community; they are oral and in this sense exist in time and go out of existence—at least out of the material existence imparted by print—as soon as they are spoken. Whereas Erks, thinking, tries to limit his world by mapping, Marlatt, writing, tries to catch herself in language. In this passage evoking a "rivering urgency," the syntax shifts without definite marker, so that the grammatical subject, the "what" that is racing past these various places, cannot be confined—it is "river" and "tide," and "fish." "Bank[ing]," "land," "reach"—nouns of place are always also verbs of extension and accumulation.

Viewing *Steveston* through the frame of *Yellowfish* points to a buried narrative in the poem. As Keeble's title claims, fish is a central trope in his novel: "His employer . . . had told him [Erks] that the business was called 'yellowfish' after a trash fish of Chinese waters eaten by the poor. Those who so entered the country were called yellowfish because they lacked the money to immigrate legally" (12). In *Steveston* the elusiveness and chance of the fishing industry defines the place. The poem is Marlatt's own chase narrative, with the haste, the careful mapping, the suspense, and the ominous, unidentified threats of Keeble's book: the writer is the pursuer pursued. Whereas the absence of the pursuer makes Erks more nervous than his presence, Marlatt finds threat in the absent presence of another language. It is marked in this passage by the untranslated term *goku*. According to *Kenkyusha's New Japanese-English Dictionary*, this word may mean: 1) prison 2) extremely, exceedingly 3) words and phrases, or 4) a votive offering. In the poem, *goku* seems to mimic the sound the river makes, and its contradictory meanings (as discovered by a non-Japanese speaker puzzl through a dictionary) are a reminder of the uneasiness of the chase.

The place names along the Steveston waterfront are noticeably territorial; they derive from surnames and imply possession. Woodward['s] Landing, for example, is named "after Nathaniel Woodward who, with his son Daniel, settled here in 1874" (Akrigg & Akrigg 340). Marlatt's writing traces the "ground choked by refuse, profit, & the/concrete of private property" (52). Keeble's verbal maps register less insistently the politics of ownership. But both are centrally concerned with trade goods and their movement, with maps that mark the nexus between transportation and cash. Marlatt maps much of Steveston with the names of businesses. Keeble repeatedly reads the highways of chase as rivers, and for Marlatt, of course, the river is everything and the world of Steveston is a river.

Both the pan-regional novel reading road maps and the village-probing poem reading local marine charts acknowledge Marlatt's "rivering urgency." The shared emphasis on river trade revises and questions any tidy list of characteristic regional tropes. Which is as it should be. I recognize regional culture, following Marlatt, as a delta, simultaneously—continuously—both eroding and being deposited, or in Keeble's terms as a gathering place and a "place of many languages" (288). The mingling and blending inherent in the concept of borderlands fits this methodology

veston and *Yellowfish* certainly work
[mo]re complex network of place,
[an]ds cultures interpenetrating,
[each] other, appropriating what the
other has lost: "A river has so many . . . things
to say that it is hard to know what it says to each
of us" (Maclean 102).

Steveston is an "island settlement": ruled
by the canning companies and dependent on
one resource, fish, it creates "islands of men"
(99). John Keeble's descrip-
tion of the communities of
the Idaho Panhandle fits the
geography of the entire
novel: "the country a wild,
craggy, hard, volcanic country, the towns—mining towns
originally, mostly lumber
towns now—built in pockets,
ravines, hollows and up
against cliffs, the people
insular, and the routes of
travel serpentine" (61).
Steveston is built literally on an island;
Keeble's description of a pattern of settlement, one-industry towns based on extraction
of a single natural resource confined in inaccessible valleys, suggests the power of the
island-idea in the wider Northwest, coastal
archipelago linked imaginatively to inland
company town (see Cole Harris).

~

Both Marlatt and Keeble pay attention to
local resources and the ways in which they
become "coin" for exchange among peoples
and cultures. (Keeble gives his protagonist a
name, Wes Erks; "W. Erks" on his rural mail
box, which puns on work.) Sensitivity to economic patterns, which extends to their potential to shape literary form, shadows nostalgia
and gives it practical anchor. Here are two
passages, by Marlatt, then Keeble, tracing
economic connections:

> . . . *the geese fly past the old*
> *Steves place & on, to dark to*
> *wherever fish come from, circling back in*
> *to their source:*
>
> *We obscure it with what we pour on these waters, fuel, paint, fill,*
> *the feeding line linking us to Japan & back, wherever, cargo ships, freighters*
> *steam up river & only the backwaters house these small boats whose owners,*
> *displaced & now relocated as fishermen can be, fishing up nets full of shadow/*
> *food for the canneries to pack, blip blip sonar & even these underwater*
> *migrations visible now as routes, roots, the river roots, out from under under*
> *brail net*
> *they lift these fishes with, reading a river gulf, Or, visibly*
>
> (Marlatt 56–57)

The place, the pair of towns, they had left behind was an
armature—the rivers its method of dexterousness, the
rivers digital—and a pivot, and prototypical, and
through time as with all gathering places, protean: its
perimeters were elastic, its form, its face, changed, mask
upon mask. The town of Lewiston—Erks knew—was
founded illegally on the Lemhi Reservation. The treaty
stipulated that no white man could erect a building on the
reservation, but the Snake River, which bounded the
reservation, was an avenue of trade, its bed, its course,
put there by Pliocene lava flow and downwarp, the

canyons later excavated by the waters of Pleistocene glaciation. Its course knitted the rugged inland country together, linked the Spokane and Coeur d'Alene country, interior British Columbia, and the Salmon and Clearwater rivers to the Columbia, and then to the Pacific. The Snake translated directly into trade, and, thus, into coin. At first salmon was the coinage, then fur, then in the 1860s it was gold—the Clearwater and Salmon River strikes. (Keeble 198)

As the fish "circl[e] back in/to their source," so Marlatt's reading of *Steveston*, which begins with a section titled "Imagine: a town," ends with this section whose title finally attaches to the circles of words its most familiar place name: "Steveston, BC" (the play on the abbreviation "BC" also suggests the town's prehistoric essence). Steveston is defined by its dependency on fish: "'salmon capital of the world': fortunes/made & lost on the homing instinct of salmon" (56). And the people who depend for economic survival on the homing instincts are ironically, like the fish, caught and vulnerable (?) on a "feeding line linking us to Japan & back." They are at once home and away on both eastern and western edges of the Pacific. "Displaced & now relocated," the culture of Steveston is both interior and coastal, an interdependence of topographies echoing Keeble's insistence that the Northwest always consists of dramatic contrasts of wet and dry. The Fraser River carries down to its mouth from the Interior the soil on which Steveston is built. The racist "relocation" of Japanese

Canadians during World War II moves upriver—but decidedly unnaturally—to the Interior. Both novel and poem, like so many books out of the Northwest, make this doubled return to Japan and back a key to knowing the place. Keeble describes the geographic imperative and the history of Asian ties at length:

The conduit between them [Seattle and Vancouver] and the Orient was the Japan Current—Kuroshio, the Gulf Stream of the Pacific, carrier of fish and seed and craft. (78)

Transformed into a cold current, it passed the coast of California and returned to its root, the mouth that spoke it first, the North Equatorial Current. A turbine action, a dynamo, centrifugal, the current looped Asia and Western America together. (79)

Kuroshio's essence lay in the atmosphere it made, in the sense it helped to shape of a certain trans-Pacific geographic skin. (80)

In *Yellowfish*, thoughts of currents and trade originate in the migration of geese—Erks carries with him the broken vertebrae of a goose as a talisman of migration. The irony here—the goose can no longer fly—also touches the geese flying past the community of Steveston, where dreams of return to Japan can never be fulfilled.

A more radical connection between novel and poem is Marlatt's enthusiasm for following what Erks thinks of as "the routes of language" (93). Marlatt reaches beyond thematic parallels (salmon and Japanese are homing), and structural parallels (circling and returning and returning to source) to poetic and linguistic connections. In the final instance, "the *feeding* line" surely also describes the fluctuating long line of words across the page which Marlatt deftly manipulates, letting it out, and pulling it in, to catch a multiplicity of impressions. The phrase "to dark to" is abruptly isolated, perhaps to suggest that the Steves place (the Steves family "founded" Steveston) looks out over the Strait of Georgia, over a "gulf"; I think she also puns on the double intensifier "too . . . too." Neatly, the prepositions which follow "Steves" ("on," "to," "to") look to be assembling themselves into a "place." The language and its ordering imply, or enact, the process that converts the name of a man and his family into a town: Steves-to-on. Now—that is in each reading of the poem—the reader puts the letters together to reinvent the town.

The language of fishing provides the language through which the poet reads the gulf. "Back waters" are necessary shelter where fishermen can keep their boats out of wind and the flow of river, away from the tug of tide. The exploited workers have no choice but to live in cultural and economic backwaters. The fishing nets are made of knots—and nots—of intricate interconnections and spaces that catch and release. The motif of nets also describes Marlatt making poetry by tying words together.

The fishermen's "sonic scan" (57) also evokes Marlatt's method of writing. She sends out the sounds in her fishing, and measures how long it takes for the echoes to come back (a measure, too, of her line). The method makes "underwater/migrations visible."

"Routes, roots, the river roots"—such sequences display the sonic method of composition. For Marlatt, fishing in language, a noun is always also a verb. Each word sounded conveys several disparate, often punning, meanings. In this case, the river is the sustaining soil for the growth of the community, but "rooting" also means "cheer[ing]" and "ship[ping]." An economy is also a language, and therefore a system of knowing the world. Marlatt roots in that language to understand the people of Steveston, and to understand her own writing in the language she is surprised to be absorbing.

When Keeble stops at the "armature" of place, he shows Erks's mind drifting from his immediate mission into contemplation of history and authoritative essay. No one economy figures *Yellowfish* in the way that fishing and canning govern *Steveston*'s form and language (unless it is smuggling). Individual islanded communities exist for and through a single

> There may be . . . a kind of merit to the center's claim to neutrality. What kind of region is the center? In America, it is the region that denies place in favor of commodity. The center has liquified all its assets, so that it does live nowhere, or at least its "where" is interchangeable with any other where or can be traded up.
>
> Bevis "Region, Power, Place" 28

resource, but the economic pattern that shapes *Yellowfish* is the exchange of coin itself: "A quintessential property of money was its synergy, its way of compounding itself, its way of tying different interests together, its ability to travel and to cause travel" (199).

In *Yellowfish*, river is road and road river. The trope is as central to novel as to poem, but in *Yellowfish* rivers are more exclusively "avenue[s] of trade" and narrative; the story of the economy is, on the surface at least, one of surrender to the flow. In this aspect, of course, *Yellowfish* evokes that restless nomadic tradition so central to American fiction, from Twain to those artistic predecessors Albert Sandman evokes early in the novel: Jack Kerouac, Allen Ginsberg, Ken Kesey (50).

But the beginnings and endings of travel in *Yellowfish* imply a narrative structure opposed to the dream of lighting out for the territory ahead of the rest. Erks smuggles Taam, Chang, and Lee between Vancouver and San Francisco, between the second and first largest Chinatowns outside of China, or, as Keeble puts it, "between the two metropoles marking the northern and southern boundaries of the region" (Newberry 7). The novel actually opens at the end of an earlier version of the same trip—and, therefore, is spatially circular, from San Francisco to San Francisco, a city both times hidden in fog. Yet Erks, at the end of the novel, returns to his home near Davenport,

Washington, a name whose suggestion of relaxing on the verandah is appropriate. Each of the shifts in place implies the Northwest as Keeble conceives it: that is, moving inland from the ocean by following the routes of water into the arid interior and, renewed or reborn, returning to the Pacific. This pattern of trade essentially defines the region, no matter what the commodity. Circulation in the Northwest is always a version of the life journey of the salmon. But Keeble's crucial summary of trade routes is "serpentine."

In this passage, one river, the Snake, forms the essential link between high country and Pacific. Movement is winding, subject to unexpected twists, mysterious, unpredictable. But, immediately after a reference to Erks's finding "no relief from such uncertainty" (198), the description of the river settles deliberately into the measured syntax of rational control—an assertion about treaty conditions, an expansive qualification in a "but" clause. The blank verbs and passive constructions suggest an *Encyclopedia Britannica* sensibility, an impression reinforced by the geological vocabulary. The information is interesting—to Erks and to the reader. Yet, read side by side with Marlatt, it is considerably less engaging in its openness to the surprise catch that might be made by letting out a line of words (or sounds)—or by the serpentine.

Whereas Marlatt listens for the particular vocabulary that makes the economy run, then exploits that vocabulary to read "the gulf" as she writes, Keeble uses a more general vocabulary of economics and trade. When Erks reflects on the meaning of the paired cities of Lewiston and Clarkson, he slides from one range of vocabulary to another, from one metaphor to another, almost willing himself to be detached from it. This intersection is a "gathering place," like Steveston, where Native Americans have come for ages to fish for salmon and, like Steveston, perhaps, it is "protean," continually shifting in shape and form, as Keeble's opening sentence does—from "armature/pivot" with their connections to machine and electricity, to the body or hands of the rivers, to prototype, and physiognomy and mask. It's a passage where Keeble reaches toward poetry, in an open syntax, the alliterated "p's" apparently becoming more important to the choice of words than their meanings or their logical associations. Keeble's choice of an epigraph from Ed Dorn provides a context in which we might have expected a more open verse of place—such as in "Idaho Out." As with Erks's thoughts of Simon Fraser's journal—"a journey through the anarchic woods and water, the stone, the dark, the cold, the land of spirits." (137)—Keeble seems to be thinking of his own style of writing and yearning to be postmodern, or at least metafictional.

Rather than push these two works apart as novel and poem, or crime-thriller and meta-linguistic play, I would like to push them together as travel books. Not that I want to diminish their independence, but I am interested in the notion that travellers may construct an understanding of a culture more perceptive and valuable than the conventional image of tourist implies. The traveller who is merely "passing through" and paying attention to surfaces may have a first-time perception the insight of which lies in its very spontaneity and crudity. But honouring the visitor's immediate reactions might promote the dichotomies that are a frequent pitfall of Canada-US comparisons: the United States is violent/ Canada is peace-loving; *Yellowfish* is a narrative of the footloose adventurer/*Steveston* is a study of a confined and beleaguered garrison. I would rather walk the border, to ask what lies in the middle, to ask one work to illuminate the shadow in another, to reveal its changing process and its fluidity—refusing to *fix* one or the other.

Reading *Yellowfish* in contexts established by Marlatt suggests that *Steveston* could be the poem of place that Erks wants to write or, even better, speak. As a traveller, behind a car's windshield, his mind drifts into neat encyclopedia-entry history. As historian, he wants to stop and go down into the sensory, layered history of a place, but he is caught in the narrative of the smuggler and outlaw. During the chase, he is frustrated by a surface of "paradox" (146, 186), "nonsense rhyme" (146), and the "incomplete syllogism" (176). In the very mystery and incompleteness of his dialogue with Taam—"It was impossible to follow a straight line in conversation with the man" (159)—Erks understands that what he's looking for speaks outside either outlaw adventure or history: in a writing of the Northwest "as [he] find[s] it," layering ethnology and geology, Confucian epistemology and twentieth-century mercantilism in a verbal "multiplicity simply there," Erks, the mechanic of words, imagines his way toward an incantation of place. At the end of the novel, he drifts "delirious," trying to orient himself to the coyotes' "cries interwoven and dense and ornate as a gospel choir, one voice scooping up and down like a gospel obbligato, but without text, without meaning, pure glossolalia, utterly abstract and yet powerfully concrete." And after the unmeaning song, "[h]e heard only the space the sound had occupied, magically empty" (310).

Steveston, writes Christina Cole, might be a "travel book about getting lost" (12). Marlatt, or the narrator, becomes trapped in the role of ethnographer. She develops such an intensely complicated hermeneutic relationship with her subject, the enclosed space and its culture, that she can't get any distance. The insistent motif of "running" implies, perhaps, a need to get away from her subject—into an adventure narrative such as *Yellowfish*. Somewhere hidden

~

Steveston is sitting on the edge of momentous changes. . . .

The company [BC Packers] recently announced it is closing its last processing plant on the site and moving the work and jobs to Vancouver, where it will set up a joint processing plant with its former competitor, the Canadian Fishing Company.

Vancouver Sun
7 October 1996 B2

in Marlatt's Steveston is another hungry, souvenir-gathering, bewildered, traveller like Erks. Unable to recognize her own story in the alluvial language of place, she is ironically in the same position as the exiled community and excluded woman worker of Steveston.

When Richard Hugo writes that "two nations own/these islands," he immediately questions the neatness of the assertion with a sequence of ambiguous possessives. The islands may be literal, or figurative; the nations may own different islands, or the ownership may be joint; the two nations may be Canada and the United States, or immigrants and first peoples, or humans and animals. And at its core, crucially, each of these island-books traces the story of "the latest run of springs." Both writers respond to ecological and autochthonous patterns that omit national boundaries. That shade of green may be Canadian, but it's more likely that the firs and grebes belong to whoever is observing them and speaking them. In their attention to the symbiosis of an individual's job, the collective means of survival (economy), and a community's language, *Steveston* and *Yellowfish* recognize in geography the shape of a community's story. The long poem layers itself into one small community (which no longer exists, except as a name) whose culture—a hierarchy built on native workers and Asian immigrant labour with European bosses—and whose singularly concentrated means of survival—fishing and canning—permeated the entire Pacific slope region. Against it place an adventure thriller whose scores of road signs and local histories impinge on, and complicate, the journey of the Asian migrant on highways that define a Northwest: coast and interior, Canada and United States, "following the water routes down" through Native American histories and explorers' journals (Keeble 289)—"the Cadillac like a boat along a channel" (275).

～

Raven File

Then there is Raven living. He had a big house. A big house Raven had. It was two-fire size. He is high-class, high-class. Raven is full of pretensions that he could never keep up. Raven lived with lots of people around him. Suddenly, Raven said (in nasal Ravenese): "I'm going by water, by water, by water."

~from "Star Child" as told by Susie Sampson Peter
(Upper Skagit, 1950) in *Lushootseed Animal People*
by Jay Miller and Vi Hilbert

We are not, or at least I am not, seeking either to become natives (a compromised term in any case) or to mimic them. Only romantics or spies would seem to find point in that. We are seeking, in the widened sense of the term in which it encompasses very much more than talk, to converse with them, a matter a great deal more difficult, and not only with strangers, than is commonly recognized.

~Clifford Geertz *The Interpretation of Cultures*

However it happened, coyote had something to do with it . . . Or this other bird, Raven. On the coast, Raven is a kind of flying coyote.

~George Bowering *Bowering's BC*

Mythtellers tell their stories to those who are listening. They also tell their stories to themselves. That is hard to do in a foreign language. When you ask a mythteller to tell you a story in your language rather than hers, the mythteller must talk only to you, not to herself. And then something is missing.

~Robert Bringhurst
"Point-Counterpoint: The Polyhistorical Mind"

41

akes my measure with one eye, letting me have it:
-whetting, chuckling, clock-winding, metallic gurgling,
.ckles and nutcracks, dogbarks and whistles,
ʝuick sotto voce lipsmacks, coos,and retchings.

Then leaving me with an impossible act
To follow, an *ars poetica* far beyond
Mere minor tricksters, he swerves to the cedar crown
And presides with lofty silence over my workroom.

~David Wagoner "Under the Raven's Nest"

JAMES AGEE BEGINS HIS PORTRAIT OF THREE families of Alabama tenant farmers with a painstakingly honest and lyrically contorted self-analysis. How do you write about what you are so evidently and impossibly unequipped to write about?

I realize that, with even so much involvement in explana-tions as this, I am liable seriously, and perhaps irretriev-ably, to obscure what would at best be hard enough to give its appropriate clarity and intensity; and what seems to me most important of all: namely, that these I will write of are human beings, living in this world, innocent of such twistings as these which are taking place over their heads; and that they were dwelt among, investigated, spied on, revered, and loved, by other quite monstrously alien human beings, in the employment of others still more alien; and that they are now being looked into by still others, who have picked up their living as casually as if it were a book, and who were actuated toward this reading by various possible reflexes of sympathy, curiosi-ty, idleness, et cetera, and almost certainly in a lack of consciousness, and conscience, remotely appropriate to the enormity of what they are doing. (12-13)

"If I could do it," Agee tells himself, "I'd do no writing at all here" (13). What he does write finds consciousness and conscience by his varying the forms, styles, and sources of his expression, by his making his own problem of speaking responsibly a constant subject, by incorporating what might be taken as irrele-vant digressions, by affixing the reverent and ironic title *Let Us Now Praise Famous Men* (1941).

The permutations of Agee's dilemma sur-face when I try to focus on a process which already shadows almost every page of this book, the translation (to be understood in the widest possible sense) of Native American/First Nations cultures. A single sentence from Walter Ong's *Orality and Literacy* (1982) sums up the problem: "Try to imagine a culture where no one has ever 'looked up' anything" (31). The enormous difficulty of cross-cultural communication suggested by Ong's challenge derives, in part, from its own tempting contradiction. Bending the mind to imagine an exclusively oral culture risks con-ceiving of that culture as some pre-literate "ruin," not a culture of "human beings, living [and writing, and reading] in *this* world."

Short of doing no writing at all here, the writer seeking conversation will have both to wrestle with the oral-print transaction and to recognize the First Nations *writer*. I need such a "both/and" to follow the flight of Raven. Raven, near the beginning of time and world, brought the light. Raven's insistent chattering announces the spiralling presence of the "timescape of the first peoples." I have not done a statistical survey, a motif-count, but I would guess that remembering another (pre-contact) time, and respecting a different sense of time, figure more prominently in Pacific Northwest writing than in any other North American region, with the possible exceptions of the Southwest and the Arctic. Prominent in Northwest writing, because prominent in the region's day-to-day living, like totem poles in public places, or Thunderbirds who play hockey in Seattle, and basketball or soccer in Vancouver.

Ivan Doig's capsule phrase "the timescape of the First Peoples" collapses place and time: suggests process rather than stasis or fixed truth; echoes Stafford's idea that place is a story happening many times. Already this book has touched on many instances where that place called *Northwest* seems coterminous with "the reach of the cedar dugout canoe" (Griffith 56).

How does this cedar canoe and the timescape of those who paddle it affect writing? I need to ask how writers have chosen and assembled the words around these subjects.

That Ivan Doig can be added to the list writers who record an encounter with the cultures of the Native peoples interests only a statistician, but when Doig finds in Bill Reid's description of Northwest Coast Indian art an attitude to shape his own syntax, the literary imagination awakes:

Scenes of this winter and of Swan's own western-edged seasons do flow together, in the way that beings mingle in one of those magical carvings of the Haidas ("They weren't bound by the silly feeling that it's impossible for two figures to occupy the same space at the same time"). (241)

Raven, shape-shifter and creator of surprise, mingles and unbounds preconceptions. A totem of translation. Unmoved that many Indians appear in H.L. Davis's *Honey in the Horn*, Raven apparently presides when "the Indian boy['s]" account of the creation comes to guide Clay's practical actions, and his ethics. The story happens again, in another space and time. Then the narrator's vernacular recounting of the story attempts to mingle the substance and magic of some native myth: "They [the people] were nothing but loose toots of vapor that went rocking around in mid-air, getting all mixed up with one another and wishing, without knowing exactly why, that they could get sorted out again" (49).

Davis intuited that some fictional form leaving people and mythologies all mixed up with one another best responded to a regional background—and it is only background in *Honey*

transformation stories. Almost [
[wr]iter mentioned in this book [
[...] or his place in a Raven File. For
[be]neath (or before) Marlatt's
Steveston [...] the home of "the natives, whose
longtime summer ground this was, coming to
fish, whole/bands whose women & children
end by working the canneries, staying in
Indian/ tenements, & it all settles down into an
order of orders." (99). The history which
speaks diminuendo in *Steveston* (First Nations
history is much more explicit in Marlatt's 1972
Vancouver Poems) mounts to a crescendo in
Yellowfish. Accompanied by a small totem pole,
Erks, in his historian's imagination, journeys
through tribal homelands, each place understood through the economy and mythology of
its native peoples. "History seems to me," says
Keeble, "to be indigenous first—if that doesn't
sound like solipsism of region—and yet one can
read a lot of history that ignores this. Maybe
this is where the novel comes in—making history
indigenous" (Newberry 8).

   In this solipsistic region, most novelists,
and a good many poets, would find a mission
statement in Keeble's comment: their program is to make place and story indigenous. A
problematic mission, more vexed, I think,
than Agee's, if for no other reason than the
array of languages, often radically different in
structure, spoken among Native Americans in
the Northwest. It is hard to tell stories in a foreign language. Hard, but necessary. Hard, but
worth trying. Raven, unfazed, keeps talking

and transforming. He is subject and story, but
also muse. Place-story requires translating the
mythteller's talk, requires appropriating in a
way that does not supplant and replace, but
borrows to understand and to give back.
Telling the story is a demanding process essential to Doig, Davis, Marlatt, and Keeble, to
Emily Carr and a host of other painters, to
sports marketers, and to Laurie Ricou writing
this book. Yet, for all the angst of this paragraph, and the entire opening of this Raven
File, I am convinced that some knowledge,
necessarily limited by cultural background and
history, is preferable to ignorant neglect.
Raven is voracious. My own reaction to this
central issue in Northwest writing parallels a
comment on the situation in Australia (which
itself points to a global interest in re-centering
autochthonous cultures):

*Current practices of popularisation have cut Aboriginal
literature off from its Aboriginal qualities by an excessive emphasis on difference, while keeping it remote
from the popular. At this stage in Aboriginal-White
relations, it is surely time to try the opposite approach,
one that tries to retain as much as possible of the qualities of the Aboriginal texts, yet confidently situates this
literature in the context of Australian culture, including
contemporary popular forms. The point of doing this is
not at all to deny differences and the history of conflict.
. . . [but] it is only by our setting up a common framework that existing differences can come into focus, . . .
instead of being masked as invisible, unspeakable
boundaries. (Hodge 277)*

Such a framework should better reveal and

speak boundaries. Within it, we could mix up the boundary-process. Within it, we should consider the integrity and responsibility of translation, and attend to what a writer's strategies of translation make alive, and to what they leave out.

Joan Crate, herself Métisse, establishes such a framework by making the difficult conversation overt, and reflecting on it, in her superb serial poem *Pale as Real Ladies: Poems for Pauline Johnson* (1989). Pauline Johnson (1862-1913), daughter of a Mohawk chief and an English woman, was a celebrated stage poet who translated Squamish stories in her *Legends of Vancouver* (1911). Crate's sequence is framed by a vignette in which the poet imagines the face of Pauline Johnson reflected in a bus window at night. The doubling of Pauline and Tekahionwake (Johnson's Mohawk name) matches the doubling of Crate and Johnson—"half-blood" (7), designating shared cultural experience, also implies a metaphor for one woman poet trying to hear and recreate the voice of another woman poet. As the sequence builds, the reader gets more involved in the family interconnections (extended to Pauline's own half-brothers and half-sisters) as well as in the intricately paced verbal interconnections: the resonance of

white and black, the reiterated colours (pink, blue, grey, maroon) seemingly picked from the "pale bruises" (12) early in the book, the sound of bone china, and the puzzle of jig-

~

bill bissett as hippie shaman chants his homage to the arbutus tree:

green wind
                numin numin numin numin niminnumin
     goldn treeeee
        eeeeeeeeeeeeeeeeeeeeeeeeeeeee

our eyez meet in th passing hallway

    green winda winda winda winda winda   goldn tree   eeeee
eeeeeeee
       eeeeeeee
          i saw a heart   flying   into th sky
   looks like yu
      lookd   like me

        "arbutus song" *canada gees mate for life* 79

saws. Crate creates verbal contexts in which even clichés are revitalized; each poem turns back to challenge a re-reading of an earlier poem. In *Pale as Real Ladies* we "climb words back to a beginning" (62) where a poet, and poetry, once fixed as "exotics," move hauntingly, challengingly, into contemporary literary life.

When the Vancouver artist Jack Shadbolt paints a Southern Kwagiutl Sun Mask, he "transcribe[s] the forms of the mask with care" but "narrow[s] the eyes to a squinting and sorrowful gaze, an amendment that both adds personality and emotion." His "Elegy for an Island" (PLATE 4) quotes "a southern Kwagiutl ceremonial curtain" (Halpin 40). Marjorie Halpin shrewdly describes the appeal of the painting: Shadbolt's strategy "locate[s] the images in time" (39) and reminds us that we deny emotion and individuality to the Native faces around us by denying their existence in time. To transform is not to destroy but to change alive. Halpin summarizes Shadbolt's impact with a quotation from Clifford Geertz: "The problem of cultural integration becomes one of making it possible for people inhabiting different worlds to have a genuine, and reciprocal, impact on one another" (1983 161). For Shadbolt, Crate, and Geertz, the ideal, cross-cultural study is a conversation, which encompasses a great deal more than talk.

The end of the opening chapter of *Klee Wyck* (1941) where Emily Carr lingers lovingly over her conversation with an old man sawing a tree effects just such a reciprocal impact:

I sat down beside the sawing Indian and we had dumb talk, pointing to the sun and to the sea, the eagles in the air and the crows on the beach. Nodding and laughing together I sat and he sawed. The old man sawed as if aeons of time were before him, and as if all the years behind him had been leisurely and all the years in front of him would be equally so. (10-11)

The lines of force shaping literature in the Pacific Northwest converge in this "place belonging neither to sea nor to land" (10), where "sea and forest were always at [a] game of toss with noises" (11). It points to the edgescape, both literal and psychological, in Davis's *Honey in the Horn*, where this book began, as it does to the location of Lionel Kearns's *Convergences* and Annie Dillard's *The Living*. The

atmosphere of leisurely lushness evokes Lotusland mythology. But in her painting, as in her writing, Carr always finds place inseparable from the Indian's knowledge of it: "I tried to be plain, straight, simple and Indian. I wanted to be true to the places as well as to the people" (1966 292). However successful, or compromised, the result, Carr knew that to write *place*, she to listen to, or see performed, the stories of the Native people. As the iconic BC artist, she became the grandmother of literature in British Columbia, if not of all the cross-border Northwest.

Carr senses the challenge and discovery that lie in crossing linguistic and cultural boundaries to the Native American perception. "Dumb talk" reverberates at these boundaries, as it does when two people on a beach point to sun, and eagle, and crow. If the term first designates sign language, the language of gesture and facial expression, it can also suggest the naively unpolished English that Carr valued—and cultivated. (I would, of course, want to exclude the colloquial sense of dumb as "stupid," even if Carr's sometimes reckless diction would suggest she is simply insensitive to this nuance.) The phrase also catches the contradiction of reproducing an oral expression in the silence of print, a paradox we encounter in Ursula Le Guin and Jack Hodgins, as in Carr. A language of image and symbol, of totems, is dumb talk too: Carr, that is, seeks a language in touch with the natural world, listening for its voices, not a language that draws its meaning only from other words. Carr dreams, ultimately, of "no language even" (1966 94), the paradox of a language, spoken or written, that conveys an unspoken knowledge. Dumb talk is, we can see, an inevitable obsession for a painter/writer: "What's the good of trying to write? It's all the unwordable things one wants to write about, just as it's all the unformable things one wants to paint—essence" (1966 116).

Echoes of the indigenous voice are, of course, but interpretations, implicit and explicit, of First Nations languages and perception. Few writers in English have a detailed knowledge of a native language, but many reach for a form, or syntax, or method that will evoke another language with its different way of knowing. In the incident with the sawing Indian, for example, Carr quotes the old man's warning when she turns into the forest: "'Swaawa! Hiya swaawa!' Swaawa were cougar: the forest was full of these great cats" (11). Transliteration of Indian words, via Chinook jargon, however approximate the translation from a language that has no written form, is one obvious way to introduce an indigenous perception into the literature written in English. Perhaps "dumb talk" is also found in onomatopoetic words, such as "swish" and "purr" (and the complementary alliteration and assonance), which speak the unwordable language of nature. Many of Carr's metaphors, suggested in this anecdote about the old man, evoke an unmediated, unworded intimacy between the people and their environment. Using an analogy drawn from the immediate setting, and even time of year, Carr seems to speak of ageing in the way the old man himself would: "He was luscious with time like the end berries of the strawberry season" (11).

Introducing Indian words and finding metaphors for the ecological imagination, Carr's aspiration tries to be "straight, simple and Indian" (1966 292) summarizes the most overt and direct translation strategy. Hubert Evans's *Mist on the River* (1954) makes communication across languages a more continuous concern than in *Klee Wyck*. Indeed, the mist of the title symbolizes, among other things, the evanescence and intangibility of language: "mist without avail rising from the river" (204).

Mist on the River is a documentary romance, whose energy lies in the tensions between coast and interior, white world and native, old and young, urban and wilderness—tensions alive among the Gitkshan people along the Skeena River. Evans knows that the Gitkshans' talk grows dumb in the most radical sense: it is, literally, disappearing, especially among the young. The only defence, according to old Paul, the village elder, is isolation: "Holding to our language is what preserves us as a people. Our language is a strong wall around us" (163).

Faced with the threat that whole languages will fall into silence, Evans's own attempts to hold to the language will seem absurd gestures. The relative crudity and obviousness of his literary adaptations of another language redefine this central artistic problem for writers in the Northwest and suggest the strengths and weaknesses of other writers' attempts at translation. Evans looks to incorporate indigenous languages into his novel in three general ways: by the obvious, occasional use of transliterated words; by various representations of dialect; and by developing metaphor appropriate to the sound and movement of another language.

Melissa, mother of the novel's central character, responds to her daughter's embarrassment about cultural habits: "'The *gum-see-wa* have their kind of smell, too'" (5). This single Gitkshan word (the one word in the text the educated reader of English does not immediately understand), repeated several times in the novel, confronts many readers (in a foreign tongue) with their own reductionist categorization by skin colour—*white*. No single word could more effectively convey the cultural bias inherent in the language itself. Evans also tries to promote appreciation by descriptions of language. He contrasts expressive schoolgirl English with June's "exaggerated native flatness" (175). Later he attempts to describe Cy's sense of the characteristic sounds of native languages: "Kitimaat with its tight-throated, clicking forcefulness: the more flowing Haida: Tsimpshean, whose intona-

tions, and some of its words, resembled his own" (19). In using an occasional native term, in attending to the sound patterns of an oral language, and, especially, in filtering the perception through Cy, Evans tries, however modestly, to break down cultural barriers.

Evans uses dialect, or Indian English, in various ways. The most exaggerated example is Marie's letter, which June reads (and then translates) to her mother: "Dear Friend, thought I drop you a line to say hello. You be surprised I home so soon but that alright because I here to help Matt till you get here" (93). However sincere the novelist's intention here, broken English seems condescending. (The dialect English in Paul St. Pierre's *Breaking Smith's Quarter Horse* (1966), for example, is much more palatable, in part because the lightly satirical tone embraces all the characters, from whatever culture.) Yet the archly correct textbook dialogue Evans uses elsewhere may be just as unconvincing. An occasional hint of ungrammatical English in Evans's own narration marks the native viewpoint more effectively: "if a person had their own truck they could get out of the village and have a little change without everybody knowing" (170). Isolated examples of native diction are more evocative than extended patches of dialect; Paul warns: "'The whites want to see all Indians in the ground, put there by the drink and the lung-sick and their other diseases'" (162). In each of these three cases—"in the ground" for "dead," "the drink" for "drink," and "lung-sick" for "tuberculosis"—the expression (we are to imagine Paul speaking in Gitkshan) is more specific, less abstract, more grounded in the senses. Evans conveys the difference of perception more subtly later, when Matt observes: "'The drink has been among us years of years,'" and Caleb echoes: "'And years of years I have made strong prayers against it'" (204). Through this metaphorical turning of the cliché "years and years," time seems to stretch immeasurable, and yet circle reassuringly. Similarly in the verb *make*, Evans implies a creative and giving element in prayer that presumably contrasts to the dominant white practice of rote repetition.

In a novel that often preaches awkwardly, Evans, at his best, can pull an element of native language out of the dialogue into his own storytelling: "No matter what she [Dot] had done to put his heart in a steep place with her wild ways, he could, and did, thank her for this moment" (101). Unlike the more subtle and continuous fusion of writer's and subjects' perceptions in Sheila Watson's *The Double Hook*, the satisfying sense of an alternative outlook emerges only occasionally in Evans's metaphors: "Old Paul would stand there and the acquiescent, reasoned arguments would drift around him like snow around a boulder" (153). But Evans will extend such suggestions of the ecological imagination to considerable length:

> It was not her fault she [Miriam] had Old Paul for a grandfather, but more and more he [Cy] was seeing that by being put to work in the boat-shed he had been maneuvered into a narrow place. It was like travelling the frozen k'Shan north to your trapping ground when you came on a place where the ice looked safe but the premonition seized you that it was not. If you were wise you backed off quickly and got your dogs and yourself on to solid ice and around by a different way. (52)

There is nothing self-consciously literary or ingenious about such metaphors (unlike, for example, some of the variations Evans plays on mist): they are drawn from the daily experience of the people, and imply a culture in which human and nature are not separate categories.

Evans's novel is important just *because* the approaches to native language are so simple and overt. Carr is more inclined to read the myths, to incorporate in her writing the images and patterns she has discovered belong to an Aboriginal world view. Her prose style, for example, often seems a contrast to the lush-

~

Their languages were mutually unintelligible, so everyone used the jargon—Chinook, the trade language people spoke on the coast from California to Alaska. Lively little Clare picked it right up, and chattered to everyone in sight. The language comprised only three hundred words, so it was simple to learn; on the other hand, Ada complained, it was difficult to say anything the least bit interesting.

Annie Dillard *The Living* 12

ness of her chosen landscape: it is economical and restrained. Perhaps her short paragraphs, the startling short sentences, the sketch form itself, and the uneasy transitions echo "the quick hushed words they [the Indians] said to each other in Haida" (18). I think Carr aims to approach silence by using as few words as possible; she tries to strip her language of anything that could be thought to be decorative, excessive, especially that might be thought pretentious. Perhaps an intuition that Native languages typically collapse English parts of speech—objects included in verbs, possessive pronouns incorporated in nouns, weak development of tenses (Haas 61)—influenced her taste for economy. But, as in Evans, the aim and the achievement are not necessarily the same: economy is not an invariable feature of *Klee Wyck*, either in diction or syntax. Carr swings back and forth between her own cultural background and the cultures she is encountering; the cloying absurdity of the old man *"luscious* with time" exemplifies the frequent turns in which she seems anything but restrained.

Carr yearns for the atmosphere she found in Skedans, where "there were no shams" and one "got close down to real things" (19). Totem poles, further, best represent such essence:

> He [the Indian] wanted some way of showing people things that were in his mind, things about the creatures and about himself and their relation to each other. He cut forms to fit the thoughts that the birds and animals and fish

suggested to him, and to these he added something of himself. When they were all linked together they made very strong talk for the people. He grafted this new language on to the great cedar trunks and called them totem poles and stuck them up in the villages with great ceremony. (51)

In contrast to Evans's, Carr's "strong talk" is more surely a "new language": governed by a conviction that the "primitive people claimed me" (1966 315) and not limited to a few uneasy transliterations, an occasional metaphor or unusual syntactic turn.

When Carr "struggle[s] with D'Sonoqua," the Northwest's most compelling female myth-figure, she insists that "[b]ig, strong simplicity is needed for these carvings and forests" (1966 160). The repetitive narrative reflects an elementary reading of an elemental pattern of native spirituality. Again, Carr remembers herself engaged in "dumb talk." When she asks Indian Tom, "Who is she?", he replies first with meaningful silence. His subsequent comments, with one exception, are laconic, as are those—earlier—of "the little Indian girl" (34-35). Carr's prose is hardly so laconic, yet the short sentences, often strategically located at the ends of paragraphs, seem calculated to evoke the same depths of simplicity: "Then he went away" (32), "Now I saw her face" (33), "Horror tumbled out of them" (35). Furthermore, through unusual verbs, Carr links "big, strong simplicity" with growth. Sentence after sentence startles with a verb that seems to fuse parts of speech: "One by one dots of light *popped* from the scattered cabins" (37;

my emphasis). The synaesthesia here gives sound and surprise to the entire scene. "Black pine-covered mountains," she writes, "*jagged* up on both sides of the inlet like teeth" (37; my emphasis). The turning of noun or adjective to service as a verb reinforces the qualities of "dumb talk"—their unconventionality suggesting a source in another language, and their implicit visual and kinetic elements perhaps evoking sign language.

For Carr, and for the native people as she understands them, a distinction between animate and inanimate has no meaning; all nature is equally alive and in shared motion. "It must be lovely," she wrote, "to be a creature and go with the elements, not repelling and fearing them, but growing along with them" (1966 241). No doubt Carr shares the central assumption of shamanism "that man and animal are close kin" (Furst 46). In "D'Sonoqua," the artist Carr apparently undergoes ecstatic initiation into the ancient mysteries of a special society. The sketch is structured in four movements: three mystical encounters with D'Sonoqua, and an interlude after the second in which Carr suffers illness and solitude. When she first sees the haunting totem figures of D'Sonoqua, Carr can describe, but not identify. The encounter comes as a surprise after sustained suspense. In a remote and desolate setting, the observer, already pushed beyond normal limits,

exhausted from lack of sleep, sees D'Sonoqua as magical: "Their [the carving's eyes] fixed stare bored into me as if the very life of the old cedar looked out, and it seemed that the voice of the tree itself might have burst from that great round cavity, with projecting lips, that was her mouth" (33). This blending and shifting between realms—sea, air, totem, forest— evoke the ready transformations of First Nations mythology. The pattern of "D'Sonoqua" is another version of Carr's "dumb talk," a representation of literal dumb talk, the silent yet speaking wild woman, the silent yet speaking forest.

In the second encounter, Carr is older and the figure is less threatening. Now it expresses "power, weight, domination, rather than ferocity" (35). Where the first D'Sonoqua breathes the spirit of tree and forest, this figure is more animal and human. On this occasion Carr's question about the figure is partially answered by Indian Tom, and she is left with a limited understanding. "Still—who understands the mysteries behind the forest?" (36).

The third and fourth movements bring Carr some understanding of these mysteries. "Tossed and wracked and chilled," journeying through the "clammy darkness" of the sea, or a gloomy forest of "black pine trees" (36), Klee Wyck's search comes more closely to resemble a sacred quest: this section might be

The Indian carvings, for all their massiveness, are verbs in wood.
George Bowering
Bowering's BC 19

read as the experience through which she earns the Aboriginal name bestowed on her in the book's opening sketch. She undertakes the shaman's solitary and perilous journey to the underworld: "the edge of the boat lay level with the black slithering horror below. It was like being swallowed again and again by some terrible monster, but never going down" (37). Her seasickness and sleeplessness mark the physical and psychic crisis that typically precedes the ecstatic shamanistic initiation. Out of her illness, Klee Wyck emerges into "the brilliant sparkle of the morning when everything that was not superlatively blue was superlatively green" (37). Her call to D'Sonoqua is answered by the most visionary appearance of the figure, now softened and less menacing. In some cultures, the shaman is also poet and rock painter: now, for the first time in this piece, Carr is able to paint/sketch. Now, also, Klee Wyck, the poet, articulates something inaccessible to other members of her community—a sense of equilibrium and wholeness: an equivalence of the "graciously feminine" detected here (40), and the "power" and "ferocity" (35) of other D'Sonoquas; a kinship of animal, human, and tree, where "wild" is both fearful and "shy, untouchable" (40).

The very structure of "D'Sonoqua" reflects the process of acquiring "dumb talk." The piece culminates in a dream-song of great spiritual power. Through persistence, meditation, intensity, and agony comes a state of enlightenment in which Klee Wyck attains something of the unspoken unspeakable wisdom of the old man sawing and gesturing: like the shaman, she has acquired a kind of "metaphysical equilibrium," uniquely able to cross over "formidable barriers of language and culture" (Furst 60).

Crossing these barriers, conversing in unfamiliar syntax, may be considerably easier in poetry, where various dictates of linearity are less powerful than in prose and narrative. Phyllis Webb's "Free Translations" in *Wilson's Bowl* (1980), makes a less deliberate approach to touch a remote language and culture. The strategy of the poem reflects the principle of freely translating—not word for word, or literal translation, but a creative interpretation of the spirit, the sensuousness, and emotion of an originating text, in Webb's case of the stories fused in the figure Raven. She recreates Raven in the language of another culture:

~

In the United States, if they hate you they tell you. It's a blatant hatred. In B.C., people are more diplomatic. If they hate you, they try not to let you know. I notice that a lot of so-called white people in B.C. are adopting Indian ways. A lot of people are turned on to our way of life here, more than whites to aboriginal cultures anywhere else in the world.

Leonard George, "A Strong Spirit Rising" in White, ed. *British Columbia* 29 hero, creator, muse, trickster.

Raven has blue eyes, like the waters of the
Queen Charlotte Islands on a good day.
He also carries a black magic umbrella.
This makes me want to sing. Caw caw.
Or cry. (56)

Through the weaving subtleties and ambiguities (a trope of Nordic purity? of the forever pending rain? a memory of Gene Kelly?), Webb even translates herself into Raven, poet and woman. When, in the sliding riffs of the poem, Raven sings Cole Porter, then thinks he's James Cagney, or plays a Chopin nocturne, Webb is choosing, and subverting, images from a *white* culture that convey the personality of the most powerful figure in Haida culture. Webb's subject is *waiting* for the ideal translation, a translation likely found not in "word," but in "eagle," animal and image; the poem talks, often colloquially, in order to translate. But then, Raven's great talent is to translate herself and himself freely from one figure to another; the parodic strategy, that is, is itself drawn from the culture it is presenting. Webb's free translation perhaps approaches most closely the spirit of Carr's dialogue with Indian Tom sawing driftwood.

Webb writes as if she has absorbed Raven's greedy motility. Unlike Carr or Don Berry, the poet subverts and invents—invents an English that has its own signature and poetics, rather than labouring to translate—although a trace of Wilson Duff's work is evidently there. Sheila Watson is a fine example: in her novel

Wyget Goes to Court

Fig. 6: Cartoon by Don Morel
Morel drew several cartoons in connection with
the Gitksan-Wet'suwet'en land claims case,
Supreme Court of British Columbia,
Smithers/Vancouver, 1987-88.
PRINTED WITH THE PERMISSION OF THE ARTIST

The Double Hook, as Bowering has shown, she not only uses Coyote as a presiding spirit, but *she*, as trickster-creator-author, becomes Coyote (1982 209-23).

The Double Hook has no central character—indeed no "character," in the conventional sense we would identify, say, in Dickens: in the remembered outlines and fragments of a story passed orally from generation to generation a small group of people searches for the essentials of its community. I am tempted to say that Watson has "gone Indian." But the phrase is misleading: we are considering not mere imitation of, nor losing oneself in an Aboriginal language and culture, but rather a creation of a personally powerful form and an English alert to the structures and images of another culture, which contains its own awareness of the limits of such immersion.

~

If Cole Porter and sacred songs seem to be straying a bit from the arbutus/madrone habitat, let me pause to recover the dynamic I have been proposing since I began. Webb's poem is not evidently or conventionally about a place or about a region. But it fits, in the sense that the Pacific Northwest exists in the translation of Raven and in the sense that place is a free translation. Raven is the emblem of the continuing necessity in Northwest writing to turn one language into another, one being into another. In Native cultures, place and ownership are more mobile and fluid concepts than in a non-Native system of individual title.

In non-Native British Columbia it is perfectly acceptable to name place after a person (e.g., Vancouver); . . . Among the Kwakwaka'wakw, however, such names sound ludicrous—as ludicrous as would a financial institution called Flo and Harry's bank to non-Native ears. Traditionally, Kwakwaka'wakw names were based on the following: (1) physical characteristics (e.g., "flat place" ['u' dzo'las]); (2) use (e.g., "winter place" [t'sa'wanxas] or "rocky place to tie up the canoe" [nuxda'ma], which includes both physical characteristics and use); and (3) historical events (e.g., "[Mink's] burial

place" ['wanamdas]). (Powell & Webster 8)

First Nations geography, if the Kwakwaka'wakw can be taken as representative, includes some concept of ownership—of communal ownership, in which particular tribes, or the constituent numayms (kinship groups), occupy more or less definable territories. But these migrated according to season, and whereas each group had its permanent winter villages, oolachan sites, for example, might be shared by several groups. Geography is mapped (although to say so is to reconfigure the concept of mapping) by gathering and processing, by potlatching and ceremonial dances, by a pattern of the "annual round" and seasonal use, rather than by property lines and husbandry. Webb's poem translates the interdependent round. Raven creates poem creates poet-Raven. Raven creates the people who create the stories which create Raven. Place creates community use which creates place.

His mind opened by study of the Haida people, and by devotion to Zen Buddhist meditation, Gary Snyder has become perhaps the most influential advocate of ecocentric thinking. When questioned about regional identity, he thinks first of Northwest coast art:

What is Northwest coast art? It's cedar, the most beautiful wood that grows naturally everywhere around here, carved. And what is carved? Ravens, salmon, beavers, sculpins—all the beings who live in Ish country. . . . The songs and the masks and the dances and the carvings made out of the prime material of the region are all a

perfect expression of what the region is. Now that's what
art does, when it's doing its job right. There's truly a spir-
itual exchange then between the physical ecology and the
mental ecology of the people. It's extraordinarily pro-
found. (O'Connell 321)

Perhaps spiritual exchange is what Raven transacts. That's what raven's saw-whetting and nutcracks speak. "Bound-aries are permeable, and the Raven is always crossing them, causing exchanges, making things happen" (Kane 119).

The Pacific Northwest is expressed in Raven. But the mainstream culture—urban, capitalist, mostly written in English—is so evidently and obviously removed from the culture of Raven. Hence, the con-tinuing need for transla-tion. From written to oral. From exploiter to exploited. Compounded by another enormous gap and chasm. From anthropocentric to ecocentric. That's where the Raven exchange is so powerful and vital. That's why David Wagoner honours Raven at the top of cedar: you're a better poet than I am—in your "dogbarks and whistles," and in your silences. Like Carr, on "land that belonged to nothing," Wagoner needs to talk

~

One thread of the tricky Raven story suggests that among the creatures (maybe including all those people who have arrived since James Cook . . .) only Raven has the capac-ity to pronounce the West Coast First Nations languages.

I heard Joni Mitchell interviewed by Peter Gzowski (CBC 29 December 1994), commenting on West Coast music. 'Sometimes,' she said—I am paraphrasing—'I go out in the daylight and tune my guitar, and write songs, to the sounds around me. On the West Coast, the bird songs at least, are not often melod-ic. Crows, eagles, hawks, ravens, gulls: the sounds are discordant, squawky. But the rhythms and sibi-lants—waves lapping, wind on cedars—are more regular.'

and be silent. Not to talk to Raven, but to think like Raven. "To write about a pine tree as a pine tree would want to be written about, from inside," says Snyder (in O'Connell 314). And Snyder again: "By opening up your mind to the point that it's empty enough that other things can walk into it, so that a rabbit can walk into your mind, so that trees or rocks can become part of your mind" (O'Connell 320).

David Wagoner studies magic and language. This conjunction perhaps makes it easier for him to transform across the unbridgeable gaps of cul-tural ignorance. In a terse and almost abstract poem entitled "Lost," he argues that a human is only lost "if what a tree or bush does is *lost* on you" (1976 182; my emphasis).

From inside a tree—if the forest becomes part of your mind—no *lost* exists: "The forest knows/where you are. You must let it find you" (182). Not surprisingly, it's Raven who shows the way across boundary:

No two trees are the same to Raven
No two branches are the same to Wren.

(Wagoner 182)

I suppose Raven speaks more often gratingly than mellifluously. Although Raven's cousin, and alter ego, Coyote presides in Jeannette Armstrong's *Slash* (1985), the novel might be said to translate Raven's most discordant saw-whetting, even retching. The novel takes the form of a political memoir, a young man's review of his own difficult awakening into his responsibility as Little Chief, obliged "'to be strong and straight for [his] people'" (*people* implying both the Okanagan nation to which Armstrong belongs, and all Aboriginal peoples in North America), and responsible "'to help them white men change'" (250). In many senses a *spare* and compacted novel, *Slash* might be found in many of the files here assembled: in its distress over industrial depletion of salmon stocks (213), in its orientation to winter dance time (208), in its homage to Sasquatch (34), a "superstition" as unsuperstitiously present in the hero's society as devils and angels in the white culture. It is also a more thoroughly border-crossing novel than most in this book: set in Denver and Seattle and on the "Trail of Broken Treaties" caravan to the Bureau of Indian Affairs in Washington, D.C., it touches on fishing rights at Puyallup (71) and demonstrations at Wounded Knee:

> He [*the president of the National Indian Brotherhood*] *said that Indians from Canada were no different and that there was really no border that was recognized by Indians. He said that we had the same objectives as U.S. Indians. I liked that.* (92)

Armstrong's novel journeys a long way from the aesthetic quest of Carr, and often the anger comes out, as it does from Slash, "in great gobs" (120). Humour and mysticism have scant place in this work, whose job of translation is to change—both the power of the Aboriginal people and the understanding of the white majority. Armstrong's strategy of translation is direct, so much so that her novel may sometimes seem more essay than narrative, more polemic than art. Yet, her translation has its own reciprocal effectiveness. In many respects this novel concerns language: it is about communicating in Okanagan—and in silences, and in ritual—and about pride that endures and grows even in people who "can't say the right English words" (86). Which seems to me exactly the point of what could be dismissed as an unsophisticated and unliterary novel. The absence of texture, of verbal nuance, of reflection, the crudely hastening narrative serve as a re-writing of the dilemma of oral culture meeting written. The limited vocabulary and plain syntax, that sometimes seem slightly patronizing in Hubert Evans, become literary strategy in Armstrong. Armstrong's writing takes the voice and effort of her community, and translates it with "yeah" and "them times," and "bullshit" (122 174 162).

She uses all manner of pro-forms, words that stand, usually indeterminately, for something specific and definite. Her writing has enough "blankness" in it that it always seems to be saying: so much lies beyond and outside *writing*; so much is unspoken:

> *It was there [in South Dakota] that I heard some pretty hairy stories of stuff going on. I saw from the reserves we visited that conditions were really bad with open prejudice by the whites everywhere. It seemed that dead or beat-up Indians didn't raise any questions by the police. A lot of drinking and fighting went on everywhere. (91)*

Armstrong's novel begins and ends with a poem. But in these sections, and in the more metaphorical passages, it is the unspoken, unsignified, that is important. So much is understood, so much community is implied in the static phrasing: pretty hairy, stuff, really bad, everywhere (twice), a lot of. Armstrong translates the impossibility of understanding through a prose that assumes an understanding.

~

If I were to give one book to a first-time visitor to Vancouver, or to choose one regional Northwest book to take as a gift to a host in Trier or Bologna or Seoul, I would choose *The Raven Steals the Light* (1984). No book, for me, quite bridges as well the ancient and the contemporary, the Aboriginal and colonial culture. No book quite so eloquently breathes the spirit of Raven, as the devious and experimenting and puckish and sometimes downright evil transformer who teaches us how to love change. And, in its combination of the art of Bill Reid, the stories of Raven, and the poetry of Robert Bringhurst, it proves that more than one art form can occupy the same place at the same time. Here is one way in which Reid and Bringhurst describe the speech of Raven:

> *And he was noisy. He had a cry that contained all the noises of a spoiled child and an angry raven—yet he could sometimes speak as softly as the wind in the hemlock boughs, with an echo of that beautiful other sound, like an organic bell, which is also part of every raven's speech. (15)*

A reader can't be quite sure who wrote this: one of the ways in which the book is so right is that you are always tricked into wondering whether you are hearing storyteller Henry Young of Skidegate, or Reid, or Bringhurst, or perhaps Franz Boas or a Haida mythteller 2000 years ago. Such synthesis, and such confusion of source and translation, inhere in the figure of Raven. This file places Raven between, or better flying across, a rain forest and post-industrial city. His voice is oxymoronic, at once natural, organic, and manufactured, as is the bell.

~

I think of this wind-and-tree voice especially in connection with the book which among contemporary First Nations writing speaks most thoroughly in Raven's gentler, perhaps Raven's female voice. The title of Lee Maracle's narrative of a Salish woman looking to find and heal a community is *Ravensong* (1993), a signal that, as important as story is, it might be permitted to resolve itself not in neat cause and effect, but in the poetry of camas root, or the courage of returning salmon, or the *other* sound of Raven. This is a book about learning to translate. Stacey, in her youth, or looking back to her youth, senses that "connectedness" (17) is so inevitable in her world, and in her Salish language, that she cannot imagine how to translate its absence in white culture. Listening to the nearly ninety-year-old Ella, Stacey thinks of the gap in languages: "The word rain [in Salish] images woman-earth, the tears of birth and endless care-giving. In English, rain is just water collected on dustballs too heavy to remain floating in the atmosphere" (21). The gap lies between the infinite relationship of family through time, or better beyond time, and the material rationalism of science, enlightenment style.

Raven, who loves to mix things up, teaches Stacey out of, or into, this gap. Maracle introduces her characters, in the first paragraph of Chapter 1, in this order: Raven, Cedar, Cloud, and then "a small girl" (9). And, as if "there were no periods in her language, just pauses" (20), Maracle has raven and cedar and cloud (and rain) and Stacey

speak and think to and through each other until sometimes the voices seem to sing in chorus indistinguishably. Raven's capacity to restore deep thinking (23) and "to shape the future of their homeland" (43) becomes Stacey's mission, expressed as the obligation of translation:

She would go forth, collect the magic words of white town and bring them home. She would try to bring them home in a way that would revitalize her flagging community. This was enough for earth and Raven. (192)

Maracle does what Stacey must do. She will take her stories, told and recreated for untold generations in the language of her village, and put them on paper in another language. It's a transformation at once impossible and inescapable, a challenge to write where there should be no writing at all:

From the depths of the sound Raven sang a deep wind song, melancholy green. Above, the water layered itself in stacks of still green, dark to light. The sound of Raven spiralled out from its small beginning in larger and larger concentric circles. . . . The song echoed the rolling motion of earth's centre. . . . Wind changed direction, blowing the song toward cedar. Cedar picked up the tune, repeated the refrain, each lacey branch bending to echo ravensong. (9)

≈

Rain File

'When frog speaks, he knows I am
not a frog; that doesn't bother him
               doesn't bother me
We talk anyway.
The love of rain is enough for us.

                   ~Robert Sund *Shack Medicine*

*A*fterwards the sky blackened and snow fell, and from that time until spring the rain never totally stopped and the light never entirely started.

                   ~H.L. Davis *Honey in the Horn*

On the mainland, a rain was falling. The famous Seattle rain. The thin, gray rain that toadstools love. The persistent rain that knows every hidden entrance into collar and shopping bag. The quiet rain that can rust a tin roof making a sound in protest. The shamanic rain that feeds the imagination. The rain that seems actually a secret language, whispering, like the ecstasy of primitives, of the essence of things.

The rain enveloped the house—the house that King Max had come to call Fort Blackberry—like a hair spray for jellyfish.

                ~Tom Robbins *Still Life with Woodpecker*

*Y*ou really should pay me a visit, Kade. There are some exciting options here, activitywise. You can stand in the trees. You can stand in the rain. You can watch the trees stand in the rain. You can watch it rain on the trees. And with two of us (true mathematical fact!) it'll be twice as great . . .

                ~David James Duncan *The Brothers K*

TO WRITE IN THE NORTHWEST IS TO WRITE about rain: to make a joke of it, to find something in it that will make you feel superior, to hide it in poetry, to assert plainly its positive effects. Naturalists tell us that Seattle's normal total annual precipitation is 38.60 inches. According to Arthur Kruckeberg's *The Natural History of Puget Sound County*, "over 75 per cent of it falls between the beginning of October and the end of March. Snowfall in the lowlands is not more than 5 per cent of total precipitation" (39). Mean annual rainfall at the Vancouver International Airport is 1055.4 mm (41.55 inches). The typical, delightfully redundant, winter weather forecast is "showers, followed by periods of rain." The editors of *Vancouver and Its Region* remind us, however, of the variability of the invariable:

> The Coast Mountains of the Vancouver region also receive heavy orographic rain. Indeed, the increase of precipitation with elevation on these slopes is one of the most remarkable aspects of the local climate. Total annual precipitation increases from 900 millimetres at sea level in Delta to about 3,500 millimetres at 1,200 metres above sea level on the North Shore slopes . . . and an estimated 5,000 millimetres at 1,700 meters above sea level at The Lions. (Oke 24-5)

In an essay titled "River Road," Kim Stafford remembers Charlie Camp, of Mapleton, Oregon, explaining the annual precipitation to two dumbfounded California tourists: "'Ladies, you see that elderberry bush down there by the barn? That's eight foot tall. If we took our year's fall of rain in a day, that bush would be under the flood'" (1986 150). Charlie's numbers may be meteorologically accurate (parenthetically, Stafford marvels that the "west slick of the Olympic Peninsula" gets twenty feet), but it's his *story* that counts: reading annual rainfall as a one-day rain makes rain forest climate manageable.

One of my favourite big rains, drenched in such tall-tale dramatics, falls early in H.L. Davis's *Honey in the Horn:*

> Even to a country accustomed to rain, that was a storm worth gawking at. It cracked shingles in the roof, loaded the full-fruited old apple-trees until they threatened to split apart, and beat the roads under water belly-deep to

~

If I were a painter, I would put the map of the Island on canvas, an ecology of color and arrested motion, the units separate but flowing together in a kind of rhythm. . . .

By October, the trunks of the madroña are almost through with their exfoliation and the tender new green that showed in patches all through late August has turned to a pinkish cinnamon tone. All through the winter, the satin-smooth boughs will keep a rich red that contrasts strikingly with the shining green of the long leaves. The madroña is an untidy tree, dropping its old dry leaves in fits and starts instead of all at once, as deciduous trees do, but it is a great reliever of gloom in the winter woods among the conifers.

Hazel Heckman
Island in the Sound 278-79

a horse. Ten-foot walls of spray went marching back and forth across the hay-meadow as if they owned it, flocks of wild ducks came squalling down to roost in the open pasture till the air cleared, and the river boiled yellow foam over the toll bridge and stumps, fence rails, pieces of old houses, and carcasses of drowned calves and horses against it. (12-13)

Such a storm is the more absurdly ordinary because Uncle Preston, busy on his "history of the early statutes of Oregon," will barely lift his head from his work to pay the "fierce flood" a moment's attention. Even the crack and boil and march of an exceptional storm is tempered toward the customary: it may be worth gawking at, but the local does not so much as glance. Maybe Uncle Preston's failure to react explains why Rain File is the smallest among these collectings. In the Pacific Northwest, you're supposed to learn not to notice the rain. Artists go out and paint in it (PLATE 2). Everybody talks about it, but nobody pays attention.

Parables of plenty outweigh the flood stories: "Charlie told me you know you're in Oregon when you can stand on the porch and grab a salmon fighting its way up through the thick tumble of rain" (Stafford 1986 150). In this Northwest troubador's mind, the tall tale mutates into a folk song. Write as rain. Northwesterners are singing in the rain.

~

The Okanagan-Colville peoples developed rituals to stop the rain. They would throw the berries of the Oregon grape into the air. Or "the bottom ends of ponderosa pine cones were set on fire and the smouldering cones thrown into the air in the direction of rain clouds to make rain stop."

Nancy Turner et al. 1980 87 34

Stafford's collective noun for rain is "glory": "Rain, a glory of rain made the river the natural ribbon that bound everything up like a purse-seine slung across the hills" (1986 149).

The glory of Northwest rain begins in play. In Earl W. Emerson's *The Rainy City*, rush hour traffic in the rain seems to be happily "splashing" (109). Still more playfully, Tom Robbins compares the rains to a "blizzard of guppies that would pelt the creaky old house until spring" (1980 203). But as David James Duncan presents it in *The River Why*, rain is also the great and, ultimately, benign, shape-shifter: "it was a rain that soothed and softened everything it touched as the river rose, taking back into its glassy Indian-summer eye the cat-eye greens it had lent to the leaves for a summer; it was a rain that hummed on the river pools and pattered on new puddles, washing the songbirds south, but bringing newcomers from the north—rain birds, water lovers." Duncan fills this passage with whispering sibilants. A rhetoric of reassurance changes song birds into rain birds, turns skeptical readers into water lovers: "Reckoning up these transformations, watching the rain that began the day I sat at the source, I realized I *had* been given a spirit-helper: I had been given this rain" (1983 252). Less reverently Duncan touches the same theme in *The Brothers K*, when Chief Yulie consoles

Everett about the rainy season: the weather doesn't "'get [] better,'" but "'your ability to see'" does. Endless rain enables some extra-visual knowing: "'Maybe [of] something in this world, maybe something in the spirit world. You'll know when you see it'" (1992 445).

The glory inhering in rain-words is the rhetoric of transcendence. In Kesey's *Sometimes a Great Notion*, the rain is a "dreamy smear" (356); Philip Teece's story "Puqmis" remembers west coast rain as "the warm, quiet curtain of isolation . . . which . . . embraced him" (1). Curtain and smear: the words incline to a permanent ambience, a presence rather than an event. "[T]he rain falls horizontally here," notes Sallie Tisdale, "sideways to the ground" (134). Horizontal rain could be said to be travelling. Such rain, for Ken Kesey as for Duncan, does not drum—it "hums" (13). We know there are words in this cosmic sound: we just cannot quite make them out. We don't remember the lyrics, but we can mimic the tune.

Glory of rain implies light. In Northwest writing, rain is light and light is rain. As the title of Ives's anthology of poetry links them: *Rain in the Forest, Light in the Trees*. Ivan Doig brings this aura and presence together:

Not winters of white steel but the coastal ones of pewter-

grey, soft-toned, workable, with the uninsistent Northwest rain simply there in the air like molecules made visible, are the necessary steady spans for me to seek the words. (103)

Doig's visible rain is a form of writing. Write as rain. The rain literally graphs the *óros*, writes the mountains. It has its own voices.

Obviously, its movement, at the mouth of the Fraser or the Columbia, repeatedly reconfigures the visible landscape. It governs what grows, how fast, and what and how humans build to stay dry. Writers are always asking themselves, in the midst of this writing/speaking climate, how to write rain. Their most frequent answer seems to lie in the notion of the uninsistent. The central challenge Northwest writers set themselves is to develop the trope of suspension. Stafford's *glory* of rain conveys no motion or violence or disruption of sunlight activity. I would guess that in a word-association test the most frequent response to the word "rain" would be "fall." Northwest writers invent ways to write the *unfalling*. "Rain doesn't fall inside this forest," marvels Timothy Egan, "it blends with the moss and then floats downward in webs of tinted moisture" (33). "The rain does not fall here," agrees David Wagoner in the poem "Waiting in a Rain Forest,"

~

This morning I drove through a steady drizzle in the valley, a form of precipitation so routine in the sodden Northwest winters that it is inconsequentially called "dry rain." It occasions neither comment nor umbrella.

Ted Leeson
The Habit of Rivers 31

it stands in the air around you

Always, drifting from time to time like breath.

(1976 259)

"[T]his drifting, silky rain" Sallie Tisdale marvels; like Wagoner, she makes rain as invisible and unconsciously essential as oxygen, "that never stops but only takes a breath now and again before it lets a sigh of moisture go" (24). Written in tropes of suspension, rain is the atmosphere itself, a quality of life, a surround: it "wipes over the land instead of falling" (Kesey 356), diffusing the world into "a picture painted by the Pointillists only done with lines instead of spots" (Thomas 22).

If "the art of a region begins to come mature when it is no longer what we think it should be," then the Northwest has not quite made it. Rain, as in this File, is repetitive, redundant, unremarkable. But Northwest writers know they should be writing it, if they are writing their region. And rain is just what readers in Wichita, Hamburg, or Corvallis, and editors in New York, would expect. I would not disagree with Kittredge (176), but I would also want to put in a claim for texturing and linkage, for the pushing of the climate cliché that writes a complex balance of rain, and temperate rain forest (said to contain the greatest density of living matter on the planet), a gas to breathe, a filter through which to see, and an Aboriginal vision time. And I would argue for the regional maturity that can cite and disrupt all these with mildewed humour:

Actually the rain has many uses. It prevents the blood and the sea from becoming too salty. It administers knockout drops to unruly violets. It manufactures the ladder that neon climbs to the moon. A seeker can go into the Great Northwest rain and bring back the Name he needs. (Robbins 1980 71)

Maybe the ravin' rain is the raven rain.

~

Kuroshio File

What is the point of the Pacific?
Somebody must be making
a statement of some kind:
in code, say,
or just many times too grand
for poor little us to read,
not being programmed, simple souls.

Anyway,
why on earth
should it be so bloody big?
And blue? It's as blue as billy-oh,
wrinkled but somehow juvescent.

~Chris Wallace-Crabbe "Ocean"

The Strait of Juan de Fuca . . . passed between the Olympic
Peninsula and Vancouver Island, the route to and from the ports of
Vancouver and Seattle. The conduit between them and the Orient
was the Japan Current—Kuroshio, the Gulf Stream of the Pacific,
carrier of fish and seed and craft: "dark blue salt," it was called,
"black current," "black stream."

~John Keeble *Yellowfish*

The Chink had been asked if he supported the American war
effort. "Hell, no!" he replied. "Ha ha ho ho and hee hee." He
waited for the logical next question, did he support the Japanese
war effort, to which he would have given the same negative
response. He was still waiting when the military police shoved him
on the train to Tule Lake.

~Tom Robbins "The Chink and the Clock People"

WASHINGTON—Acting to redress what many Americans now regard as a historic injustice, the Senate today voted overwhelmingly to give $20,000 and an apology to each of the Japanese-Americans who were driven from their homes and sent to internment camps in World War II.

The vote was 69 to 27 and followed an emotional debate. The bill's principal advocate, Senator Spark M. Matsunaga, a Japanese-American from Hawaii, almost wept as, recalling the suffering of internees, he related the story of an elderly man who crossed a fence to retrieve a ball for his grandchild and was machine-gunned to death.

The intensity of the debate, and Mr. Matsunaga's sorrow, seemed to symbolize the agony of conscience the nation has undergone over the internment issue—and the impossibility, despite the best intentions, of making more than a token apology now.

~The New York Times 21 April 1988

OTTAWA—Saying Canada must "put things right," Prime Minister Brian Mulroney today apologized and announced a compensation package that will total almost $300 million for the surviving 12,000 Japanese-Canadians interned during the Second World War.

The financial package will include a $21,000 payment to each of the surviving internees, of whom about 6,000 live in BC.

"All Canadians know apologies are inadequate," Mulroney said.

But apologies are "the only way we can cleanse the past, so that we may as best we can and in good conscience, face the future."

"We cannot change the past but we must as a nation have the courage to face up to these historical facts."

Mulroney also vowed Canada will never again do to any minority what it did when it wrongfully interned almost 22,000 Japanese-Canadians after Japan entered the war in 1941.

~Vancouver Sun 22 September 1988

FROM EARLY IN ITS POST-CONTACT HISTORY (and perhaps in the most ancient reaches of its human history), Pacific Northwest culture has been a trans-Pacific culture. Consider that in 1880, 16,004 Chinese were recorded in the US Northwest, more than double the number of Germans, Irish, or English, the next largest ethnic groups. Seattle's Japanese population grew from 125 to 6,127 between 1890 and 1910 (Schwantes 187-88). Along with multiple configurations of Asian cultures in many languages went an equally durable feature of Northwest society, anti-Asian bigotry of many shades, from the anti-Japanese riot of 1907 in Vancouver to Oregon's Alien Property Act (1923), which prohibited Japanese from owning and leasing land (Schwantes 126 298). During and immediately after World War II, the cultural stereotypes were at their most simplistic and vicious. As Paul Fussell points out, the organized killing of World War II demanded that the enemy be dehumanized; the "Japs" became animals, usually feral: "'They hide up in the trees like wildcats. . . . They take to the jungle as if they had been bred there, and like some beasts you never see them until they are dead'" (116-17). Always alert for cultural clichés, especially in his Northwest home territory, Tom Robbins punctures the racist assumptions, both overt and implicit, by inventing "the Chink," the omnibus Asian American. Robbins explodes all the dismissive epithets by collapsing two cultural stereotypes into one: "As are many of the best and worst contributions to the human race, the Chink is Japanese. With their flair for inventive imitation, the Japanese made the Chink" (1986 320).

Robbins's bemusement at cultural generalizations should set me on guard. And were it not for three decades of expository habit, I might try to avoid the pitfalls of oversimplification by writing in burlesque. I can, however,

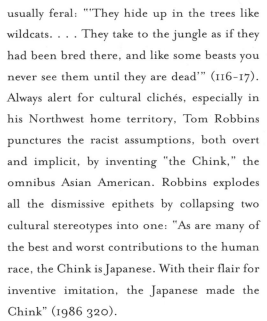

stop to listen carefully to another voice, to recognize (again) a polyphony of Northwest regions. The place is a story of trans-Pacific negotiation happening many times. We have heard the story of the strawberry fields of San Piedro in Guterson's *Snow Falling on Cedars*, and of the rivers of traffic connecting San Francisco to Vancouver in Keeble's *Yellowfish*, of the mysteries of the catch in Marlatt's *Steveston*. And we have not talked of the negotiation with East Indian, with Malaysian, with Filipino, with Vietnamese cultures that might be added. The place is also a story of the Northwest Passage, of an undiscovered, and then impossibly unnavigable, sea route from Europe to Asia, a story that has no place for the place we now call the Pacific Northwest. In *Yellowfish*, Erks thinks of himself travelling an "isthmus," a contemporary version of "the strait of Anian, the trade route to China" (164-65).

When I introduced H.L. Davis's Clay in the "Island File," he stood at the end of the land, thoughts reaching toward the next human community to the west. Going West, he finds East: the Northwest Passage in mind. History roots the trope as well, both in the anthropologists' speculation that the First Peoples migrated across a land bridge linking Asia and North America, and in the humble and curious legend of the voyage of Hwui Shan and a party of Buddhist monks in the fifth century CE. The idea of an Asian connection often appears closely interconnected to ethnopoetics and ecotopia. As Kenneth Rexroth points out, Gary Snyder was a leader in urging "an ecological aesthetic, a blending of American Indian and Far Eastern philosophies of cooperation with, rather than conquest of, nature" (273). Moreover, where form is concerned, Rexroth observes a suggestive resemblance between the patterns of gaps in Native songs (as translated)—and the ideographic method.

Japanese literary forms carry both seed and craft: the extreme conciseness of the *haiku* and *utanikki* as they appear in the work of Fred Wah, the nonsensical riddling of the *koan* in Phyllis Webb, and the meditative tautology in the poems of Robert Bringhurst: "[w]e were keenly suspicious of the dominant immigrant strain [European]," Bringhurst writes: "Asia looked like a promising moral and intellectual counterweight" (1989 189). In the visual arts, the formal connections are more overt: the popularity of landscape prints by Takao Tanabe, Peter and Traudl Markgraf, Rachel Gourlay, and especially Toni Onley, who is inspired by Zen Buddhism, show the raincoast appropriateness of blurred outlines and thin washes bleeding into one another

~

That the arbutus is common from Vancouver Island through to California—as Andrew Scott reminds us, among the longest north-south ranges of any North American tree—emphasizes the Mediterranean element (the tree seems to exude sun, even in the greyest drizzle) of the region. But Archibald Menzies refers to arbutus as the Oriental Strawberry Tree, thus linking the tree verbally to its frequent aesthetic trans-Pacificness as a bent and twisting overgrown bonsai.

(PLATE 2). In the most familiar iconography, the shapes recede vaguely in the mist:

Many who live in the Northwest may not know Picasso from Andy Warhol, but are learned in the nuances of color and texture in nature: the color of pebbles, mustard green kelp, pine cones, and fir branches, silvered dead trees, plumed ferns, sea moss, scallop shells, gulls' wings—all these tones of white, gray, green, and brown. (Griffith 58)

One of the Northwest's most important abstractionists, Mark Tobey, studied Chinese calligraphy in order to discover a different brush stroke and visual texture. Morris Graves extended Tobey's evocative "white writing" toward Dada and Zen Buddhism (PLATE 5, 8). Tobey, not entirely incidentally, travelled to Victoria in 1928 where he ran classes in Emily Carr's school and contributed his influence to her shift from representational to more abstract forms (Shadbolt 62-64).

Recklessly blurring Japanese and Chinese, Robbins apparently can use the racist slur "Chink" with such insouciance because the attendant pun is so attractive. Any *chink*, he suggests, also provides an opening, a place of vulnerability, an unintended space in a myth and barrier of impenetrable homology. In the cracks and through the fissures, alternate regional icons appear: not cedar canoe but Dragon Boat, not arbutus but bamboo. Between the literary models of extractive entrepreneurial romance and salmon migration narrative, intrude the grand gestures of Cantonese operas, the literary framework for SKY Lee's *Disappearing Moon Cafe* (1990). Region itself seems to exist not in territory or geography, but in community and social interaction. Through an armour of smugness, we glimpse the very absurdity of reductive generalizations, be they regional or cultural, Pacific Northwest or Japanese Canadian. In the gaps, a comic questioner chortles "Ha ha ho ho and hee hee" (1986 321). Robbins's version of an Asian language is laughter.

The Pacific Northwest shares, collectively, the experience of the Nisei, born in North America, preferring English, and then coming to seek the meaning and personal significance of a Japanese connection—knowledge, that is, gained largely at second hand, through books and hearsay, rather than from direct experience (even where the parents are Issei). Momoko Iko's play *The Gold Watch* (1971) presents many versions of this pattern as the thirteen-year-old son Tadao dreams of returning to Japan and taking up the Imperial Way, a possibility strongly rejected by his father:

TADAO: *You think you know so much Papa. You think I don't see anything. You think because you don't talk about things. ... You think because I can't read the Japanese papers. ... I can read* (He's ready to cry

but can't stand the thought.) *the Herald ... and those signs in town ... and I can hear what they say. ... If they hate us so much, why don't we go back to Japan.* (111; author's ellipses)

This need to study, to negotiate some understanding with another culture, is almost as strong across the Pacific as it is toward the Haida, Salish, and Lushootseed. And in the late 1980s, responding to an increase in immigration from Hong Kong and Taiwan, and the geographical displacement (in Eurocentric view) to a Pacific marketplace, the Northwest culture launched on a new pop ethnography to understand the new-old neighbours in its midst, as in glossy magazine articles on *feng shui*.

In May 1999, Vancouver celebrated Asian Heritage Month, in part to mark the fiftieth anniversary of universal enfranchisement: federal and provincial elections in 1949 were the first in which "all Chinese, Japanese, South Asian and Aboriginal Canadians could vote." The brochure describing the program runs to thirty-two pages: it alone should be sufficient warning against the disposition to enclose in the term Asian American some pan-Asian identity, a disposition I am only beginning to unlearn. One way of doing so is to give the title "Kuroshio File" to this portion of the book, rather than highlighting the more reductionist terms trans-Pacific or Pacific Rim. An ocean *current*, with its more unpredictable predictability, might better imply that Vietnamese Canadians and Korean Canadians, not to mention Seattle's Japanese Americans and Steveston's Japanese Canadians, belie some homogeneous identity. Kuroshio, also known as the Japan Current, translates roughly as "Black Stream" (*Kodansha* 318); it originates east of the Philippines, and flows north past Taiwan, into the East China Sea, and northeastward past Japan's Pacific Coast (*Rand McNally* 162). A narrow current, flowing at "speeds of more than 93 miles a day," it eventually flows east as part of the great North Pacific Gyre. (Kuroshio's northward flow—it splits near the Columbia into the south-flowing California and north-flowing Aleutian current—pushes the Columbia delta's sands, now much diminished because of dams, to compose Washington's Long Beach.) This huge churning, affecting climate, vegetation, ocean nutrients, fish population, and beachcombing can stand for the gyrations of cultural mingling and the richness of upwellings.

I take Kuroshio, with John Keeble, as a dynamic metaphor for "the creative synthesis

~

I think the early Chinese pioneers actually started "going bananas" from the moment they first settled upon the West Coast. They had no choice. They adapted. They initiated assimilation. If they had not, they and their family would have starved to death. I might even suggest that all surviving Chinatown citizens eventually became bananas. Only some, of course, were more ripe than others.

That's why I'm proudly a banana: I accept the paradox of being both Chinese and not Chinese.

Now at last, whenever I look in the mirror or hear ghost voices shouting, "You still Chinese!" I smile.

I know another truth: In immigrant North America, we are all Chinese.

Wayson Choy,
"I'm A Banana and Proud of it"
The Globe and Mail
18 July 1997 A20

out of two or more traditions. . . . It i[n] reflecting from within two or more cul tures. . . . . This imperfect immersion does not matter too much: what matters is the illuminating character or otherwise of what emerges" (Smart x).

Asian ancestors and ancestry blossom as the most visible—after the Native peoples—un-British other in British Columbia. In the chinks of the dominant culture in the American Northwest appear versions of Robbins's "Chink." This background or foreground may explain why teaching Joy Kogawa's novel *Obasan* (1981) has been unlike any other experience I have had in teaching Canadian literature. Many novels and poems document social injustice, and ignite political analysis, even anger. But *Obasan* elicits a reaction closer to bewilderment and amazement: poverty and corruption concern my students, but behind their concern lies often a slightly weary sense that "we've always known about that." *Obasan* reveals legislated racism, a historical and political fact that, especially for

uver, seems staggering news.
ing I do am I so aware of how
unquestioned is the assump-
n tolerance and generosity.
dresses this assumption when
Aunt Emily tutors the young Naomi about the
obvious contrast in the way the United States
handles the "evacuation" of Japanese-
Americans:

> *"I hate to admit it," she said, "but for all we hear
> about the States, Canada's capacity for racism seems
> even worse."*
>
> *"Worse?"*
>
> *"The American Japanese were interned as we were
> in Canada, and sent off to concentration camps, but
> their property wasn't liquidated as ours was. And look
> how quickly the communities reestablished themselves
> in Los Angeles and San Francisco. We weren't allowed
> to return to the West Coast like that. We've never
> recovered from the dispersal policy. But of course that
> was the government's whole idea—to make sure we'd
> never be visible again. Official racism was blatant in
> Canada. The Americans have a Bill of Rights, right?
> We don't." (33-34)*

Nothing upsets Canadians more than to
be told they are more racist than Americans.
I suspect that the reaction of my students,
multiplied in university and high school
classes across Canada, significantly accelerat-
ed the redress movement. (The novel has
been a standard of Canadian literature courses and at my own university, of first-year
introductory courses since 1983.) As if rec-

ognizing the importance of the novel, Ed
Broadbent, then leader of the New
Democratic Party, read from *Obasan* as he wel-
comed passage of redress legislation in the
House of Commons (22 September 1988).

Robbins's Japanese Chink is a laughing,
self-aware, self-confident representative of a
Northwest community, whose story is most
often the story of victimization and guilt. But
it is wise to remember that not all Asian
American history is the story of invisible
acquiescence. Resistance to the evacuation
orders came in the courts, the most influential case being that of Mitsuye Endo, who peti-
tioned for a writ of habeas corpus in July
1942, and eventually won her case in the US
Supreme Court, although not until December
1944, when the war was nearing its end
(Kitano 39-40). The figure of the defiant
no-no boy expresses resistance most overtly.

John Okada's *No-No Boy* (1957), published a generation before *Obasan*, did not have
the immediate impact of the Canadian novel,
although *A Literary History of the American West*,
articulating the current received view,
describes it as "powerful, uncompromising,"
and "[p]erhaps the finest single novel by a
Japanese-American" (Chan 1128). When it
was reissued in 1976, this account of a
Japanese American man who refused military
service and attempted to reintegrate into the
life of Seattle, promised the same influence
on readers' attitudes as *Obasan*. In his
Introduction, Lawson Fusao Inada wrote that

"[w]hoever reads this book will never be the same. Whoever reads this book will see, and be, with greater strength and clarity" (iv). As the newspaper clippings included in this File's epigraphs show, recent politics have to some extent affirmed Aunt Emily's differentiation of national policies: the United States completed its redress settlement with citizens of Japanese ancestry significantly ahead of Canada (and, thus, prompted the Canadian settlement?).

Two novels set in the two largest cities of the Northwest, 200 kilometres apart, tell the story of the Japanese North American community's coming to terms with its own dispersal following the bombing of Pearl Harbor, 7 December 1941. A map of the "exclusion zone" in the two countries would provide one uncomfortably ironic imaging of the limits of the Pacific Northwest. This place is an exclusion zone. Let me compare the two books by reflecting on their storying of place, and on the motif and formal strategies of silence in communities where forgetting is the strongest temptation—probably the force is stronger than the word "temptation" implies: "The walls had closed in and were crushing all the unspoken words back down into his stomach" (Okada 3). As in Raven File, we will discover a sense in which the region is written, paradoxically, as a squawk, as a choking on unspoken words, as well as of silence as a positive value.

Lost mothers dominate the child worlds in both novels: in *Obasan* the primary perspective belongs to a female child, although Naomi is framed and formed by her own adult-self remembering; *No-No Boy* is narrated from the perspective of a male arrested in adolescence, no longer a child but still looking for his independent adulthood. In Okada's novel, Ichiro Yamada must escape from a mother

Fig. 7: *Men play softball at Minedoka [Idaho], a Japanese Internment camp that was hot and dusty in summer and very cold in winter (1943)*
COURTESY THE OREGON HISTORICAL SOCIETY

driven mad by the conviction that Japan could never be defeated. In *Obasan*, Naomi Nakane must find the mother who disappeared in the conflagration of Nagasaki.

Okada presents the immediate aftermath of the internment as a male quest, almost an urban on-the-road novel, its aimless series of incidents mirroring Ichiro's frenetic lassitude (Rigal-Cellard 99-100). Kogawa imagines the continuing adjustment to the internment (twenty-seven years after the war) through what we might read as a woman's journal, incorporating a montage of documents and pseudo-documents, of differing styles, which serves to bear witness to the experiences of the Canadian Issei.

Each novel is the first in its own national literature to treat the consequences of the internment. *No-No Boy* jumps tensely from one encounter to another, following a chronological line, with occasional flashbacks: its fictional present is concentrated into a few months in 1947 and 1948. *Obasan* is more of a poet's novel, its metaphors of knitting and nets (20-21) an implicit guide to Kogawa's concern to make connections, to hear echoes, to trace patterns of community rather than primarily to tell story. These differences assert themselves, almost startlingly, even as the lesser similarities emerge: the narrative importance of the letter in both novels, the occasional overlapping images—of stone, of tree. Amidst the interplay of similarities and differences, the novels' multiple evocations of silence organize ironic resonance.

Contexts of silence surround the novels. Prominent among them is the observation, mentioned on the cover blurb of the University of Washington reprint of *No-No Boy*, and repeated in some form in most commen-

tary on the novel, that Okada's novel was ignored, especially by the community which forms its subject. Okada's title, with its double negative and implicit racist appellation, suggests a universal and repeated denial. The Japanese North American community countered the supposed shame of the internment by refusing to speak of it: "The horror would die sooner, they felt, if they refused to speak" (Kogawa 236). Bewildered silence fronts an inability to understand such monolithic rejection, but uneasy silence worries that a more active, articulate resistance was demanded of the community (Kim 237).

Kogawa and Okada, writing of their protagonists' relationships with their mothers, provide the details of their silences:

Silent mother, you do not speak or write. You do not reach through the night to enter morning, but remain in the voicelessness. From the extremity of much dying, the only sound that reaches me now is the sigh of your remembered breath, a wordless word. How shall I attend that speech, Mother, how shall I trace that wave?

You are tide rushing moonward pulling back from the shore. A raft rocks on the surface bobbing in the dark. The water fills with flailing arms that beckon like seaweed on the prow. I sit on the raft begging for a tide to land me safely on the sand but you draw me to the white distance, skyward and away from this blood-drugged earth. (241)

How is one to talk to a woman, a mother who is also a stranger because the son does not know who or what she is? Tell me, Mother, who are you? What is it to be a

Japanese? There must have been a time when you were a little girl. You never told me about those things. Tell me now so that I can begin to under-stand. Tell me about the house in which you lived and of your father and mother, who were my grandparents, whom I have never seen or known because I do not remember you ever speaking of them except to say that they died a long time ago. Tell me everything and just a little bit more until their lives and yours and mine are fitted together, for they surely must be. There is time now while there are no customers and you and I are all alone. Begin from the beginning when your hair was straight and black and everyone was Japanese because that was where you were born and America was not yet a country beyond the ocean where fortunes were to be made or an enemy to hate. Quick, now, quick, Mother, what was the name of your favorite school teacher? (104-5)

~

Dear Mom,

Mr. Lam is not a bad man. He lets me work in his pickle factory when it's raining outside. Japanese women and girls my age work there too. They pick out big and small sizes and put them in bar-rels. My job is to take away the big and old ones with a cart. They are polite people and nice. Mr. Wong taught me to say good morning and thank you to them *o-hi-o* and *ah-le-ga-tor*. I like to talk Japanese because it is not hard to know. I don't think Mr. Wong knows much because often he talks Chinook to them. He gets mad when they talk too much. He says *hy-iu-wau wau* and *halo skookum* when they want him to lift heavy things. That means "enough talk" and "not strong."

Sing Lim *West Coast Chinese Boy* 37

interior monologue directs the reader to the fundamental silence of an often too noisy mother.

Interior monologue structures *No-No Boy* and animates its alienation. Chapter Five (the source of the passage here) begins typically with the briefest setting of the dramatic scene, followed by a page of dialogue between Ichiro and his mother. This dia-logue records talk, but absence of communica-tion. Ichiro responds to a mother's questions—"Where have you been?"—curtly, monosyllabically, grudg-ingly. He doesn't dare reveal how deeply he hates his mother's obsession with true Japaneseness. A rather awkward authorial descrip-tion of Ichiro's emotions follows. Turning on two questions about the past which fill Ichiro's mind, the chapter shifts, as almost all Okada's chapters do, into present-tense interior monologue. Some interior monologue approaches stream-of-consciousness, draws on intense sensory perceptions, and suggests the fleeting clutter of varied mental images. But Okada stays close to the speech register—his interior monologues represent the words

The passage from *Obasan* makes direct reference to the literal silence of Naomi's disappeared mother. Kogawa mentions silence on almost every page of the novel, as she plays variations on the theme that opens her lyrical "preface": "There is a silence that cannot speak" (ii). Although the passage from *No-No Boy* makes no direct use of the word "silence," Okada's use of which want and need to be spoken, but which halt and choke on themselves. Many of the sentences in this passage could, in another context, be evidence of urgent pleading: "You never told me about these things. Tell me now so that I can begin to understand." The poignancy, and the intensity, of the interior monologue rests in the readers' knowledge that these speeches are *potential* only. Ichiro *cannot* converse with his mother: the reiterated imperative "tell me" is futile—there will be no telling.

Other phases of the monologue, less akin to the conventions of recorded quotation, reinforce the sense of cultural aphasia. The opening sentence depersonalizes the thinker to "one," and, in an apparent echo of the use of kin terms in Japanese speech, imagines Ichiro only in his role as "son" (Suzuki 89-90 102-109). Revealing the mind's voice to the reader is a fictional device to convey extremity—psychological or emotional stress. Okada handles this dimension delicately by juxtaposing phrases which could come from direct speech, with a more strained discourse: "my grandparents, whom I have never seen or known because I do not remember your ever speaking of them." Such grammatical correctness ("whom," "your") signals a more writerly, less vernacular discourse—a sign of a mind agonizing with the formalities of relationships. Elsewhere, the author is less concerned to correct grammatical oddities ("a little bit

and a little bit," "because that was where," or the overused connector "and"). Thoughts break out, pile up, and are much too frenzied—too vague and unverbal—to be refined into grammatical precision.

Further, unspoken discourse is removed to the conditional. The words "cr[y] to be spoken" (105), but not even a possibility exists: "*If he had been *about* to say something.*" (105; my emphasis). Words are, of course, silent on the page. In the imagined world built by the fiction, they are hoped for, but also silenced in the mind. The urgent final question of this passage seeks for specific detail—significantly, Ichiro needs a person's name, and a sense of a teacherly relationship. His mind reaches continually toward the discrete personality latent in the individualizing detail. Ichiro's world can only offer him the type of the Mother, no American individual.

The complementary passage from *Obasan* appears where Naomi begins to glean some details of the horror of her mother's being caught in the atomic bombing of Nagasaki. Although something of the interior monologue might also be felt in this passage, Kogawa's are not sentences likely to be spoken in dialogue. In their varying and complicated syntactical structures, and in their shifting images, they imply writing more than speaking. We might be reading from a letter or a journal; we might be reading Kogawa representing Naomi's dreaming. The uncertainties raise questions about narrative—about how to tell this story with its huge silences. When Kogawa's phrasing takes an interrogative turn, it challenges Naomi to "attend," to "*trace*" a "wave" of "speech"; not, as in Ichiro's case, to find some scrap of normalcy in the madness which is obliterating his mother, but to bear witness. Naomi does not plead "tell me," but declares: "you do not speak or write." The observation implies that Naomi *must* speak or write, and the form of the novel—especially Aunt Emily's diary posing some challenge to Naomi—has a more political face than Okada's monologues. Whether we are to imagine Naomi writing a journal, or to follow Naomi imagining how she might write, the book we are holding replaces all those journals in Japanese that cruel, unfeeling authorities destroyed during the internment years for fear they concealed military secrets.

Kogawa approaches silence through waves of metaphor. She makes a concrete of the abstract—"the voicelessness," "the extremity." The sound of silence is a sigh (the *si* in silence), which is immediately redefined by oxymoron: "a wordless word." The idea of tracing a *wave* of sound leads to a paragraph of more concrete metaphors. At first the silent mother's presence swells and ebbs as the tide, although in the final sentence of the paragraph she is (more appropriately?) the force of the moon. Whereas Okada makes passing reference to the "country beyond the ocean," Kogawa works the metaphor throughout the novel. At their limit, the accumula metaphors are nearly "failing," implying tha Naomi too is silenced—in her own intense and frustrated sensitivity.

In Okada the silence of an inaccessible mother moves in a series of interior monologues. Proposing that his title is "both a restatement of and a rejection of the term 'Japanese-American'—'No' to Japanese and 'No' to American," (xxxv) the editors of *Aiiieeeee!: An Anthology of Asian-American Writers* salute Okada for recognizing a distinctive language belonging to a unique community evolving in its own North American place. They are profoundly uncomfortable with the stereotype of the silent Asian American: it is a vehicle of white racism guaranteeing invisibility. Okada counters the silence, in their view, by responding to a "new language" that articulates in "old words" the new experience of a new land: "John Okada writes from an oral tradition he hears all the time, and talks his writing onto the page" (Chin xxxvi xxxviii). This assertion makes a vital polyphonic craziness of Okada's text, which is invigorating, although it suppresses the ironies implicit in the interior monologue convention (Chin xxxix). Words spoken aloud between individuals are planned or imagined, but not delivered, until the intensity of Ichiro's dilemma is summarized in a drifting solipsism of unanswered questions. When the writing corrects itself, awkwardly, into linear narrative, with normal conversation, its banality and tedium measure the

hat normative world, and that
:ican narrative, is unavailable
has twice said no.

nveys the silence of the lost
mother ... a dream vision in which an
intricate stream of images
reify the wordless word. To
the child whose favourite
reading is fairy tale and
fantasy (not newspapers
and political documents),
sea and mother, even
silence, form themselves
only in similes. Even when
Naomi claims "I tell her
[her mother] everything"
(60), none of that *telling* is
obviously, or overtly, recorded in the novel. Avoid-
ing articulation amidst
traceries of metaphor contains the ultimate
irony of silence in *Obasan*. Naomi, who is called
to bear witness, can only write herself into—or
imagine herself writing—ever-tightening circles
of words whose preciousness alone highlights
the terrifying political force in the positivist
legal language of the documents appended to
the narrative. Or could it be, and I think again
of the impact of the novel in the classroom,
that Kogawa insists that ideals exist and thrive
and move society more powerfully in poems
and dreams and traceries of metaphor than in
any report, or legislation, or petition?

Viewed through these two novels, set in

> Don Yamamoto, head of the Washington State Patrol's crime lab, is a criminalist of the first water. He's one of those second-generation Japanese who, as a kid, was incarcerated along with his parents in a relocation camp during World War II. He spent all his spare time during the years they were locked up reading the only book available to him—a Webster's unabridged dictionary—and he came out of the camp with a far better education than he probably would have gotten otherwise.
>
> J.A. Jance *Trial by Fury* 101

the region's two principal port cities, the
Northwest is so pacific it has no voice. It is psy-
chically, intelligently articulated—but cannot
speak. From Lee Chin's body hanging incalcu-
lable in Annie Dillard's *The Living*, to the Sikhs
held off-shore, confined to
ship, in Sharon Pollock's
The Komogata Maru Incident
(1978), to the brooding
accused in *Snow Falling on
Cedars*, the place is a story of
the wordless word. Of guilt
and shame in a minority.
Of a dominant society not
daring to name its racist
belief. Of an official, legislated racism that the society
fifty years later still seldom
acknowledges. And, yes,
Frank Chin to the con-
trary, it is also about layering into the story of
a place the narrative of silence enabling meditation leading to understanding:

*Asymmetry, incompleteness, tranquillity, the simplicity
of shibui, and the empty spaces of painting, the blank
whiteness, the empty silence, the non-distinct background sand in Zen rock gardens—each is expressive of
the ground of all, of the unseen "beneath," of the "lining," of nothingness as undifferentiated. All art emerges
from and leads to this deep reserve. The almost imperceptible movements in the Noh drama are gestures
towards the stillness. The serenity on the faces of the
ubiquitous statues of the Buddha engender and encour-
age this tranquility. This "beneath" is a saying without*

saying, yet for one who can hear it is as loud as thunder.
(Carter 121)

No-No Boy and *Obasan* are set in the cultural region of the part of Canada and the United States most directly affected by the internment of the Japanese during World War II. *No-No Boy* is essentially an urban novel, and in its urbanness a reminder that the opportunity to return to home and business after the war was much more available to Japanese Americans than to Japanese Canadians. *Obasan*, in its fictional present, is set in southern Alberta—to which many citizens of Japanese origin were removed as labourers from camps in the interior of British Columbia. In a novel of double exile (the Canadian Japanese are sent to Slocan, BC then to Alberta), the geography embraces the setting of the two novels, and the coast/interior tension so frequently structural in Northwest writing. In the child's world of *Obasan*, prairie air is "fist" while "mountain air" caresses with "watery fingers" (191); the prairie is "dust and grit" (194), while the mountain coast is "oil" to lubricate the joints; the prairie is invisible "prison" whereas Vancouver is sea and home (196). In *No-No Boy*, camp and prison are only a memory, and resisted at that; Seattle is an urban job market, a grid of street names and blank buildings having little room for the supposedly unpatriotic.

This passage from *Obasan* evokes the places of Naomi's journey:

We are leaving the BC coast—rain, cloud, mist—an air overladen with weeping. Behind us lies a salty sea within which swim our drowning specks of memory—our small waterlogged eulogies. We are going down to the middle of the earth with pick-axe eyes, tunnelling by train to the Interior, carried along by the momentum of the expulsion into the waiting wilderness. (111)

The sea image of Naomi's dream of her mother again draws the adult's imagination. In the physical features of a wet climate, Naomi discovers an emotional empathy—the air is "weeping" for the expelled. A bizarre conceit—"pick-axe eyes"—links the history of the Japanese Canadian labourer to the economy of the BC Interior. Building railroads and working in mines are crucial to the community's experience and historical contribution. In Vancouver, or in New Denver, British Columbia, or in the coulees of southern Alberta, Kogawa always remains alert to turning an external feature of landscape into a metaphor for a human condition and historical connection to place. In this sense, we see Naomi trying to write her way into a connection with place, to root herself through naming. She is, perhaps, writing subconsciously into a regional tradition (be it Prairie or British Columbia) or into a Canadian tradition of the landscape novel.

But American literature has a similar and stronger tradition, configured by Emerson and Thoreau, and prominent in most writing of the Northwest. Yet, the reader of *No-No Boy* is startled to come to this description at the beginning of Chapter Ten:

It was the sort of morning that non-Seattleites are always ascribing to Seattle—wet without being really wet and the whole city enveloped in a kind of dully, grayish, thin fog. The rain was there, a finely speckled spray which one felt against the skin of one's face and which clung to water-resistant garments like dew on a leaf. The temperature was around forty and the clammy chill of the air seeped through the outercoats and past the undergarments and sucked the warmth from the very skin. (215)

I wrote "startled" because this is almost the first and certainly the only passage of this length which can be said to describe place overtly. When Okada attempts to define the peculiar no-rain of a rainy Seattle (a "no-no" perspective?), he presents a persistent regional distinction, apparently to signal change in Ichiro's perception.

Although Okada gives a number of Seattle street names to locate Ichiro's wanderings, when he and Kenji drive out into the surrounding country (83), we realize how directionless, how unlocated this novel is. When a passing reference to endless rain appears (175), it again is a reminder that almost nothing in the novel gives any texture of place. This odd (in the Northwest tradition) absence of locale and setting reveals an essential feature of *No-No Boy*. Here is a novel about becoming American, about an arrested adolescent's overwhelming need to be seen as American. This desire embodies a universal, trans-continental dream of freedom, which it would diminish to locate too precisely in one city, one state, one differentiated region. Perhaps the passage I have quoted counters this observation. Coming late in the novel, it may suggest that an identity—in place—is beginning to emerge for Ichiro. As he grows, he glimpses for the first time his own place.

According to a recent book on Japanese Canadian literary connections, in traditional Japanese literature "the quest for selfhood has reached its paradoxical conclusion when the isolated 'self' as such has ceased to exist, allowing the protagonist to merge with an all-encompassing flow"

~

In the majority of cases in this book, the American in Asian American refers to the United States, but it must be stretched to mean "North American" in reference to Canadian writer Joy Kogawa's *Obasan* (1981). The practice of including Kogawa in the Asian American roster is standard in the field. Perhaps it is because scholars feel that *Obasan*, so exemplary in its integration of political understanding and literary artistry, is simply too good to pass up: it has proven equally effective as an eye-opening course reading, ... and as a powerful weapon to defend minority literatures against uninformed charges of inferiority. Under other circumstances and for other purposes, Asian Canadian literature can and should be differentiated from Asian American; perhaps, as publications become more numerous, a separate Asian Canadian critical tradition will arise. In the meantime, this book will continue to draw on *Obasan* as a key text in Asian American literature.

Sau-Ling Cynthia Wong *Reading Asian American Literature* 16

(Tsuruta & Goossen 17). *No-No Boy* perhaps echoes this narrative pattern in the final chapter: Ichiro does not emerge from his ordeals with a confident sense of an independent self (rather he is a blurred amalgam of other characters in the novel—most of them dead), but seemingly merges with the flow of society endlessly chasing some "faint and elusive insinuation of promise" (251). Certainly Kogawa's dominant metaphor of sea and tide, her two (or three) alternative endings, and the novel's kinship network of aunts and grandmothers work to diffuse individual personality into an all-encompassing community.

Using the term "Japanese *hyphen*" in such designations as Japanese Canadian, as I noted uneasily at the beginning of this file, inevitably "envisions a . . . discrete, neatly bounded culture" (Handler 171) which I know does not exist. Perhaps to end this file with a few obvious differences, and a meditation on the paradox of reception of the two novels, will resist the tendency to shape the impression of a homogeneous community.

The Nisei in *Obasan*, after all, is a school teacher in small-town rural Alberta, conditioned to see herself as an old maid, whose role is perhaps especially trying to teach, with all the evasions and difficulties that task implies. The Nisei of *No-No Boy* is a he, a dropout, an unemployed drifter who loses his lover, brother, friend, and mother. He chases desperately (251) after hope like some latter-day Gatsby. Both novels conceive of Japan as mother: in Okada that mother is lost to the male; in *Obasan*, which links the sexual abuse of a female child (and its guilt and violence) with the secret violence of the state, the mother is re-established in a kinship network of aunts and grandmothers and single women, a network of guiding and supportive women.

This feminist dimension in Kogawa probably accounts, more than anything else, for what I term the paradox of reception. While *Obasan*, with its perspective from Alberta, yearns to reconstruct a West Coast home in memory, *No-No Boy* plunges sharply back into a barren Seattle and the need to assimilate, to become American. As such, Okada's narrative is a strong reminder that anti-Asian racism, more entrenched in Canada, as Aunt Emily observed, did not even permit Canadian internees to return to their coastal origins until 1949. Yet *Obasan* immediately became a canonized text in Canadian literature, and added significant impetus to the redress movement, while *No-No Boy*, then and now, is an ethnic curio, read almost exclusively in Asian American or regional contexts. Both ways, the novels deserve and reward attention, both at home, and in the home across the border.

⁓

Salal File

On leaping from the boat, the first object which attracted our notice, was the *Gualtheria shallon* growing in abundance among the rocks, and covered with its beautiful roseate flowers.

~Dr. John Scouler 9 April 1825
Botanical Exploration of the Trans-Mississippi West

IN FICTIONAL COMMUNITIES FALLING UNDER the influence of Jack Hodgins's *The Macken Charm* (1995), the castles and forts a child finds among decaying ten-foot stumps, are more real than the "grey cement" of Vancouver. A fallen log becomes a "pirate galleon, ploughing through the waves of buttercup and salal" (1995 66). Navigating oceans of salal defines a way of looking at life, and if Toby Macken is ever looking for a title image for the film he will one day make to interpret his coastal world, he could not do better than to zoom in on this shrub.

I, too, would make salal into a title image, if only for this brief interlude—even though I cannot find the same sus-

~

[T]he Kwakwaka'wakw ate the ripe berries at large feasts; they dipped the berry clusters in Grease and ate the berries one at a time, then threw the stems in the fire.

The usual procedure for preparing the berries for winter storage was to mash them and either boil them in boxes using red hot rocks or allow them to stand for a day or two. The thickened "jam" was then poured into rectangular cedar frames set on Skunk Cabbage leaves and dried for a few hours on a rack over an alder-wood fire. The cakes were about 3 cm thick and could be as large as 30 cm wide by 90 cm long. The cooks folded or rolled the cakes and stored them in cedar boxes in a warm area of the house.

Nancy Turner *Food Plants* 77-78

tained narrative of salal as follows the salmon, or the explicit iconography that identifies the Northwest with cedar or slug. Perhaps salal's everywhereness at the beach's edge, or on the rainforest floor, makes it ignorable. But its very commonplace fecundity also compels attention. Hodgins takes notice, and uses salal as localizing detail; but he also finds another significance, perhaps hearing in an expanse of salal the slip-slap of the sea, the metaphors of dissolving and reforming transpiration that often write the wet coast.

Salal (*Gaultheria shallon*) belongs to the Heather family (*Ericaceae*), the same family as arbutus/madrone. Its popular name, unlike arbutus or cedar, has a Native American origin: it may originate in the Makah or Chinook or Musqueam language; it was transmuted in Chinook jargon as *kikwu-shala* (Turner et al. 1983 106). The word sounds differently in Canada (which prefers the "sal" of *salad*) than in the United States (where the first syllable is "*shall*," perhaps closer to the Ish river pronunciation).

One of the first shrubs to succeed the pioneering succulents, weeds, and beach grasses in a sand-dune environment, salal at the edge stabilizes the shifting sands. In turn, its roots are host to the parasitic herb Ground Cone (*Boschniakia hookeri*) (McConnaughy & McConnaughy 70-71). But salal also thrives in forests of all age classes: it suggests a year-round green thriving in conditions of very low light. Salal grows best in shade, in filtered light: its astonishing green implies another mist-story. Guidebooks, slightly desperately, describe its flowers as "urn-shaped," its berries as "rather tasteless" (Kathleen Smith et al. 66). Arthur Kruckeberg resorts to pragmatic abstraction: "Though common and thus taken for granted, it is an elegant evergreen in leaf, flower, and fruit" (1991 161).

Salal cakes were highly prized. The Kwakwaka'wakw would only use the pure cakes for a family meal or for chiefs at feasts. Cakes made to trade or sell and those given to commoners at feasts were usually mixed with currant or Red Elderberry cakes to make them last longer. Salal berries of poorer quality, or not yet ripe, were used in these "cheap" cakes.

To prepare the dried cakes for eating, the cook soaked them overnight, . . . kneaded them until they broke into small pieces and mixed them with Grease. Feasters ate them with special black spoons made of Mountain Goat horn, which would not show the berry stains. Guests were not permitted to drink water after a Kwakwaka'wakw Salal feast.

Nancy Turner *Food Plants* 77-78

Much of the world beyond the Pacific Northwest appreciates the elegant leaf of salal, although few would know its name. Salal provides the gleam and green for bouquets throughout North America. The gathering of florist greens makes a fascinating understory in the Pacific Northwest economy. Hazel Heckman tells the story best—of gruelling work, of secret places, of solitary independent labour—in *Island in the Sound* (154-61).

Gathering greens for the floral trade (ferns and huckleberry, as well as salal) seems to be the perfect edge-economy. Although said, even in 1967, to generate over five million dollars a year (presumably in the US), and have a history stretching back to 1915, brush picking—a mostly solitary vocation pursued by people hidden in dense bush—is as unacknowledged as salal. Choosing her title "The Happy Brushpickers," Heckman seems tempted, despite knowing the rigours, to people this story with wanderers, even minstrels. She writes of gathering salal as "individual," "independent," and kin to "beachcombing" and "clam digging" (154).

Like many a story of the Pacific slope economy—searching for gold is the most obvious— the dream of ready pickings, gathered when you want, where you want, hides the less glamorous stories of hard work, scarcity, and market realities. Thirty dollars for a day's work is surrounded by the conditional:

[I]f the brush is plentiful, if it grows in the proper shape, if it is bright green, showing no frost damage or russet color, if the picker does not have to pay too high a fee to the owner of the land, if he can get his brush to market before it begins to deteriorate, and if he has access to a road of sorts, so that he need not spend more time lugging his brush out on his back than he spends in harvesting. (Heckman 156; author's emphasis)

Although Heckman does not single out "brush picking" as a predominantly female activity, stories from the Canadian Gulf Islands, where brush picking has, not surprisingly, a different name, or no name, suggest that salal is key to an underground female economy. "Cutting greenery," writes Howarth in *Treasure Island*, is a "good job" because it "almost makes you part of [the wilds]" (27). Harvesting the evergreen provides an extension of the Pacific Northwest as

[T]he journey from Jordan River on was a disquisition on green: iridescent-, glaucous-, sea- and aquamarine-green mountains flowed into an ocean the colour of olive, pea and sage. Greens folded into one another, blurred, melded, shifted with the light. Hallucinatory greens, greens never seen before. Passengers stumbled from the *Maquinna's* outer decks overwhelmed with green, yarded on the doors, lurched inside . . . and faced the Christly green chairs. It was a green trip to a green land.

Tom Henry *Westcoasters* 100

economic region: it extends to wherever florists sell greens.

In April 1825, David Douglas, of the Royal Botanical Society, began his furious eight-year search to collect mature seed for possible propagation in England. When he landed at Cape Disappointment, the "first plant he took in his hands" was *Gaultheria shallon*: "'So pleased was I that I could scarcely see anything but it,'" he wrote excitedly in his journal (McKelvey 328). And so begins the troping of salal: this shrub will stand, in many instances, for an overwhelming greenness and impenetrable growth.

Trask encounters salal twelve feet high (Don Berry 106), and Pojar and MacKinnon note the height can vary from point two metres to five metres. Salal berries were important food for all Coastal First Nations; patient, or adventurous, home canners continue to use them for jellies and jams, and even a wine, with little flavour but very "intense aroma" (Underhill 81). For the Nitinaht and Hesquiat Nootka (Nuu-chah-nulth), salal leaves give extra flavour to steam-cooked foods; among the Nitinaht, they are chewed to relieve hunger; Nuu-chah-nulth dancers ate them to improve their performance (Turner et al.

1983 105-106). Hazel Heckman's islanders might know something of this pungency, since they call salal *lemon* (157), which may evoke the yellow-green stain that can be squeezed from the leaves. The berries yield an intense purple stain (Turner 1998, 212). The colour of berry and flower could also be connected to salmon; the Haida used salal berries "to thicken salmon eggs" (Turner 1995 78). Among the Nitinaht, more intriguingly, the leaves are

Fig. 8: *Elegant leaf and flower*
Photo by Laurie Ricou

chewed by couples "who wanted their firstborn baby to be a boy" (Turner et al. 1983, 106).

Salal, which can float a pirate galleon or grace a side table in Lincoln, Nebraska, could be a title image of the Northwest's intimacy with nature. "Never before," writes Bernard Malamud, summarizing the newness of *A New* [Northwest] *Life*, "had he lived where inside was so close to out" (53). I suppose this seductive mythology of proximate nature so dear to Mountain Equipment Co-Op and to Weyerhaeuser could explain my own pausing to file this short report on salal. Would it be too much to imagine not only a tossing sea of salal, but the sea in salal? Mark Tobey's "white writing" connects patterns of city light and through "rock, or bird" the "concentrated energies" flowing (Kingsbury 18)—or leaf. In Ruth Kirk's *The Olympic Rain Forest* the

~

Cherry-flavoured Salal Pie

pastry for 2-crust pie

750 ml	salal berries	3 cups
250 ml	sugar	1 cup
50 ml	flour	¼ cup
2 ml	vanilla extract	½ tsp
2 ml	almond extract	½ tsp
	pinch of salt	
125 ml	water	½ cup

Line pie plate with pastry and prick with a fork. Mix the salal berries, sugar, and flour together. Add flavourings, salt, and water. Mix well, pour into pastry shell, cover with top crust, seal edges, and prick the top with a fork. Bake at 200° C (400° F) for 30 to 35 minutes. The almond extract gives the pie the flavour of fresh cherries.

Turner and Szczawinski
Edible Wild Fruits and Nuts of Canada 83

al is the close-up of but one [?]tare at it closely: its patterns [?] and river deltas, [?] visible green. A [?] about salal is a reminder that reading a region through the writing of its indicator species gets the outdoors in: into our overheated homes, and into our minds.

Explaining the "tentativeness" of Canadian writing, Faludy suggests that words don't go very far to articulate "primaeval nature." Travel inspires much poetry, he muses, but "downright botany, as far as I know, none at all" (103). So far as salal is concerned—although not, I think, arbutus/madrone—Faludy seems, for the moment, to be right. But botany is its own poetry to an ecocritic. If we learn the word salal, and the story of its growing and harvest, then we will learn from a growing in place. In Nitinaht the fruits are named *keyicapx* (from *keyick*, the word for "blue") and August is *k'aʔiːtsapaxpɬ*, the season of salal berries (Turner et al. 1983 104-106). And, then, we would try to learn more names: for example, sk'it'gaan, the word for salal berries in Haida. One of my informants advised that another term would be taan ghaan-gha, the northern Haida (Masset) word that loosely translates as "black-bear berries," tempting me to understand salal as an interdependency of animal and food, with a bear-y colour and "hairy" berries. Robert Bringhurst later told me the words are not synonyms. So even when we have learned all the names, we will, of course, not have learned a definitive word, but a set of limits and possibilities—possibilities that will exceed limits. So we will keep reading to get the outside in.

Sasquatch File

*Y*ou have to know a country intimately to have lost all fear of it and all doubt about your ability to survive in it, before you can whole-heartedly make a jackass of yourself in it.

~H.L. Davis *Honey in the Horn*

*W*e need the Sasquatch to find our place in the universe . . . "Sasquatch is good to think."

~Marjorie Halpin

*T*here is a sense, here, living at the edge of the continent, that this is also the extreme frontier of the world. Old realities can be thought of as left behind in old countries . . . and new realities can take their place, the realities of Lotus Eaters perhaps. Writers here, concerned with the new interior realities of their private visions, sometimes require unusual forms of their own, . . . a logic of their own, . . . and a spelling of their own.

~Jack Hodgins *The West Coast Experience*

A BURLY HALF-BEAR HALF-HUMAN SHAMBLES through the Pacific Northwest, leaving enormous footprints, blurred photographs, and fearful affection. The Sasquatch file does not concern itself with Sasquatch, the way the Salmon file focuses on salmon, or the Woodwords file on the language of logging. We don't know much about its lifestyle or mating habits; we don't know much about how it communicates with other sasquatches when they work together, or even if there's more than one, or if they need to work. Bigfoot—again we have a shift in dominant name at about the 49th parallel—for all of the metaphorical potential that rests in rain or the great blue heron, is more exclusively figment. When it comes right down to it, we don't have a body, living or dead, to study.

A regional literature takes root when writers begin rewriting antecedent place-texts, in homage and parody combined. I have enthused about Ivan Doig's re-imagining the an in *Winter Brothers*. Daphne woman's version of Martin r's *Woodsmen of the West* (and a books) in *Ana Historic*. This uality, the process by which one work will ..._.e on an enhanced and echoing presence within another, could extend to the diffusion and transformation in written texts of entirely or mainly oral material. Kim Stafford, for example, is an important regional writer whose respect for oral history, gained in summer student-work projects, permeates almost everything he has written. I would call Stafford's a sasquatchian disposition. Take the spoken stories seriously enough to play with them.

So sasquatch here, whatever its overt presence in Eden Robinson's first novel or in beer commercials, is primarily a trope for things sasquatchian. It's a way to name the things that can't be seen, for speaking the beauty of terror. Sasquatch stands for the oddball, the bizarre, the predilection in Northwest writing for the crazily off the edge. And it stands, still more broadly, for the folkloric, for all that intensely personal, passionately amateur writing, and signmaking, and singing that makes the landscape and soundscape. H.L. Davis and Jack Hodgins, exuberant creators of the regional novel, keep looking and listening for this material. They take on the sasquatchian.

Chapter Four of Davis's *Honey in the Horn* has Uncle Preston swinging through a story about Joab Meacham, carpenter turned preacher, who, having lost two horses to spring flooding on the Little River, stopped to turn his water-soaked corn meal into loaves of bread. After three days baking, Joab hears the call of the Lord—to stay at Little River, then to preach. The narrator muses that the mysterious celestial voice may have sounded remarkably like the "wheeshing noise" bursting from horse-carcasses rotting three days in the hot sun (55). Now there's enough stretch in these details, especially the business of the divinely exploding horse, to convince me that Davis is retelling some well-circulated pioneer fable. But my best effort and the work of two diligent research assistants have not turned up a parallel in printed sources. Our frustration may, of course, simply confirm the oral basis of Davis's extended windy. The same might be said for the "courtly" niceties surrounding the three-quarter-hour fights between sheep herders (344), or Preston's romance-novel *Wi-nem-ah*, "in which an Indian chief's daughter ran off with a high-strung young warrior from a hostile tribe, and [relates] how, when the vengeful pursuers were closing in, she hove herself over a bluff to keep from being parted from the man of her choice" (17).

"It was founded on solid statistics, too," intones the narrator. Well, very likely, sure, and who could argue? But, the impasses facing those readers intent on solid statistics, inevitably push them to where they likely want to be, and to the aspect of folklore I want to write about: an invented folklore, I suppose, whose appeal I would sum up by proposing a motto that would suit the best-selling of the Northwest tall-talers, Tom Robbins: it would be something like "LOVE LANGUAGE, CHERISH THE GOOFINESS." Davis mentions the "windy" often enough in *Honey in the Horn* to signal that we might understand the whole novel as a wheeshing, bloated version of this genre. In writing of "Northwest Regional Folklore," Barre Toelken gives "windies" a special place, noting that the "'hero'" they "enshrin[e] . . . is the local character, the village liar whose self-proclaimed exploits are known primarily to his own small community and are locally thought to be clever tall stories" (29). The label I have placed on this file stands for all these self-proclaimed exploits. Three nights ago, driving back down the logging road just about dusk I had to slam on the brakes to avoid hitting this huge—must've been ten feet high—hairy figure. It couldn't have been a bear; I've seen enough bears in my time to know one when I see it.

Of course, I made this up. I have never fished for salmon, or gathered Sasquatch tales on the backroads of Vancouver Island, or been to a Loggers' Sports Festival—much less climbed a spar-tree. So I keep asking myself: how does this or that subject *read*? And how is it written? And trying these questions tells me something about place and culture. Or about the place I want to make up. Writing (and talking) stores at least some of the guesswork, and

THE FAR SIDE By GARY L[ARSON]

More tension on the Lewis and Clark expedition.

Fig. 9: *The ideal region according to Gary Larson*

aspirations, the anxieties and habits which are implicit in a place, and which affect our perception of it. In the case of Davis and Hodgins, I am inclined to ask *how* they write fiction that persuades us that it incorporates the locally oral and, hence, pushes the word "folk" to the tip of our tongue.

Writing the oral begins with quotation marks to mark directly quoted speech. Clay Calvert, in a minor dispute with Payette Simmons, the "boss herder" (38) threatens: "'If anybody goes, it'll be you, and if you take ary other step at me you'll go packin' your innards in your hat'" (46). Let me hypothesize writer would be content to ech with a few contractions e "g" on a slightly ter would sense the nicety of the euphemism "innards," as much for its nuance—as a variant of *inwards*, it connotes not only literal guts but an emotional and spiritual self—as for its cheerful informality. But Davis extends this compact distillation of his character to the stumbling pronunciation "ary" (is it a combination of "any" and "every"?) and the deviant use of the preposition "at" (where "toward" would be standard). We don't need to know if anyone *really talks like that*, but we at once appreciate that Davis's writing

Hank and Judi Mangis started the tradition of homemade pies in 1937 in a small building located on old Highway 99 in downtown Marysville. Wholesome country dinners and "Mile High" meringue pies soon made this a popular stop for travellers and local residents alike. . . . Mr. and Mrs. Wayne Cross had purchased the business in 1954 and operated it until its current owners Ray and Tina Thorsen bought the tradition in 1976.

Very little change has occurred in the pie recipes over the years except the pure lard used in the pie dough has been replaced with vegetable shortening. We are honored with your visit to the Village Restaurant and with the responsibility to carry on the tradition of wholesome country dinners and "Mile High" meringue pies.

Menu, Village Restaurant, (as recorded 18 November 1995)

only an intermittent sympathy for and-then-this-and-then-that linearity, and little taste for the public and political events that sustain most newspapers. Call it fictionalized social history, perhaps, resting in the accumulation of characters and the stories implicit, and volunteered, and bursting in the distinguishing tics of their appearance or, especially, of their speech. Each of them has the potential to become legend, to haunt us like Sasquatch. Davis's copyright-page disclaimer apologizes, with casual irony, for falling short of his original ambition "to include in the book a representative of every calling that existed in the State of Oregon during the home-

conveys talkiness to the point of defining the pitch of a personal voice print. It's a Dickens of a technique, compressing whole gobs of personality into an incidental line of speech.

Honey in the Horn piles up a swad of Northwest history (II 58). That's one reason it has remained in print. But Davis seldom attends to history, in the chronological textbook sense. The novel has no precise dating,

steading period—1906-1908." But the texture of these intersecting stories, the sketches of a character's past, his current obsessions, her visions of the future, go a long way to convey a community's economic history, although the primary narrative—the wanderings of Clay Calvert on the lam—has little historical breadth.

Honey in the Horn compiles history or histories, but it has a very relaxed, even careless grasp of time—at least as conventionally measured by clock and calendar. In refining the applications of the word folk, professional folklorists often turn to notions of the oral: "restriction to oral circulation is characteristic of Folk speech" (Richmond 149). That circulation configures *Honey in the Horn*—history, as it might be in the purely verbal, framed by *a few years ago*, or *along about the time that*, or *I think it was early in the Spring*.

As much as we have oral history without the exacting textbook time-line, so the novel meanders toward an oral geography without the exactness of atlas or surveyor's transit. The underlying narrative is the picaresque: on-the-road reckless and restless. A dependably American (or "USAmerican" as George Bowering has taught us to distinguish it) narrative structure, the on-the-road pattern, although scarcely extinct, certainly has less hold in Canadian writing: consider the single small town in *The Resurrection of Joseph Bourne*, or the adventures confined to a homestead in Hodgins's *The Macken Charm*.

Names such as Looking Glass Flat (330) or Drift Creek (79) are as likely to have been used by "real" pioneers, as to have been invented by Davis. "Geographical names," he notes in the disclaimer, "are in general altered as to topography." Davis's places, via such alterations, have a touch of the story happening many times. As surely as his dateless oral history, they seem to negotiate two

perceptions—indigenously Native; Amer~ and yearning-to-be-indigenous. In post-contact white culture, Sasquatch becomes the nostalgia for a native American self-knowledge through land-knowledge "without the complexities and confusions brought on by the whites," and a dream of "living in the more durable society of the sea and mountain and forest" (Don Berry 131). This intersection is often implied in Davis's ecological locationing, his preference for trios of plant names. Much more prominent than place names, change in compass direction, or elevation, the shifting, mobile place that composes Davis's Oregon is its network of flora and fauna.

I began this book by remembering Davis's Clay on the "very last land of the continent," and by defining some edges that run nervously through and under the North Pacific Slope. One such edge is a liminal Canadian presence. Davis's Oregon reminds of an era of shared history in the Northwest, but does so with a rawhide caricature of national character:

There was a settlement of French-Canadians—pink-cheeked, shapeless people with bristly black hair and oxlike expressions—who stuck to one modest quarter-section apiece and farmed it so diligently that it fetched them from forty to fifty bushels an acre regularly. (433)

This bit of border-crossing in Davis is at least one more indication of his aspiration to be inclusive. However cartoonish his version of a mythology of the North—and Canadians have

being shapeless—the compar-
another hint of prescient envi-
The Americans, by contrast,
sand or three
thousan... res, and still
"yearned for more land."

But to return now to the novel's attention to the smell and kinesis of place is to recognize that Davis imagines place as the interdependence and coexistence, the mutual illumination, of plants and animals. The difference between "little knoll" (243) and "black-mud marshes" (242) would not, in itself, likely impress a reader as more than narrative convenience. But Davis shows us what lives and dies in these places:

[F]locks of black wild ducks cruised low over the mud, and pale-blue herons stood one-legged, peering into the swamp water for eatables and, as far as could be noticed, not finding any. (242)

There was a rise over a little knoll covered with fallen spruce logs and dwarf myrtle-bush and madroña. (243)

Nothing, not mushrooms, not ferns, not moss, not melancholy, nothing grew more vigorously, more intractably in the Puget Sound rains than blackberries. Farmers had to bulldoze them out of their fields. Homeowners dug and chopped, and still they came. Park attendants with flame throwers held them off at the gates. Even downtown, a lot left untended for a season would be overgrown. In the wet months, blackberries spread so wildly, so rapidly that dogs and small children were sometimes engulfed and never heard from again. In the peak of the season, even adults dared not go berry picking without a military escort. Blackberry vines pushed up through solid concrete, forced their way into polite society, entwined the legs of virgins, and tried to loop themselves over passing clouds. The aggression, speed, roughness, and nervy upward mobility of blackberries symbolized for Max and Tilli everything they disliked about America, especially its frontier.

Tom Robbins
Still Life with Woodpecker 129

Triplets are most usual; they indicate strength and a system of reciprocal support. Where we find the less usual doublets (just ducks and herons, though the herons are doing three things at once), we sense Davis asking: what is the third that complicates and confuses this binary?

As Davis noted in an essay, "Some of the country's most common and useless-looking types of vegetation have stories back of them" (1986 26).

This storying bias is at work here, I think, not so much in the orality of the triplets, but in their constantly conveying a sense of what lives, thrives, and dies in a place. Might these places consist of stories of birds flying and standing and peering in the mud, of madroña as a companion of spruce and myrtle-bush? Even in the compact phrase I have quoted, Davis tells the marsh as living in air, on land, and in water. His account acknowledges the specialness of habitat, in the necessary dependencies of the food chain: crucial because they are often beyond human noticing. What story Davis might have had in mind in describing the knot, if any, I have no idea. But his studious triangulations of plants do insist on some interpretation. Madrone grows on dry, sunny, even rocky sites, and spruce on moister sites. The spruce logs are out of place: perhaps deposited on this higher ground in flood conditions. A Straits Salish story tells us that madrone was the tree used by "survivors of the Great Flood to anchor their canoe to the top of Mount Newton" (Pojar and MacKinnon 49). Maybe this knoll is a sacred spot. And storying place provides a way, maybe the only way, to approach some sacredness in place. That's the connection Marjorie Halpin articulates when she urges that sasquatch is good to think (Crockford 18). The prominence Davis gives to the verbs *to notice* (or not) and *to happen* might apprehend such knowing. As if anticipating Kim Stafford, at the end of Chapter Seventeen the narrator makes the crossing of story and place explicit:

Except for what had happened he would never have remembered them [the wire grass . . . the slate-blue

~

Bernard had advocated the planting of blackberries on every building top in Seattle. They would require no care, aside from encouraging them, arborlike, to crisscross the streets, roof to roof; to arch, forming canopies, natural arcades, as it were. In no time at all, people could walk through the city in the downpouringest of winter and feel not a splat. Every shopper, every theater-goer, every cop on the beat, every snoozing bum would be snug and dry. The pale green illumination that filtered through the dome of vines could inspire a whole new school of painting: centuries from now, art critics might speak, as of chiaroscuro, of "blackberry light."

Tom Robbins
Still Life with Woodpecker 129-30

doves . . .]; but that fixed them in his mind so clearly that in course of time he found he was able to give much more precise account of them than of what had happened. (376)

Rusty Macken, the narrating first-person storyteller of Jack Hodgins's *The Macken Charm*, island-bound, late-adolescent, sees his world and dreams his future as a Hollywood film. He might, from his confined community and confining family, be imagining the high drama of the Clay Calvert story, a gentle outlaw, constantly in motion, his life a blur of adventures and jackass characters. In their sparest form—Rusty worrying through one long day at his aunt's funeral in 1956; Clay brawling all over Oregon in 1906—the two novels are the sharply contrasted exemplars of two national literatures: the "stockade-rim[med]" mentality of a stay-close-to-the-hearth family (Hodgins 1977 21), and the lighting-out-for-the-territory impatience of a pioneer society. But they share a sasquatchian enthusiasm for getting "a full wind of brag up" (Don Berry 131) and a predilection for circulating the "cracked loopy cuckoo" (Hodgins *Resurrection* 1979 27).

The Invention of the World (1977), Hodgins's best-known novel, opens in the midst of a festival, the annual Loggers' Sports, and ends with Canadian literature's most spectacularly excessive wedding reception. The novel's action occurs within the parentheses of two wild parties. Predictably, the "action" consists largely in talk: burbling, unguarded, exaggerated. And subversive, perhaps: Hodgins's novel seems to have absorbed the folk "texts" that unselfconsciously give group identity to Vancouver Island, yet incorporates them with a taste for parody. Trust the local, his novels seem to urge, by never quite trusting it.

The photos of Sasquatch may be blurred, or faked, but Sasquatch is very real in the mind of the Northwest. Sasquatch is the necessary presence of the unknowable but still potentially human. Sasquatch is the atmosphere in Don Berry's *Trask*, where mountain men venture to the land "where the god walks" (127 134). In Hodgins, Strabo Becker—the traffic director on the ferry between the mainland and Vancouver Island—serves as a shifting mediator between the commune where the god walks the Revelations Colony of Truth (and its successor trailer park), and the outside world. The tech-

~

Eugene Oregon can claim to be the region's most regionally clichéed city: it is both interior and rainforest, mellow fertile valley but logging dependent. J.D. Brown in *The New Pacific* lists some features: ecothinking, joggers, shrinking lumber revenues, bike trails, new age medicine, track and field, and orthopaedic surgeons. In Eugene in 1994, I noted this quintessential shop sign:

> RAINBOW ZEN
> Naturally.
> Vintage Bakery. Juice Bar

nology of the tape recorder provides a guide for the oral folk novel—the fiction of the form amounts to: turn on the recorder and transcribe the results. To Becker the tape recorder is "magic," but he wants everything: "he has chosen to nest in a certain piece of this world" (viii), and that nest consists of his tapes, his scrapbooks, photographs, and notebooks hoarding a history that will not be shaped, and all the time never quite realizing that his nest is fledging a folklorist. His attempt to accumulate everything possible about the colony is an adventure in going down into history, local knowledge, artifacts, and folk-legend. As parody, Becker's quest must be both trusted and mistrusted. The desire to know his own place is both futile and heroic, which is to say essential.

This venture of the gigantic local nest joins the debris and trailings of a thousand and more bits and fragments of legend, of dialect and story and artifact, Weight Watchers and Emily Carr and arbutus, into a nurturing place deep within which can be hatched a new and soon to be soaring being. *Invention* assumes the form of the local narrative, and invents a crucial "place" in Northwest writing. But that claim is firmly established, and many have written well about it. I would like to concentrate here on *The Macken Charm*, especially because its story of growing up makes such a neat pairing with *Honey in the Horn*.

Other novels by Hodgins would do almost as well. In *The Resurrection of Joseph Bourne*, a radio talk show provides a stimulus similar to the carnival on tape: we witness the peculiarities of local inflection taking over the narration, without quotation marks.

Of course, the tsunami that submerges and transforms Port Alice is itself a folk motif in the fault-line culture. When the Great Flood comes, tie up to an arbutus. Tsunami are mainly known through legend. Just as with the eruption of Mount St. Helens (18 May 1980), everyone living within ground shock has a story to tell. (I remember, we were just getting ready to go out to church . . .) We cherish the affiliation without the actual experience. Talk shows, too, so easy to sneer at, signal just the sort of unfiltered spontaneity of talk that makes Hodgins a region.

You might say, you know, that all of Hodgins's fiction is a talk show. Hi, Jack. Love your show. All the novels talk excitedly, with the possible exception of the most explicitly researched, most deliberately historical of them—*Innocent Cities* (1990). That novel is

~

Daphne: This is the greatest misconception that landlubbers have about mariners. I am not a passive island the day weaves its way thru. You mis-understand, mis-represent. If you must think in generalities, think of fishers as voluble, multivocal. Imagine 3 or 4 radio telephones, all within reach of the skipper. Think network and networking.

Joel Martineau
"Fishing for Texts" 15

Hodgins's post-Saussurean novel, mos[t] consciously concerned with the physical nat[ure] of language itself, with how meaning is produced. Newspaper, letter, and stories engraved on stone push the prattling Chaucerian band of pilgrims, whose presence is never far distant in Hodgins, slightly to one side of the road. But still, it has a marvellous jest of dialogue, and especially and most important, impetuous monologues which hide and take over, unsuspected, within dialogue.

Despite the memory of *The Canterbury Tales* that lingers in much of his writing, Hodgins does not usually assemble a series of stories, character by wonky character. In contrast to Davis, who allows his characters to tell their stories in sustained monologues/passages, Hodgins, from *The Invention of the World* to *The Macken Charm*, seems inclined to accumulate folk moments. Details separated from the complete events, scraps of dialect—these are occasionally stretched into narrative shape, but more often they are stretched just enough to hint at irony, or to fuse one myth and another legend, or to open a fissure where a rewriting might be possible. The Loggers' Sports and the small-town wedding are such folk moments, themselves filled with moments. The Vancouver Island chainsaw wedding which caps

ation is itself an opportunity
the bric-a-brac of pop cul-
yering,
s to be
. Even the communal utopias whose West Coast dreaminess provide the novel's larger structure, function not in their implied narrative—the founding, rise and fall of each anxious invention—but in their pervasive mocking of a culture of communal utopias that shapes Pacific slope politics from idealizing First Nations social systems to Hazel Heckman's summarizing her *Island in the Sound* as all "temperate climate and a fastness stocked with natural resources, blessed with rainfall and lovely to look at into the bargain" (10).

Hodgins is not so much weaving the emerging folk materials into the texture of the society, as Davis does, but sending up the clichés (two generations later, more surely entrenched) in an imitation of the tall tale's affectionate exaggeration. As Hodgins explains in an interview with Geoff Hancock, he is less interested in "'getting the region right'" than "in getting the people right" (Hancock 51).

Madrona gives its name to a Victorian Country Guest House on Vancouver Island, an independent elementary school in Vancouver, and a Seattle neighbourhood.

"Flesh-coloured and almost human," it engenders legends:

> "Islanders directed me to a curve on Foster Point Road where the behemoth stood alone, its mossy base festooned with young fronds of sword fern and loops of honeysuckle. It was a shock to see an arbutus with a trunk five metres in circumference—as thick as old-growth fir or cedar. However, if a stalwart stem is what defines bigness, then a Humboldt County, California giant has more than twice the girth of the Thetis tree." (Scott 1998 33)

People talking *in* place, I suggest, rather than *about* place. Hence, the interest in the folk, in the origins of the local, largely oral, legend, as in the muddled and contradictory accounts of Brother Twelve. And, hence, the persistent features of what we might term letterpress orality: Hodgins, in print, emphasizing knowledge that is discovered and circulated without writing.

Sasquatch is humanoid, definitely furry, almost stumblingly awkward, but damn difficult to catch up to. He, or she, is afraid of cameras. But ideal for stories. So Toby Macken and Glory get placed in the Sasquatch File: because they're bigger than human, hard to get into focus, but people love to tell stories about them. Hodgins loves to tell stories about people telling stories. His favourite, slightly jaundiced, clandestinely eager version of the oral folk tradition is gossip, a form he is happy to associate closely with the writing of fiction:

> *Storytelling and the tradition of the storyteller is telling people about their neighbours, and in its lowest form, it's backyard gossip that concentrates on vicious inside information that shouldn't be repeated. But, I'd also*

like to think that in serious fiction, it's telling tales about your neighbour, but in a way that isn't exposing him so much as revealing him or exploring the mystery that's in him. (Morash 16)

Rusty Macken tells his story with enough comma splices to signal the allure of gossip: "Old Man Stokes was a silent man, he hadn't spoken to anyone for years" (148). And, in the same breath, alluding to Uncle Toby's gossip (parents hide it from children), Rusty/Jack relies on comma splices: "[H]is temper was legendary. Parents were vague about this, but Toby supplied the details: he'd tossed a disobedient spaniel into the upper branches of a cedar, he'd killed a workhorse with a fist to the head, he'd lifted loggers off the ground with one hand while breaking their noses with the other" (148). Joining sentences with commas shortens the pauses, suggesting a hurried, pell-mell, unthinking haste to get the story out before being interrupted, or overheard. And, if not vicious, this form of telling certainly intro-

~

1950 Loggers' Sports

The Loggers' Sports got under way shortly after noon with the men's bucking contest. Five men competed for the hundred dollar first prize with Alan Woodrow of Courtenay winning. He cut through the 24 inch log in a time of one minute and forty seconds. His filer, Herman Carlson, won twenty dollars. Sid Sayce, also of Courtenay, was second when he completed the task in two minutes and one and one-half seconds.

D. Currie of Ladysmith made the marlin spikes fly to win fifty dollars and the eye splicing contest. He did the job in a remarkable two minutes and fifty-five seconds. Runner up was Bill Ford of Camp 5.

Mrs. V. Norvack won the ladies' bucking event and ten dollars by cutting a 12 inch log in only 42 and four fifths of a second. Mrs. Sam Henderson of Campbell River was second and was awarded a special prize, a ten dollar credit note valid at Millers' Ladies Wear.

Isenor et al. *Edge of Discovery* 410

duces one of the novel's blackest moments: Stokes kills his own son by throwing a rock at him. But we can sense how Hodgins might, even here, be pausing over the mystery: the silence of a man in a relentlessly talking society; the touch of affection, perhaps, as talk turns Stokes into a legend. ("Can these stories be true?" the reader will wonder. Has a society which reveres such bravado caused the very crime it laments?)

As prime storyteller, as narrator, as putative author of his own unfinished *bildungsroman*, Rusty indulges himself, unwittingly, in the snippets and threads of gossip that wrap him up. The novel's action is pushed into one long day, the focus on Glory's funeral and subsequent picnic-come-wake, where the capacious and elastic Macken family (extending across the US/Canadian border to Uncle Curtis, the ironically taciturn one, cornered by the tyrannical lust of his American landlady) trade stories of Glory, Uncle Toby, and the zest to climb to the highest point in a landscape, which is one version of the Macken charm. But how reliable a gossip is Rusty?

At loggers' sports he [Uncle Toby] was always the fastest to scale the spar tree in his climbing gear, but he was never content to ring the bell and come down. Instead he climbed onto the sixteen-inch top, where he teetered, and swung his arms, and broke into a little dance. (Hodgins 1995 11)

Toby provides the definition of the landscape, an exuberant upright extension of his internal rhythms. His story—on roof peaks, in helicopter, on Forbidden Plateau—is an adventure in defining an insistently vertical and vertiginous topography. It is also, it seems, the performance of his community's story: not only at the peak, pushed to the limit, but in the colloquial sense definitely "over the top." So, when Rusty (Hodgins), scrabbles and strains for the extravagant analogy, we sense the tall-tale simile is the gossip's signature, or voice-print. A creek bed, for instance, is "a crooked slice like the sort of unnerving fissure an earthquake might leave" (189). To Nora, on her way to the outhouse, Caro shouts a warning: "'Plug your nose and grab the Airwick, Nora. Someone ate a crate of prunes and dumped everything but their lungs'" (46).

In the stories that give the family, and the *Island family*, proof of its existence (31), the listener both loves and wonders about Rusty's account, not always eyewitness, of the heroic building bee that attempts to rebuild Glory's/Toby's shack and hotel. Jump-cuts leave the project not quite finished. Tall tale reaches its apogee with one more climb to the top, where Toby waves a flag of possession from the peak of his rebuilt home. Yes, it's all just a bit over the top. Like gossip. Which is just where Hodgins wants it, I think. Where he can best pay homage to the people, get them right, celebrate their language. Gossip works to build legend and hence, a sense of being in place, that is, like comma splices, just outside the bounds of "standard" grammar, like gossip, just on the edge.

Writing the gossipy implies isolation and suggests the narrator never quite understands what is going on. Gossip especially honours what the dominant culture—in Hodgins, often that of the Mainland—considers "unimportant" or "irrelevant." And ducking the

~

If in Frost's New England "something there is that doesn't love a wall," then there is also something in the Northwest that doesn't love a porch . . . .

And perhaps that's the whole point about porches: you are watched on a porch, no matter how wild or proper the behavior. Porches are society set smack dab in our own front yards. . . .
Not so on Northwest decks. Set sturdily in the back, shielded by shrubbery or trees, the Northwest deck is more often than not a sanctuary or haven.

Brenda Peterson
Living by Water 69 73

curiosity of the dominant culture, as in "'Oh, we're just gossiping,' . . . avert[s] attention from topics of conversation that are in fact crucially important to the speakers" (Radner, Lanser 421). Like the tall tale, gossip as form creates a "tension between insider and outsider," a particularly productive tension in the relationship of the reader to the reading. Reading Hodgins is not knowing which is "true" and "false," yearning to be in on the gossip, yet recognizing that we are being marked by the text as outsiders (Carolyn Brown 33 9).

Frank Davey, in writing of Hodgins's *Invention of the World*, urges that we "should seek vision rather than shelter within inherited forms" (43). *The Macken Charm* leaves that possibility both in the *bildungsroman* barely launched, and in the dreamed of, unmade film, which mainly shapes Rusty's version of his own locale and of the big world beyond. Gossip as an unofficial language, a loveable lingo, is a form of seeking alternatives. And, as elsewhere in Hodgins's work, it points to a subversive, heroic female, in this case to the gentle tutor with the grandest name, Glory, and, then, to a muted respect for his own mother and father embodied in the way their own speech, freely, indirectly, comes to tell his own story.

The charm of the Mackens is their "taking [every] advantage of an opportunity for excess" (245). In "Waterville," or *"Warrvul"* as it is locally spoken, Glory's, or Rusty's, "tone of voice" might "suggest [. . .] that none of it was real" (Hodgins 1995 63). But never mind. The story is essential.

~

Salmon File

The old ones buried here once called themselves
Duwampsh—the people living on water;
they used to dance the rhythms of the Sound
and praise all moving waters to the moon.

They used to call the salmon in the fall
and sing for tides to bring them up the reach,
and rains to raise the river bringing down
the ancient messages to guide them back.

> ～R.P. Jones "Duwamish: Remembering Richard Hugo"

Then fell a miracle. The waters knew
Some deep sea call, and their swift tides became
Incarnate, and sudden incarnate grew
Their shifting lights—Argent and azure flame
Drave through the deep. The salmon pilgrims came.

> ～Clive Phillips-Wolley "Autumn Salmon Run"

As a cultural talisman, wild salmon have demonstrated their
power as they have diminished in numbers. . . . Salmon fishing is,
and long has been, political; it is ideological. It is about staking a
defensible social claim to a share of the catch and calling that claim
a defense of nature: the fewer the fish, the more intense the fight.

> ～Richard White *The Organic Machine*

I suppose
all said, this is my soul, the salmon rolling in the strait and salt air
loaded with cream for our breathing.

> ～Richard Hugo "Letter to Wagoner from Port Townsend"

There's an awesome dedication to ecological stability in salmonid evolution. Small fish living in fir- and pine-shaded streams of sixty million years ago took to salt water, made ocean-wide migrations, grew to giant size, ascended turbulent rivers—and for what? So they could continue to spawn in fir- and pine-shaded streams. I don't think any group of animals has shown a stronger attachment to the ancestral, north-temperate forest than the salmonids, even though the most they know of the forest is the taste of pine needles in the water and perhaps a glimpse of green boughs against the sky. Their evolution has been like a quest, in which desert, tundra, and ocean are crossed in search of the talisman of clear water running over clean gravel.

~David Rains Wallace *The Klamath Knot*

A salmon is a "little man," a penis
A spent salmon is a limp penis
salmon with his tail down
bear with tongue hanging out
Raven with a limp beak
When a salmon comes, he dies.

~Wilson Duff *Bird of Paradox*

She stands scaling salmon,
while glistening flakes fall
becoming stars on the earth

~Earle Thompson (Yakima) "Afternoon Vigil"

IN 1978, I LEFT BEHIND THE SURPRISING cactus in the coulees running down to the Oldman River for the unlikely arbutus trees clinging to the rocks above Howe Sound. The change to a Pacific Coast landscape took a lot of getting used to. My difficulty rested in a paradox: I never felt the place required getting used to, yet I continue to feel as if I have just arrived. Three years later, on the banks of the Goldstream River, my family witnessed a migration that felt like a rite of passage, an initiation into a new home. The deathward struggle of the spawning Pacific salmon flashed glimpses of the essential Northwest story. The story runs simultaneously at two radically different paces: "Quick and yet he moves like silt," notes poet Richard Hugo as he stares at the steelhead. And always the glint

spectrum: "call it chrome,
side like apples in a fog,
ish the colours of arbutus.
: of the
sed you
could define a place in
salmon. The migration of
the Pacific salmon marks
the limits of an eco-region.
"The secret of life in the
Northwest," muses Timothy
Egan, "runs in packs of
silver; as with most mysteries, it lies just below
the surface, evident to anyone who thinks it
important enough to look" (180). The mystery quickens in a life story that encompasses
both fresh water and salt, interior desert and
coastal rainforest, and, yes, "landbound two-
legger and sea-touring giant" (Egan 184-85).
The salmon's ecosystem is an interdependency of Pacific Ocean, forest, desert, river, and
mountain—ideal linkages for Egan's regional
rhapsody:

An outsider has trouble understanding this infatuation
with salmon. They're just fish, or lox on a bagel. But then
you go to a waterfall deep in British Columbia's high
country and see leaping sockeyes, worn and battered, with
long green snouts, struggling the final miles to their alpine
lake. Now you think of them as athletes. You check the
elevation, nearly 3,500 feet above sea level in the
Chilko River, and they become alpinists. What kind of
fish climbs a mountain? (185)

Egan's term "outsider"—used here affec-

They [the Vancouver Island Coast
Salish] cooked the [camas] bulbs in
steaming pits usually 1 to 2 metres
across and almost a metre deep . . . .
Sometimes they mixed them with
Red Alder or Arbutus bark to give
the bulbs a reddish colour.
        Nancy Turner *Food Plants* 43

tionately, and self-consciously alert to his own
immigrant status—implies a boundary. But the
region bounded is evidently not primarily territorial, as in the range of
Sockeye salmon during its
lifetime, but fictional.
Region moves in the shar-
ing of this story. The place
finds its form in the awesome migrations of the
salmonid, that ancient story
happening many times.

Region defined by landform, or political
boundary, is inherently territorial and implies
possession. (The Latin root, *regere*, means to
rule.) International regions—here we might
think of them as river-regions—are defined
primarily by story: they are dynamic and
unstable, inflected with the personal. The
impetus behind regional allegiance is not
property rights, but imaginative rights, the
need of a community, expressed in story, to
take care of itself.

Fish stories jump out of many waters: one
of my favorite versions of the salmon adventure
is the Atlantic version found in Charles G.D.
Roberts's "The Last Barrier" (1905). But in
the Pacific Northwest the salmon's story defines
a culture: its "commercial value," combined
with the appeal of its "mysterious instinct to
leap rapids," explains Carlos Schwantes in his
regional history, "caused the fish to become as
closely identified with the wild Northwest as
cod was with New England" (164). Such iden-

tification has much to do with the paradox of "quick" serenity amidst tumble, with the reassuring determination of the salmon "[h]unting, in the thresh and welter of creek mouths/and shifting channels, the one true holding place" (Wagoner 1976 137). And as often as the salmon is visible—in the magenta flowers and pale orange flesh of the salmonberry, for example—it is a shadow just below the surface: Ken Kesey juggled the paradoxes as he prepared to write that encyclopedic novel of independent logging *Sometimes a Great Notion* (1964): "The river flows out to sea[.] The sea is surrender. . . . We made it up out of the sea, stormed around on land for a time, now the sea is bent on reclaiming us" (Kesey Collection Box 2). In the Northwest, space gets its human face, becomes culture and a *place*, through cedar and mist, and especially in salmon. I personally find fishing tedious, and an allergy usually prevents me from eating salmon, but I *must* write about them. And how I articulate and realize salmon is itself part of the subject which lures me.

Salmon is cultural talisman, its story the Northwest's regional narrative. The salmon story—the story of attachment and quest—happens more times than one file, or book, can contain. (Just one spawning system, that of the Fraser River, covers over 230,000 square kilometres.) But here are some instances. Salmon is, and has been for millennia, an economic staple. Physical practicality curbs regional sentimentalism. The salmon story calls for hard work. One of the North-west's two greatest salmon novels is Bertrand W. Sinclair's entrepreneurial romance *Poor Man's Rock* (1920). Sinclair pulls one strand of his novel from pure melodrama. Jack MacRae sets out to avenge himself on Horace Gower for offences against his father. Neatly, the plot reverses itself: Jack becomes wealthy as surely as Gower slips into penury, and falls in love with the forbidden Betty Gower. In one sense, the less said about the formulaic plot the better. Joel Martineau, friend and former commercial fisher, notes that the plot's required line through conflict to climax and denouement fits poorly with the seasonal rhythm (6)—very active summer and dormant winter—in the fishing

~

"Do you really think the Creator sends fish because Orville and some of the other old-timers catch them according to the old ways?"

Willis squinted at Danny, as if surprised he had even asked the question. "When the first fish comes up the river every spring, you have to treat it right—say some words over it and lay it on the rocks with its head pointing upstream so others can follow. It's always been that way on this river. In the old days, the men got their spears and nets and waited on the platforms. Some listened to the old singing river channel because its voice changed pitch when the fish came upriver. My father said they'd first see the fish way off downriver. Gulls wheeled overhead, and in the water, the salmon gleamed like ribbons of light."

Craig Lesley *River Song* 182

industry. But if Sinclair slips with the narrative line, he shows a sure touch in carefully documenting the market economics of the trolling industry:

> The salmon, now, were running close to six pounds each. The finished product was eighteen dollars a case in the market. There are forty-eight one-pound cans in a case. To a man familiar with packing costs it is a simple sum. (Sinclair 107)

Sinclair also gives instructions about how to fish blueback, and details of the competitive strategies of the canneries (221-23). These particulars, in unornamented prose, imply discontent with the stock plot: it is not very congenial to the economy of salmon—the topic Sinclair seems most to want to write about. It may be that Sinclair, like David Duncan, parodies the very romance conventions on which he relies by insisting that we recognize the simple needs (and, perhaps, the spare writing—as in a ship's log) of those people who are his subject, and with whom he shared a vocation: "They were primitive folk, these salmon trollers" (107).

Poor Man's Rock endures as a historical novel: it's still worth reading, if seldom noticed among the many rhapsodies for salmonid "ribbons of light" (Lesley 182), for the story of getting the salmon from boat deck to market. Yet, like the fishermen to whom it is tacitly dedicated, Sinclair is alert to the toponymy of a restricted local area, the inti-

mate knowledge of which is essential to survival. Poor Man's Rock is not on any chart or map, but it is known to the people who fish:

> [T]here are places where the salmon run and a gasboat trolling her battery of lines cannot go without loss of gear. The power boats cannot troll in shallows. They cannot operate in kelp without fouling. So they hold to deep open water and leave the kelp and shoals to the rowboats.
>
> And that is how Poor Man's Rock got its name. In the kelp that surrounded it and the greater beds that fringed Point Old, the small feed sought refuge from the salmon and the salmon pursued them there among the weedy granite and the boulders, even into shallows where their back fins cleft the surface as they dashed after the little herring. The foul ground and the tidal currents that swept by the Rock held no danger to the gear of a rowboat troller. He fished a single short line with a pound or so of lead. He could stop dead in a boat length if his line fouled. So he pursued the salmon as the salmon pursued the little fish among the kelp and boulders.
>
> ~
>
> Poor Man's Rock had given many a man his chance. Nearly always salmon could be taken there by a rowboat. And because for so many years old men, men with lean purses, men with a rowboat, a few dollars, and a hunger for independence, had camped in Squitty Cove and fished the Squitty headlands and seldom failed to take salmon around the Rock, the name had clung to that brown hummock of granite lifting out of the sea at half tide. (Sinclair 22-23)

Sinclair's salmon story pivots on chance rather than chase, on paying attention rather than pursuit, on respect rather than reckless accumulation. Sinclair gropes toward what we might now label a conservationist message, long before Northwest writing was self-consciously urging environmental stewardship:

> "Oh, the canneries made barrels of money." Stubby shrugged his shoulders. "They thought the salmon would always run in millions, no matter how many they destroyed. Some of 'em think so yet."
>
> "We're a nation of wasters, compared to Europe." MacRae said thoughtfully. (215)

In his concern about prices and the methods of fishing, and the monopolies and the breaking of monopolies, Sinclair writes the region whose limits and character derive from a particular economy. The romance rests in a story of love and revenge, but his salmon story rests in the economics of recovery from a world war, and in the risks of hunting food too close to the rock.

To fish salmon near Poor Man's Rock, it is necessary, Sinclair shows, to *become* salmon. The salmon that make the place human stretch back to the first story. The First Peoples of the North Pacific Coast all took their identity from the Salmon People (PLATE 9). Each spring, the Salmon People put on the guise of a fish, and come up from their home deep in the ocean to offer themselves up as food (Bruggman 40). Each tribe from northern California to northern British Columbia and Alaska had its version of a ceremony celebrating the return of the salmon in the spring and ensuring—through honour—the plentiful run of the salmon. The ceremony of the Wishram peoples is described by Leslie Spier and Edward Sapir:

> The first salmon caught (sometimes the first few) was carried home by the fisherman and laid aside. No further fish could be taken until the proper rite had been carried out over this one. No one might touch this fish except a shaman (any shaman), who cut off the two flanks of the fish, leaving the head, backbone, and tail in one piece. He made incisions at short intervals in each flank piece, inserting bits of dry cedar wood to hold them open. The backbone-piece was also prepared for roasting by cleaning it. Stones were heated in a shallow pit and arranged to form a flat surface when the wood was consumed. A thick layer of choke cherry leaves was heaped on this, on which the pieces of several salmon were laid covered with mats. From time to time the covering was raised to see if the fish were baked.
>
> All the people of the town attended the feast. Other food had been prepared and spread out on the ground. Old people came to take some of it home. Everyone, even children, was given some of the salmon to eat. (Sapir's information stated that "all the old men eat it, each a small piece," but this does not preclude the others). Prayers were said at the feast by anyone. "He prayed over water, salt, fish, etc.," to the accompaniment of drum and bell. (248-49)

This ceremony marks the beginning of the annual "ritual" calendar, culminating in the winter ceremonies (and, therefore, the renewing death of the year) (Bruggman and Gerber). Whatever the variations in the first salmon feast among greatly varied cultures, all ceremonies, in basic form, recognize the sustaining ecology by returning all or part of the remains of the salmon to the river/sea. Each ceremony includes a prayer, or series of prayers, reverencing the honoured guest. An undifferentiated fusion of the spiritual and the practical economy of community sustenance is enacted in a ritual. The integration of prayer and economic know-how continues to be central in the ceremony of Northwest fiction and poetry. Sherman Alexie makes this connection most compactly in an eight-word poem titled "Communion":

> we worship
> the salmon
>
> because we
> eat salmon
>
> (n.p.)

Tim Bowling finds a more ironic sense of devotion in an unbookish library:

> My family's only first editions,
> slime-stained, wind-cracked,
> opened and read in all weathers,
> tossed down on the boot-printed floor
> of our moving library. Each year,
> new copies, and the same story told
> with only slight variations; low water
> on the fourth of August that much lower,

> 37 sockeye delivered instead of 46:
> but we were co-authors with the river
> of that second book and filled its pages
> with the nerve-ends of our hours.
>
> (1995 57)

Trying to express the implicitness of the salmon in shaping a sense of place, Tom Jay recognizes that the term "symbol" is inadequate—as presumably are such phrases as "shaping" and "sense of place":

> [S]almon . . . are literal embodiments of the wisdom of the locale, the resource. The salmon are the wisdom of the northwest biome. . . . The salmon were energy: not "raw" energy, but intelligent perceptive energy. The Indians understood that salmon's gift involved them in an ethical system that resounded in every corner of their locale. (112; author's emphasis)

The visual arts frequently depict the salmon in a circular configuration, tail near mouth, as if its own leaping inscribes an arc of its extravagantly cyclical existence (PLATE 10). Frequently a human face forms part of the salmon's design, making the integration of salmon and human complete.

~

Reading the place bounded by the salmon story recognizes a region that is both salt water and fresh (and has a life both in and out of water), of rain forest and desert, of metropolitan centre and hinterland inter-depending. Salmon ecology is a complicated mutually sustaining transaction among animal, plant, water, atmosphere, and world. At its best, the human element of a salmon economy integrates with this cycle: at least, art and literature model such integration (PLATE 12). The story of the migration of the Pacific salmon extends to Russia and Japan, another reminder of the historical and contemporary importance of trans-Pacific cultures, art forms, and aesthetics in Northwest culture. It is also a reminder of the crucial importance—and exploitation—of Japanese and Chinese immigrants in the salmon industry. As well, it is a story of a demand in Asian food cultures for salmon and salmon roe. The salmon's river-ocean-river region figures a trans-national region both of biological and cultural interdependence.

The salmon narrative, the sequence of its life-story, begins with a reversal of the evolutionary trope, downstream back to salt water, and ends with the salmon reverting to something resembling its prehistoric progenitor. The salmon's sole act of reproduction is also the final act of its life, a detail of particular note in a lingeringly puritan, sex-obsessed, society. Salmon's upstream migration to spawn accelerates transformations. The salmon fast from the time they re-enter fresh water until they die, and as they migrate they turn colour (a bright red), and shape (the male growing a large hook nose). Successful migration depends on a combination of superb fitness and luck (the "chance" so conceptually central to Daphne Marlatt's *Steveston*). Only the strongest mountain-climbers survive to

reproduce. In sympathy with thi[s] stamina and desire, Hubert Evans's sincere *Mist on the River* (1954) figure[s] of the Gitkshans' struggle to sustain t[hrough?] ture through their migration down and up the Skeena River: to Prince Rupert to work in the canneries in the summer, upriver to their homelands and the village called the Junction for the fall and winter. *Mist on the River's* hesitant relationship to its subject is very evident to a contemporary reader. Even the attempt to link the Gitkshan to the salmon's "nomadic urge" (21 218), as necessary as it is, shows the sentimentalism to which my own writing is vulnerable: "'Whose maps? What maps?'" challenges the elder Paul Leget, "'our maps are in our minds and in our memories, and our memories are long'" (151).

Evans works into his novel a good deal of documentary material on the process of canning and the contrasting Native methods of preserving the salmon. These accounts provide some of the novel's most engaging moments: the stories that are supposed to keep the attention—the story of the evolving relations between sister and brother, June and Cy; the love story of Cy and Miriam; the story of Cy's growth into the chieftainship, are not as haunting as those of the returning salmon. Many of the novel's political and sociological messages we read dutifully, but now almost always aware of the author's and our own ethnocentrism. When he touches on the likeness of the "people" and the "run of salmon" (202), Evans's

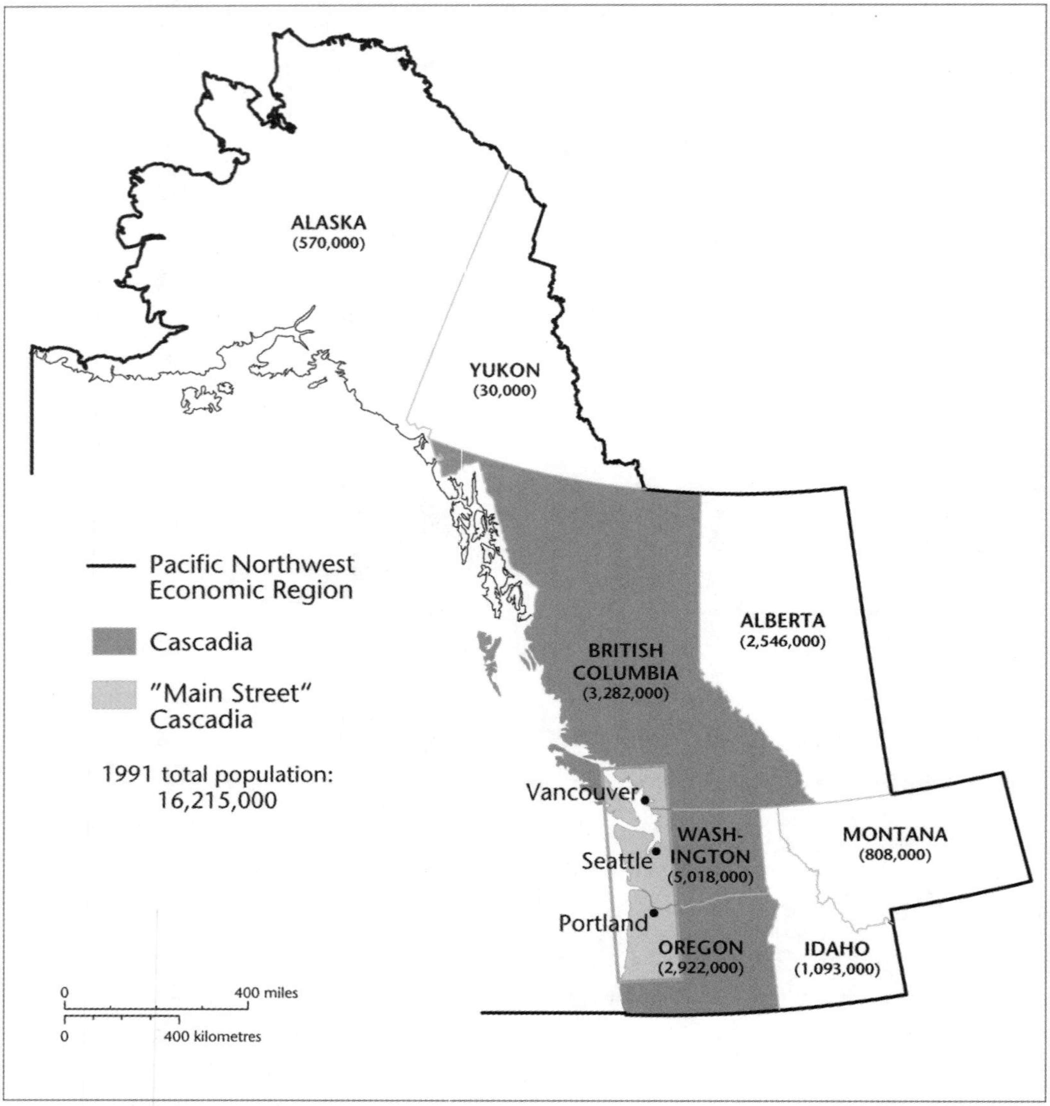
ALASKA
(570,000)
YUKON
(30,000)
ALBERTA
(2,546,000)
BRITISH
COLUMBIA
(3,282,000)
MONTANA
(808,000)
WASH-
INGTON
(5,018,000)
OREGON
(2,922,000)
IDAHO
(1,093,000)
Vancouver
Seattle
Portland
Pacific Northwest
Economic Region
Cascadia
"Main Street"
Cascadia
1991 total population:
16,215,000
0
400 miles
0
400 kilometres

Fig. 10: *Regions overlapping*. Cartography by Eric Leinberger.
Adapted from maps by David Edgington and Alan Artibise.

PRINTED WITH THE PERMISSION OF THE ARTIST

prose seems to move into a different register, more confident, more resonant, more attuned to the map in the mind. This crucial understanding gradually takes hold as the characters themselves gain in self-awareness and confidence. It figures in the sexually charged scene where Cy and Miriam work together to net the spawning salmon (213-15). And it is evocatively summed up in a passage that I assume articulates Evans's plan for the novel's form. Certainly, read in retrospect, it becomes pivotal both to the narrative and its politics:

> The salmon were born here, the people were born here, and no matter how far they traveled they always came back up river when their natures called them home. They had to; that was the way it was. There were things you counted on which did not turn out, just as, thinking back, things had not turned out as Mr. Lloyd said they would. But all changes were not good changes. And most things did stay the same; the same summer days, the same night breeze as when he was a boy, the day's warmth held in the ground when you stretched out before your fire. These things would never change, and the salmon and the people dying, and the salmon and the people being born. (229-30)

Evans's writing on salmon and Salmon People is unusually daring: he throws together comma splices, abruptly truncated sentences, a series of rolling parallelisms, and then foregrounds the conjunction "and" where its connecting function is uncertain. Evans is trying for a prose whose rhythms catch both the compulsion of the salmon migration and the inevitably predictable cycle. For me, this passage stands up to most of the best expressions of the energy and ethics of locale that have appeared in Northwest writing since.

Most north Pacific coast peoples have a story of Salmon Boy. Franz Boas summarizes the key elements of this multiple and complexly internal story in *Tshimshian Mythology*:

> 1. (a) A boy is scolded because he has performed some action on a salmon which is considered as offensive, but which really benefits the Salmon chief.
>
> (b) The Salmon take him to their village, and his life in the village is described. This part contains particularly the incident of obtaining food by killing a Salmon boy, who is restored when his bones are thrown into the water or into the fire.
>
> (c) When the time for the salmon-run comes, the Salmon take the boy back. Incidentally it is described why the various salmon go to different rivers, and why the salmon appear in a definite seasonal order. . . .
>
> (d) The youth returns with his Salmon wife and many presents.
>
> (e) The salmon taboos are described.
>
> (f) The boy becomes a great shaman. (771)

Of course, any such summary, or even re-telling, *in print, in English*, can claim little authenticity. Without diminishing these urgent limitations, I think the continued speaking and writing of salmon promises a way beyond the repression implied by appropriation. That Boas identified thirteen versions of the story of Salmon Boy, and there are certainly many more, justifies David Wagoner's own continuing transformation of the story in song, in speech as record. Wagoner's poem "Salmon Boy" is one of his most successful reimaginings of Native American story because its transformations in language (the essence of any good poem) respond so sympathetically to transformations biological and narratological. He conflates three stories, so that the boy's flight to the sun becomes one with the more oceanic versions. He takes turning over as a theme, and as a principle of construction:

> Salt water came from his eyes,
> And he turned over and over. He turned into it.

So he turns the words over and over as salmon and people and river fuse in ecological interdependence:

> He was breathing the river through his mouth.
> The river's mouth was in his mouth
>
> (1978b 66).

He turns Boas's staccato, periodic sentences into song. He turns water into wind into water. He turns statement into jubilant exclamation as the poem becomes his own first salmon ceremony.

The story of the salmon—the movements and major transformations of its life cycle—is always and everywhere on the north Pacific coast the story of the Salmon People and the legend of the Salmon Boy. Reverent worship and habitual humanizing follow the salmon upstream and down. I wonder whether the exact balancing of upstream and down has a great deal to do with the magic (PLATE 9).

The salmon narrative makes a paradox of survival uniquely visible: the nearer to death a generation is, the nearer it is to spectacular renewal. The life of the hatchlings, known as alevin, begins usually in February and begins hidden beneath the gravel. The salmon fry eventually push up through the gravel into the sunlight. Many begin their migration to the ocean in May or June, while other species spend a year in freshwater. The spring runoff helps to carry the maturing salmon, now called smolt, to sea. For a few weeks they remain in the estuary of their native river adjusting to salt water and ocean diet. Then they spend from three to five years in the ocean, growing, in the case of kings, to as much as thirty-five pounds.

Defining a region as the salmon lives it involves considerations of habitat value in very different, if interdependent, topographies and climates. A novelist relying on the salmon narrative to define a sharing of place—as Craig Lesley does with the Columbia system in *River Song* (1989)—recognizes a region which includes both Coast and Interior, rain forest and desert, baseland and hinterland. Sockeye have been recorded migrating—they are thought to migrate virtually continuously—over 3,700 kilometres in open ocean. Their story, in Roderick Haig Brown's *Return to the River* (1942) for example, includes both seagoing adventure and riverrun.

That Asian and North American populations of sockeye interpenetrate in the mid-North Pacific figures social history—if ironically—in both the success and the shame of the Pacific Coast canning industry. Initially, a large percentage of the labour force in the canneries were First Nations workers (as in *Mist on the River*), but in the 1890s and later, Chinese cannery workers and Japanese fishermen replaced much of the Native work force.

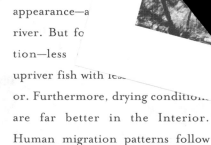

These points may seem to be drifting rather wide of the salmon narrative. But I introduce them to make the point that any approach to region based on fish (or trees) will take into account not only human impacts on natural habitat, but also the economic patterns generated by the resource. The stories of the Salmon People are so multiple and widespread because salmon was always an economic staple. Because salmon could be relatively easily preserved and, therefore, used year-round both for food and as a trading commodity, Northwest coast peoples were able to develop "dense populations, complex social organization[s] and elaborate material culture[s]" (McMillan 182).

Here salmon gather. Again, the salmon story shapes a human story—and a fluid relationship to place. At the initiation of their upstream migration sockeye average 15 per cent body fat reserves; almost all this reserve is used up during the upriver journey to spawn.

From a human point of ? their best condition—in appearance—a river. But fo tion—less upriver fish with i... or. Furthermore, drying conditio... are far better in the Interior. Human migration patterns follow salmon ecology, a movement significant in Don Berry's novel *Trask*. Coastal peoples moved inland to fish, where drying conditions were optimum or, in another season, to trade with people who had a larger supply of better preserved fish.

Any dedicated biologist will conclude in *wonder*, "much remains to be learned" (Groot and Margolis 100). Of the salmon's secrets, none is more fascinating than the homing mechanism—or more suggestive to writers, as in the lyrical celebration of the salmon's return in Momoko Iko's play about the Japanese-American dispersal, *The Gold Watch* (1970). At the end of their ocean life, during which they may swim as much as twenty-five kilometres a day, they return to the mouth of the home river and begin the long climb upstream to the place of their birth. Here they spawn in a nest called a redd (a nice, if accidental, echo of the fire so often connected to this fish); the female lays her eggs while the males fight for the right to fertilize those eggs. Within a day or two of their deaths, the male and female must come together. The eggs and

Fig. II: *Landscape Cascading: Multnomah Falls, 1867.*
Photo by Carleton Watkins

Duncan likely does not know Sinclair's book; it is long out of print, and Sinclair virtually unknown even among unversity teachers who specialize in Canadian literature. Duncan's novel has enough to do with environmental advocacy that it was originally published by the Sierra Club. Eclectic, self-reflexive, ambitious, learned, humorous, and encyclopedic, it assembles forms as well as facts and quotations. Its primary form is *bildungsroman*, the adolescent-growing-up novel, but shaped by the droll tension between the narrator's father, Henning Hale-Orviston (whom the narrator calls H$_2$O), dedicated to fly-fishing, and his Ma, equally committed to bait-fishing. Here, too, is a love story that depends for its resolution on the migration of the salmon. The novel eddies and swirls toward an embedded narrative in which the hero, hooked to a migratory Chinook salmon by the lightest of lines, follows it upriver in an intuitive synthesis of human and fish:

milt (sperm) must fuse within *one* minute. The gravelly riffle which is their redd (nest) must be free of silt, whose presence would prevent essential exchange of gases. Even a log boom overhead can inhibit the production of phytoplankton and deprive the hatchlings of food. The mortality schedule, according to zoologists, is two spawners from 3,500 eggs. And the salmon dying. And the salmon being born.

David Duncan's *The River Why* (1983) develops this love story while extending the environmentalist impulse of *Poor Man's Rock*.

It had always been my way to approach the river like a wanded magician out to work deception. But this night, thanks to Eddy, thanks to love, I came as a blind man led by a seeing-eye salmon—and it showed me a world I'd believed was destroyed, a world where a man could still walk unfeared among the animals and birds he calls "wild." (1983 275)

Fish, river, and human run together: "The angler/fish, hunter/quarry paradigm began melting away like blood in water" (1983 275). I have given just a glimpse of the six-page-long migration of love that defines what Northwest writing has always aspired to in its love affair with the salmon: a bond of trust and companionship and tutelage with the seeing-eye salmon.

Although *A River Runs Through It* concerns trout rather than the Pacific salmon, its poetics of fly-fishing and its commitment to reading the language of rivers give Norman Maclean's fictional memoir honorary status as subtext, intertext, reference text for any writing on Northwest rivers. Perhaps, he muses, the fisherman's phrase "reading the water" describes the process of telling the fish story. "I did not know," he says, elaborating an analogy which could easily describe Hubert Evans's salmonoid syntax, "that stories of life are often more like rivers than books. . . . a sharp turn, deep circles, a deposit, and quietness" (63). For Maclean, as surely as for Ethel Wilson, the mystery dictates an interrogative syntax: "it is not fly fishing if you are not looking for answers to questions" (42).

~

Prophecy

the salmon have built mansions
at the bottom of every ocean

thousands of rooms
thousands of rooms

the salmon have sent ambassadors
to live among Indians

thousands of salmon
thousands of salmon

these ambassadors are teaching us
how to breathe water.

Sherman Alexie
The Man Who Loves Salmon n.p.

The same could be said of trolling for salmon: Edith Iglauer's *Fishing with John*, a portrait of her husband John Daly, pivots on the intellectual questioning that is inevitable to the romance of the salmon story. "Why do you stay out so long?" she asks John. Because "I love it," he responds:

"The romance of the thing is so thrilling. The salmon start from six or seven hundred miles up the McGregor River or Skeena River, wandering as fingerlings all the way down through log booms and pulp mills and booming grounds and pollution in the Fraser River until they finally make it to the Gulf of Georgia, out among all the dogfish and seals and every other kind of predator, into the Queen Charlotte Sound; and then they turn around and go back through the trollers, sea lions, seals, gillnetters and sewers, and two hundred thousand sportfishermen in the Gulf of Georgia, up through all the pollution of the Fraser River, into the hundreds of creeks on this coast, to spawn. Think of it! And I've got to outguess the depths they feed at, and when to speed up and slow down, the color and shape of the lures, the size, type and weight of the hooks, and the color of the water. I have to remember patterns of runs of various previous years. What I don't know is what's going on under the water." (119)

Variations on the word *through*: the chorus

sings continuous, uninterrupted movement; a process extending, from one to the other, always between and among. To explain the attraction of fishing for salmon is to marvel at running through it—and end with a question.

John Daly was a union man, and as sentimentally as he is portrayed in this passage, he never for too long forgets the economic and political pragmatics of his means of livelihood. Remember that when I use the word sentiment, I do not always take it to be pejorative—certainly not where it concerns environmental understanding, and where it attaches to the genre of romance, which implies celebration—and discovery. But when I was reading the crudely handwritten minutes of the Lower Columbia Fisherman's Protective Association, with their obsession with penny-a-pound differentials in what canneries pay, with creating policies for cooperatively removing snags on the river, with their attempts to have cannery workers join with

~

WITNESSETH: That the party of first part, for and in consideration of the sums of money and other considerations hereinafter mentioned, hereby contracts, stipulates, agrees and binds himself to clean, split and can by hand, and cook such salmon as the said party of the second part shall offer and deliver to the said party of the first part for that purpose, and keep cannery clean, during the entire fishing season of the year 1898, all to be done at the cannery building of the said party of the second part, located at their fishery in Wasco county, Oregon, and lacquer, label and wrap the cans and pack the cans in wooden cases and nail same ready for shipment, and box all scrap tin, load and unload all cars of tin and fish, all to be done in a good and workmanlike manner and satisfactory to the said party of the second part.

Indenture between On Hing & Co. and Seufert Brothers Company, The Dalles, State of Oregon, 18 March 1898 Oregon Historical Society MSS 1102

them to effect change from the companies, I realized how little the workers' side of the salmon narrative has touched Northwest fiction and poetry. The few exceptions—Bowling's *Low Water Slack*, Marlatt's *Steveston*, and Sinclair's *Poor Man's Rock*—suggest the possibility of a cross-border distinction. The business end of fishing and canning seems to be more a concern of the Canadian writers, whereas the romance of the catch lies closer to American concerns.

Paradoxically, the novel and poem that adopt the salmon narrative seem more recurrent in Canada, whereas the American versions are more likely to approach the form of meditative essays, something not all that far from the inheritance of Walden Pond, even if a continent removed.

Of course, like any convenient national differentiations, these generalizations immediately reveal their limitations. Craig Lesley's *River Song* (1989) goes a long way to making fiction of the marketing and eco-politics of salmon. And it was an American journalist with the *New York Times* who coined the most striking expression of the persistent analogy between the psychology of gold rush and salmon mining: the frenzy of greed that was the growth of salmon canning complete with salmon wheels (and today, driftnets) Timothy Egan calls "Klondike on the Columbia" (187). In fact, many ex-miners did build salmon canneries (McKervill 48-49).

To depend on the seeing-eye salmon is to admit you don't know what is going on under the water. Salmon do not recognize the international boundary between Canada and the United States, in swimming either through the Strait of Juan de Fuca or up the Columbia River system. The salmon is a totem of region, its territory—or aquatory—and story defines a region, distinct and with different resonances from that defined by homogeneous land mass, or geographical boundaries, or political borders.

The salmon returns (with the exception of a very small percentage of strays) to exactly the same gravel bed in which it originally spawned. At the core of the salmon story is a mystery that continues to defy precise scientific explanation. How do they get back? How do they find home? The questions, and the story, are so inevitable to being in place that it seemed right to put the Salmon File somewhere near the centre of these readings. There it might signal a rest after the Kuroshio turbulence, and a trope more compelling than Sasquatch, and an anticipation of the forest understory and overstory, and the future of arbutus itself.

Homing, in fresh water, is surely olfactory in good part. But what of the ocean migration? Most of the biological writing on this phenomenon is speculative: salmon apparently use a complexly interrelated combination of migration mechanisms—an ability to detect the earth's magnetic field, the use of sun and polarized light for celestial navigation, a strong calendar sense, and an imprinting on the odours of the home stream, what has been called a chemical memory (Groot

~

Meeting in Portland, the Northwest Power Planning Council unanimously approved the region's first salmon-rescue plan. The proposal sets minimum springtime water flows in the river and calls for experimental lowering of reservoirs by 1995, to determine how major dams can be modified, and be made easier for fish to traverse.

But the plan stops short of other proposals sought by environmentalists. It reduced water-flow requirements for the two rivers to appease Montana interests. To meet irrigators' objections, it removed a deadline for lowering the Columbia's longest reservoir, at John Day Dam, a measure intended to help flush young fish to the ocean faster.

Larry Lange, "Salmon-rescue plan sets flow rates, calls for lowering reservoirs"
Seattle Post-Intelligencer
12 December 1991 A1

and Margolis; R.J.F. Smith). And as sockeye move back upriver, what has been an ungendered story (the male and female are very difficult to distinguish) becomes a story of "marked sexual dimorphism." Both change from silver to green and bright red. The male develops a fleshy hump and a hooked nose (changes that appear to favour the survival of the female). The salmon fast from the time they re-enter fresh water, hence the frequent association with the spirit quest. And when the female sets down her eggs the male simultaneously fertilizes them. It is the one and only sexual act in a three- to five-year life, and it comes within two to five days of death. It is a story made for poetry:

> salmon spawn, then die
>
> lovers
> who love without a morning after
>
> poets
> whose utterance is consummation
> who do not wait for echoes
>
> my words pulse out like blood
> like straining bodies
> leaping in the sun
>
> i send them to you
> written upon water
>
> (Eadie n.p.)

The salmon story, in one sense, concerns an area smaller than region: it focuses on the peculiarly unique smell of the local, of a particular stream, of a specific bed of gravel, of the birthplace. (The imprinting of the odours of the home stream has been called a chemical memory.) Northwest topography is extravagantly mixed (and if arbutus were its indicator species, it grows mainly on dry rocky outcrops), but the salmon story is ubiquitous because it makes a connected region of the disparate region. It is a major political force. And, as anticipated in the Rain File, it also shapes tall tale and song:

> Charlie told me you know you're in Oregon when you can stand on the porch and grab a salmon fighting its way up through the thick tumble of the rain. That turned into a song as I drove home:
>
> Step to the porch, a salmon flies by—
> Hook him in out of the rain.
> You're pretty far gone, pretty far gone:
> You're clear out here in Oregon.
>
> (Stafford 1986 150)

In the flying salmon story, we approach a fusion of folklore and regional awareness (PLATE 7). Similarly, David Wagoner's "Riverbed" is not a regional poem in some of the overt senses we might expect—that is, place names, or meticulous descriptions of landscapes—but in the insistent story of the salmon happening to escape to die.

~

Vessels travelled . . . across the Pacific . . . and dumped their ballast . . . before loading salmon. Consequently the Steveston waterfront has Chinese sand as well as sand from the Fraser River.

Stacey 2

R i v e r b e d

1

Through the salt mouth of the river
They come past the dangling mesh of gillnets
And the purse-mouthed seines, past the fishermen's last
strands
By quarter-light where the beheaded herring
Spiral against the tide,

. . .

Out of our smoke and clangor, these miles uphill,
We come back to find them, to wait at their nesting hollows
With the same unreasoning hope.

. . .

The river turns its stones like a nesting bird
From hollow to hollow. Now gulls and ravens
Turn to the salmon stranded among branches.

They lie in the clear shallows, the barely dead,
While some still beat their flanks white for the spawning,
And we lie down all day beside them.

(1976 137)

As in so many Northwest stories, the poem follows the ascent from salt water to fresh, then through faster and faster water (to a climax and a bed). Wagoner gives enough turns to the poem's syntax—"Downstream a foot at a glance"—that the upstream narrative also remembers the birth journey in the other direction. And, in developing the inevitable Salmon-people analogy, the poet discovers that the humans, the "we," must follow and replicate the journey "out of our smoke and clangor" "uphill" to our own satisfying death.

    I would urge, however, that to appreciate the poem with some measure of [understanding] Wagoner brings to it, we need [to rec]ognize not only the variations on the fam[iliar] narrative, or the bravado of a thirteen-line sentence, or six stacked prepositional phrases, but also the ways in which everything connects to everything else:

1) the memory imprint of unique stream odours from the mix of rock and tree and shrub at the holding place;

2) and the hypothesis that there must be a sequential series of imprinting processes corresponding to each change in order;

3) and that the salmon from a single spawning ground separate in salt water and must use a whole different system, (electrical fields?—science does not know) in the Pacific;

4) and that the nutrients released from rotting salmon are needed to process litter from the forest canopy to keep the stream running clear;

5) and that dead and dying salmon provide food for

        eagles
        raccoons
        bears
        mink
        shrews
        skunks
        mice
        bobcats
        chickaree squirrels

...iirrels

 ouzel

ay

r's jay

rea-tailed hawk

and winter wren.

(Groot and Margolis 82-83
100 passim; Kirk 100-101)

The items filed here don't begin to cover the full cultural ecology of the salmon: the fish-flesh pattern in baskets and ceremonial robes, the taste of the salmonberry, the continuing consequences of the Boldt decision (1974), or the use of dried salmon skin as ingredient in the paint for rock painting. But I have tried to suggest that approaching regional writing through the salmon narrative implies topography and turbidity, tides and water temperature, bears and gulls, and ratios of dissolved oxygen.

In the mythology of salmon, a regional culture finds its self-made instructions.

~

The Pacific Northwest is simply this: wherever the salmon can get to.

Timothy Egan 22

~

Salmon is the guide on how to relate to where we set ourselves and touch the earth (PLATE 9). The *economy* of salmon shapes a functional region which includes in the Pacific Northwest the food boutique in Harrod's. The *life* of the salmon tells of a region where water is a territory and land is fluid (PLATE 7). It is no surprise that in Jack Shadbolt's painting of his own garden and home, the returning place (*Place* 1971-72), you can just detect, if you look closely, just beneath the surface, the artifact that organizes his location: a salmon-drying rack (Halpin 1986 21). And when Gordy Tweit, retired pharmacist in Fairhaven, Washington, took the students in English 492 to his basement museum, they discovered, as backdrop for herbs and tinctures from the 1890s and a rusting machine to make suppositories, a display of 250 labels from cans of salmon spanning ninety years of canning, and in their brand names, 250 more poems for salmon (PLATE 11).

~

Woodswords File

Logging's a bit like writing poetry.

~Peter Trower 1974

"Who's a whistle-punk here?" Kitty said. "How many peeps to say 'quittin' time'?"

"There's no quittin' time for loggers, you know that," my mother said. "Put two of them together and it's 'spar tree' this and 'rigging slinger' that until they drop."

~Jack Hodgins *The Macken Charm*

The actual harvesting of timber is conducted with surprising efficiency, considering the general laxness of Ecotopian work habits. There is much goofing off in the forest camps, but when a crew is at work they work faster and more cooperatively than any workmen I have ever seen. They cut trees and trim them with a strange, almost religious respect: showing the emotional intensity and care we might use in preparing a ballet.

~Ernest Callenbach *Ecotopia*

The whole country was more peaceful than he had expected. But there was this odd . . . *volatile* feeling about the new country that struck him the very day he arrived, struck him and stuck.

~Ken Kesey *Sometimes a Great Notion*

PETER TROWER—WITH EMOTIONAL INTENSITY and care—defined and continues to sustain a tradition of logging poetry on the West Coast. His claim that logging is a bit like writing poetry should probably be read with strong emphasis on the word "bit": for the most part it is difficult to imagine two more disparate occupations. But Trower so casually splices

117

logging cable and line of poetry that he produces this odd *volatile* feeling that sticks to logging, and writing about logging.

Something at least theatrical, if not histrionic, struts in the word "show," which loggers use to indicate a stand of mature, accessible timber ready for the cutting. I found my first show of logging poetry (other than the legends of Paul Bunyan that penetrated my prairie childhood) in a prose work, Martin Allerdale Grainger's *Woodsmen of the West* (1908). Both its language and random form link logging to poetry. Stories long and short, trivial and utilitarian, don't quite follow one another in "wondrous zig-zags" (77). The narrator can say "perfunctory" and "soogey-moogey" (33) in the same breath. At least in casualness, if not in volatile odd metaphors, Grainger's *Woodsmen* now looks like the book that first made Northwest woodswords literary. Carter, the boss-logger, is entrepreneurial hero on the resource frontier. The unreliable narrator, in bursts of extravagance that parody the macho adventure tale—happily disparaging the entire category of "West-describing novelist" (45)—portrays his boss

Our home, in an upper middle class residential area of west-side Vancouver, sits where once a dense rain forest must have flourished. More recently, it was a neighbourhood of small orchards: on a few lots ageing fruit trees still twist themselves alive. Ours is a wood-frame house, with cedar shakes, and cedar siding. The wood windows and trim are varnished not painted, so that the grains mix and complement (so we think) the pine and oak furniture we brought with us from Toronto and Quebec and Victoria Beach. It's a house, I suppose, which speaks of a love affair with wood, where wars about trees, and who has the right to cut them (and about the significance of trees in different cultures) continue to be waged daily.

operating with "charming brutality" (122) in "sack[ing] the woods"; taking "wild risks in starting business as a boss" (55), a business that is as much "child's carnival" as "anarchy" (68).

Carter has held so many jobs—as miner, trapper, railroad foreman, and saloonkeeper, among others—I imagine him as a composite of Northwest (male) economic history. Grainger knows it is a history of "sacking": Carter's steamboat is *Ima Hogg*, and each of his jobs includes some form of pillage. (The verb "sack" derives from the French *mettre à sac*, implying throwing all the loot in a bag and running.) My colleague Bob McDonald makes the novel required reading in his course on British Columbia history, in recognition of the book's strong documentary appeal. Down among the stories of adventure and plunder lie caches of "pure" information: lists of essential tools and provisions (50), an itemizing of the massive breakfast spread out in the cook-house (88), or a blackboard advertising the exact wage offered a rigging slinger (14). To an outsider, logging often seems all spontaneous sprawl. Grainger's documentary side especially appeals where he counters this impression, as in his account of the geographical and climatic considerations necessary to selecting a hand-logging site, by revealing the job's technical subtleties (51-52).

But I most often tend to the outsider's view (or accept the myth), and read a sprawl and spontaneity of language. Attempting to outline a sustained narrative in the book would not likely result in anything very detailed, or very convincing. *Woodsmen* might be thought of, from one angle, as Carter's biography, or as a variation of the journey story—beginning in Vancouver and moving up to the head of Coola Inlet, from which heart of Carr-ness a return is promised but never achieved. Or we might recognize that the narrator moves, in time-honoured fashion, from innocence to experience, from feeling a "conspicuous foreigner" (29), through several trials by suffering, until the wilderness becomes to him a home (129). But readers will have to strain to detect these structures: they are at best vague traces of books that Grainger might have written. The absence of transition between chapters and their titles suggests a collection of

~

We live in the profound ambivalence about trees that is the daily contradiction experienced by millions and millions of Northwesterners, at once spellbound by the forests, and yet dependent for many pleasures—and, at least, indirectly for income—on their being cut down. "How one feels toward trees," writes Sallie Tisdale in her interpretation of a Northwestern tree-home, "both singly and in forest, is a large measure of how one lives here— literally *how* one's life is spent. I think it is possible here, where so much of our history is in our trees, to feel more strongly toward them than seems quite proper elsewhere. (And that improper depth of emotion is true for the logger as well as for me.)" (207)

separate stories. And embedded within these stories are more stories. The business of the novel (as Mikhail Bakhtin has theorized it), like the business of logging, mixes child's carnival and anarchy. Grainger's title designates woods *men*: there are many of them, and they all have stories to tell; the loggers' stories are sometimes directly quoted, sometimes retold by the narrator and, in one case at least, told by an anonymous storyteller (Grainger 64 ff). Grainger knew he could best tell about the woodsmen of the West in bursts of narrative that evoked loggers gathering to trade hyperbole: every page or two a new anecdote is turning toward tall tale. Grainger's own background—he was a scholarship student at Cambridge (albeit in mathematics)—suggests that he could have written a book to satisfy more conventional literary criteria—more adventurous in its metaphors, more allusive, more complex in its characterization, more alert to its own narrative strategies. Yet, he gives us several clues that his ingenuousness and random form are deliberate. My colleague Joel Martineau would go so far as to call the book avant-garde postmodernism, its very unconventionality necessary to questioning the get-gut-and-git plunder of the West.

When the narrator finds himself with no facts, and scarcely any hearsay evidence (concerning Carter's career as saloon man, for instance), he feels entirely free to make up a story, to "imagine" what "would be his style" (47), or to leave the story to his audience: "you can, *if you like*, picture the boat trips" (50; my emphasis). Imprecision about origins of stories, about geography, and especially about dates snag the narrative lines. An incident happens "*about* five years ago" (49; my emphasis), or the narrator laments "I wish I could remember" (51).

Given the narrator's grasp of story, you could believe he had caught a touch of the Northwest epidemic Ken Kesey diagnoses: *tranquilitis* (453). Inexperienced in living such novel adventure and strenuous physical activity, Grainger's narrator is often only half awake, or half in dream, and able to put together only a piece of one story and a fragment of another: "I would listen awhile to what the man said, and then I would doze again. Sorry I was afterwards that I did not keep awake. For Carter was telling

~

Costlier tree-removal fees and an insistence that developers relocate garages to save significant trees are among a raft of tree bylaw amendments city council will look at Thursday. Council is also expected to support a reduction in the minimum fine for offences against the Private Property Tree Bylaw—from $5000 to $500—to offer judges more flexibility and reduce the number of failed prosecutions, as well as the launch of several programs aimed at encouraging tree preservation.

Alison Applebe, "Council Considers Tougher Tree Bylaw" *The Vancouver Courier*, 9 July 1997 13

me the history of his life" (38). The whole book registers on the reader, as on the narrator, with such casual uncertainty.

The movement of storytelling, and listening, which is not-quite-awake, complements both the life and psyche of the woodsmen. Carter's own "careless methods," and the mirroring "carelessness in the men he dealt with" parallels the woodsmen's sense of time: "the future and its days of payment do not weigh heavily upon the logger's mind: he lives much in the present" (69). Grainger implies that obliviousness to lack of skill is characteristically "Western" (108), and rigs the book's narrative to embody "the Western art of makeshift—the art of rough-and-ready and never-at-a-loss" (110). In apparently stumbling in his writing, Grainger is giving literary (or, better, *a*-literary) shape to the logger's "punctilio" (deliberately paradoxical term), an inclination best revealed in his "yarning": "At any moment you may be puzzled by some touch of the quaint, the unexpected, in the way the man is said to have acted; something you fail to see sufficient reason for in the story" (107). I say "apparently" stumbling to acknowledge how adept Grainger is at makeshift: Mart's inability to remember, his valued self-deprecation, surely register the pace and diffidence of male storytelling, especially with loggers who cannot dare to talk smoothly. Grainger's methods seem "careless," but only because they convey something "carefree." Careless "yarning" is far from inconsidered. Lounging about in the midst of scraps of conversation and story is practical; tranquilitis is not mere idleness but essential to economic survival in the logging business:

To get the latest news about the demand for logs, the trend of prices, or the rate of wages, or the supply of men, Bill just drifts into the hotel or the store, and sits on a box within spitting range of the stove, and chews. Talk will be going on; all sorts of news that has an important bearing on his business will come out, in casual, desultory fashion, from time to time. (80)

Grainger invites his reader to be a good listener, invites all of us who have not been loggers to learn something. Mart realizes that the greenhorns, from cities bloated with power, can not stop talking when they come to the edge. And all their yammering alienates those who could teach them about wood and work. Mart wisely listens, tentatively yarns a bit, pretends to doze. In

short, he learns woodswords. And h makes the book worth reading.

Grainger extends the "makeshift" cc struction of his book, which attempts to put the reader in the midst of this essential but desultory talk, by using the vocabulary of the loggers. He sprinkles his prose liberally, if intermittently, with "Timber-cruisers" (35), "donkeys" (60), or with men "blowing-her-in" (14) at endless saloons. Sometimes he pauses to footnote or gloss one term or another. After describing extensive preparations for hand-logging, he reports: "Their 'boom' (in loggers' speech) was 'hung'" (52). It's as if Grainger bounces between appreciation of the go-for-broke vigour of the unique logger talk

Fig 12: *Highballers in Heaven: Felling giant spruce trees near Tillamook*
Photo by Wesley Andrews

remote it will seem to his
ience. Languages clash:
\glish public school jos-
rds. Grainger explains
" is a "lock-up" on a
˻ ˻˼, ˻o my ear, relegates the
term to mere curiosity by continuing: "To it
the first mate of the *Cassiar is wont* to shoot too
noisey drunks" (20; my emphasis). To be sure,
the narrator frequently apologizes for his
ignorance, but the formal diction (and the
predictable, for 1908, eliding of the curses)
sometimes reduces the loggers' language to
local colour. But Grainger goes well beyond
Jack London, or Robert Service, or the scores
of adventure writers whose formulas he mocks,
pushing loggers' speech toward the resonant
literary language it becomes for the logger
poets, and for Ken Kesey.

~

The title of this file makes a micro-poem. The
term *woodswords* comes from Walter McCulloch,
who used it for the most comprehensive glossary of Northwestern logging vocabulary we
have. To my mind the title puns on a pun—the
grade-schooler's grumpy parody of an ode by
Wordswords or Worstworst. This echo com-
presses both mocking irreverence (the violent
edge to timber-talk contrasts with the pastoral
beauties of hosts of golden daffodils) and
affection for the users of woodswords.
(Wordsworth is the prime mover of the unending post-romantic attempt to write poetry in
the language such as is spoken by ordinary people in their everyday talking.) For all their
involvement in the woods *wars*, the loggers
themselves speak a respect for trees and the
forests which would not be out of place in
Wordsworth's most rhapsodic recollection of
tranquility. On the tongue, McCulloch's
phrase is a blurred and tangled compound, as
if borrowed from a language made *exclusively* of
squeezed and alliterating formations, that read
the wilderness as an "explosion of terrain," a
language whose vocabulary itself explodes, as in
the bluster of Peter Trower, until flying words
smash into one another and stick:

Explosion of Terrain
> *greengray*
> *fogfingered*
> *desolate*
> *forests beyond feet*
> *heights beyond hands*
> *rainridges beyond reckoning*
> *wild to the horizon.*

(1978a 48)

Grainger himself seemed to recognize the
industry's poets: in the final scene of *Woodsmen
of the West* the loggers drunkenly sing a ballad
with this bumpy refrain:

Grainger was a-firing, and the donkey *throwing fog,*
Cully at the throttle, and he had *a big log;*
Bill blew the whistle when the line it broke,
For Joe was slingin' riggin', and Carter tending hook.

(144)

At the end of the book, where rhetorical emphasis supposedly falls most strongly, Grainger follows this song with several paragraphs of explication. In some sense, it's a surprisingly banal way to end the novel, but in giving such weight to understanding hook and riggin', he anticipates many Northwest writers telling us that to know the forest you need to understand the language of the woods as workplace.

Getting to know woodswords sweeps you well beyond understanding the forest or the economy. Much of the loggers' lively vocabulary has found its way back into the general speech. Some terms commonly used without much thought to their origins in the woods include: a raft of, highball, haywire, skid road, hang up, in a jam, and hooker. Not surprising that all these terms are linked to deviance, instability, and a little craziness, staples of all logging poetry. You can tell a Northwesterner, often, not by the number of years she has lived in a place—many are recent arrivals—but by his cringing at the term "skidrow."

To this desk-bound Northwesterner, at least, it makes sense that Grainger's pioneering novel of logging builds toward a loggers' ballad. Grainger's early attempt to make literary form echo the speech-patterns of logging

Skidroad is the proper name. It originated in Seattle some seventy years ago, when logs were hauled through the town over an actual skidroad made of logs laid crosswise . . . of recent years a corruption has appeared as "skidrow," but its use is confined to those who wish to be known as men of the world, and who patently don't know what they are talking about.
Stewart H. Holbrook
The Far Corner 226n
(PLATE 6)

surely anticipates the development of an identifiable body of logging poetry: his (tentative) acknowledgment of the perceptions to be discovered in woodswords recognizes a regional lingo. Logging poetry comes in three flavours, but, as on the tongue, they may be happily confused with one another.

The mocking ballad near the end of *Woodsmen of the West* signals the first category: poetry—often songs—created by the workers themselves, or with an audience of workers (certainly not literary critics) clearly in mind. In Grainger, the men drone on the names and work assignments of those in their own "show." They sing harmony, simultaneously sounding and tracing an easily followed narrative line, and thumping out a dramatic and mnemonic style that is readily recited. The memory of repetitious work, done to the accompaniment of song—as in a sea shanty—governs their pace.

The most prolific, or at least most published, of the logger balladeers, is Robert E. Swanson, whose three books *Rhymes of a Lumberjack* (1943), *Rhymes of a Western Logger* (1942), and *Bunkhouse Ballads* (1945) provide the booming ground for any sorting of loggers' verse in the Pacific Northwest. In his opening "Warning" to *Rhymes of a Lumberjack*, he claims an audience among those who are his subject:

> *My songs are songs for the outdoor throngs,*
>> *In the Great Wide Open Spaces,*
> *Where the mountains soar and the axes ring;*
> *Where the rivers roar at the call of spring,*
>> *When the log-jammed freshet races.*

(60)

Swanson's songs for the throngs, such as "The Death of Rough House Pete," remind us of Grainger in their drawing specific attention to the narrator, and in their careless storytelling:

> *"When the bull teams all were finished and the*
>> *ground-lead donkey came,*
> *And the line-horse days had gone beyond recall:*
> *I had hired to do the hookin'—up at Simoon*
>> *Sound of fame,*
> *But the camp and cook were haywire—grub and*
>> *all.*
> *On the table-top jumped I, and made the dishes fly,*
> *You can bet my old caulk-shoes weren't very*
>> *slow.*
> *Then the Cassiar I boarded, and I bade that camp*
>> *good-bye,*
> *And they stowed me with the cattle down below."*

(79)

Simple rhymes (usually based on monosyllabic words), stock epithets ("gone beyond recall"), and a history related in direct speech mark the ballad tradition. Traditional logging poetry, exaggerated masculinity everywhere, loves to set one powerful man against the whole world, and subject him to sharply contrasting emotions joined in a single quatrain. Within two lines, Pete goes from leaping on the table with his caulk boots to being "stowed" ignomin-iously below decks with the cattle. Pete's story is, after all, an *envoi*, after his days of carousing are done. (With so much kicking and flying in the poem, we're sometimes surprised to remember the elegy.) But it's also a memory, or a necessary fiction, of the "roughest, toughest kid," in rough tough verse to match. Logging poetry seldom neglects the opportunity for hyperbolic action, subtlety of characterization be damned.

The sense of action and style of excess are compressed in the loggers' vocabulary Swanson glosses at the end of each of his collections. Exaggeration and physical force permeate his writing: the logging camps were "jungles," and Pete "hit" them: in this one rant Swanson uses ten or twelve terms which are unique (or have unique meanings) in the jargon of the industry: hang-up, bull-team logging, skid, swell, ground-lead donkey, line-horse, hookin', haywire, caulk-shoes. As Swanson's glossary recognizes, we need to understand that "hang-up" does not mean inhibition, but refers to a fouled "turn" of logs (188), a tangle in the group of logs being yarded out of the woods in a single load. (A good deal of the pleasure of learning logging jargon lies in discovering the metaphorical potential now drained out of the commonplace colloquialism.) The imagery behind such terminology ("hang-up" also describes stuck rigging, or a tree stuck against another in falling: a current usage, "don't get hung up on that," is close to the sense found in logging) intensifies the sense of precariousness which permeates this vocabulary. But Swanson only uses these terms incidentally, in order to speak from the soles of his caulk boots to the audience of loggers themselves.

As he does in the admiring ballad "Life in the Western Woods," which opens *Rhymes of a Lumberjack*:

> There to hear a donkey's whistle; feel the yarding
> donkey shiver;
> See the main-line stretching skyward; watch the
> soft ground heave and quiver;
> See the mighty logs come walking—crash through
> windfalls as they hurry;
> Hear them thud beneath the spar-tree; watch the
> chaser jump and scurry. (61)

Again Swanson juggles the logging vocabulary enthusiastically and thuds along with gusto. This poem, with a weaker narrative line than "Rough-House Pete," jumps with more character as Swanson tosses into his lines as many verbs and verb forms, and as many sound images as possible. The relentless imperatives reinforce the verb-ness of logging: the poem quivers with the frenzied action and "jangling" noise of the loggers' work site. The speaker continually commands the reader to do something: poet is boss, reader is bossed.

Of a dozen logging terms in the first two stanzas of the poem, seven—"yarding," "wind-falls," "chaser," "loaders," "rigger," "hooker," "choker"—are formed from verbs. The last five all designate the various workers in the camp— identity rests for each worker in a single repeated action. Again, Swanson looks to the vocabulary not for the literary, but to identify with his community. The metaphorical energies of his given language, the doubled meanings in terms from donkey to duplex to hooker, presumably never occurred to him as they would to me. Swanson's doggerel may not be high art, but other poets honour attributes of his poetry (exaggeration, alliterated doublets, strong verbals). And anecdotes and logging vocabulary are recognized by other poets as necessary to their own version of logging poetry.

The contemporary significance of such relatively unambiguous anecdote is primarily political. To sing the life of the worker in the language of the workplace—song fuses pride and articulateness— implicitly urges political power for the worker. As Bruce Bennett, paraphrasing A.G. Stephens, described the "prolific versifiers" of the Goldfields region of Western Australia: "[T]heir voices often sound tribal rather than individual, expressing group feelings, values and attitudes; hence their

~

California must be a magic place. Not only will it be the first state in the US of A in which the minorities combine to outnumber the white folks, but her colours dot our northern landscape. Pinks, pastel blues, and rose-hued beiges colour new homes and apartments, diluting the powerful deep green of our mountains almost as though we needed some of the soft colors of California's desert to tone down the depth of our green.

Lee Maracle *Sojourner's Truth
and other Stories* 108

preference for the ballad form" (79).

Ballad has less appeal for the poets whose subject is work (the balladeers are more likely to include, or emphasize loggers' play and relaxation), and whose theme is almost invariably the physical violence and danger of logging (not the romantic heroism of the "steel-nerved rigger" swinging his axe with ease). A good introduction to this "documentary" aspect of logging poetry—at least because of its preoccupation with industrial violence—is Howard White's *The Men There Were Then* (1983). White acknowledges an intimate connection between his "formal concern . . . to explore the genius of common speech" (11), and the subject of accidents. His introduction might serve as a manifesto for all logger poets:

> *Every job I've ever been on I've seen the same thing happen: people sit down to talk and sooner or later they end up talking about accidents. The stories are usually offered as eyewitness accounts and told with such hairraising detail you'd think they must be; but more often than not they're ones you've heard before with different victims in different places. I have long been intrigued by this phenomenon. I see it is an authentic legendary tradition flourishing right in the midst of modern industry, a species of oral literature that rivals the written variety in its refinement of effect. (11)*

"Group feelings" are again crucial, even if the "genius of common speech," as White interprets it, and Grainger honours it, is far different from the formulaic phrasing which shapes the Swanson ballad. A storyteller's casual bravado when talking to the insider group understates the scream:

> *Uppit Englewood there one time*
> *I was blowin whistles, scaler*
> *busts out of the bush   hollers*
> *get a stretcher—fallers bin burned*
>
> *was cuttin upwards on a big leaning fir*
> *gascap unscrewed   doused im down is front*
> *then lit im up*
> *just black goo from is ribs to is knees*
>
> (22)

The common speech, as represented by White, with the diffident haste of its contractions, counters the horrific vision of a man burned to "goo," and demonstrates what becomes a theme at the end of the poem—the "trying to think," the struggle to say anything about either cause or effect. Thus White's poem, like others of its type, necessarily makes analyses look ridiculous at the same time as it covertly contemplates its own achievement of effect. The repeated message embodies a proletarian vision: anger and shock for the lot of the worker whose violent injury or death seems casually disregarded by those in power.

This paradox of power explains why relatively little specialized vocabulary inflects White's poems. Only one or two suggestions of a particular dialect, as at the beginning of this poem, evoke a particular violent profession. For the rest, White does not attempt to make extended use of the distinctive vocabulary, despite an interest in the workers' voices.

His emphasis is on variations of story—the story common to all workers. Though he knows logging jargon, he makes a literary decision not to draw attention to it: thus extending the social comment beyond one incident or industry.

David Day's *The Cowichan* (1975) similarly collects stories in the loggers' own voices, dwelling again and again on the violent accident and the indifference of the machine:

> We are slugging against the cold
> but it is going badly:
> the lines burn, chokers break
> the logcount is poor
>
> and late in the afternoon
> the chaser holds up a broken hand
> bright blood coming down
> the white flesh of his arm
>
> his slow scream
> lost in the diesel roar
>
> (n.p.)

As in White, the workplace speech emerges poetic, although the terms might not be isolated in glossaries: "cuttin upwards," "gascap," "doused," "logcount," "diesel roar." With that roar, the poem, titled "Storm," ends—with its own resignation to the brutality of the industry or, perhaps, with its own "slow scream," the impossibility of speaking out.

Patrick Lane, writing of work associated with logging ("Thirty Below," "Mill Cry," "Quitting Time") also avoids any "literary" interference with the folk grotesqueries of his narrative. The poem "After" tells of a man who has lost his forearm in an accident and is reduced to telling endless stories about the incident "until he ran out of variations, and no one would listen to him," and then to pounding pins into his deadened limb, "the dead piece of meat," in return for glasses of beer (46). The phrase "gyppo show" touches the event with the loggers' language. "Gyppo" refers to the small independent loggers' operations, with inevitable perjorative connotations according to Swanson. In current usage, when independent loggers are scarce and multinational corporate logging overwhelming, gyppo often has a more fondly nostalgic association. (When Joel Martineau, whose father was a gyppo logger, read this chapter, he informed me, with a logger's directness, that equating gyppo with a cheating outfit underpaying its workers was "bullshit.") Opening with this term (the one *odd* word in the poem) implies the aimless wandering (that is, itinerant, gipsy), the cheating, and poor quality or pay of "gyppo shows" remembered in the bar. But to the speaker "gyppo" is not odd: unselfconsciously, he relies on a word that *belongs* in his vocabulary, and shows his belonging.

Canadian poets have learned from Al Purdy to tell stories of physical work in an open, self-questioning, and usually self-deprecating manner, which itself is poetically productive—that is, the language in the poem registers both as something you understand

and that is interesting in its own right. Logging poetry in which the workers' register is also an aesthetic vehicle tests the resonances and metaphorical potential of the language. This process is, I think, just emerging in the poetry of the Northwest. We still await—we may never have—the poet who will do with logging and its verbal forms what Robert Kroetsch did with the languages of the prairie farm in *Seed Catalogue* (1977). The most significant poet, so far, to give us some sense of the literary possibilities of the loggers' verbal universe—and, also, the British Columbia poet most like Al Purdy—is Peter Trower.

Trower's "Caulk-Boot Legacy" defines the literary tradition to which he wishes to belong. This short essay reveals how logging is a bit like poetry. As a logger poet, Trower has written a great deal on the subject. Like Martin Grainger, he had a British childhood, but he became absorbed in writing about logging, whereas Grainger turned, after one book, in the direction of the policy-making if not the politics of logging. Yet, the straining artlessness of *Woodsmen of the West* could contain the poetic jumbles of Trower. "Grease for the Wheels of Winter" is one of his best-known, most anthologized poems:

Grease for the Wheels of Winter
Quickening in the valley, the white flutter
blurs the road-slashed relief map   The valley floor
tips in the salted distance   Such damp confetti
will wed these boondocks to quiet

. . .

No one will unlock these doors again until spring;
rigging will hang like forgotten laundry from
*   clothesline-pole spar-trees.*

Only the wind will come then to croon in the spared
*   boughs*
of trees too high or meagre to kill   The white, the white—
flutter and smile of silence will spread from ear
*   to ear*
and nod this place calm like a mother.

(1999 65)

Trower loves to throw together the extravagant metaphors in the loggers' jargon, as when, in "Booby Trap," the "mule-kicking alder barberchairs back—/catches me clean in the crotch" (27)—or, mixing workplace and bookish vocabulary, he toasts "Bill, you old sky-hanger" and his "subliminal savvy" (36). From time to time he writes explicitly about the inherent poetry of his work lingo, most memorably when he hears "The Last Handfallers":

They have crinkled Swenska voices
like wind in the branches
of the countless killed trees
who have given them their tongues. (26)

He writes an entire poem about a fellow worker whose tongue has discovered just one perfect phrase:

There were a lot of dead trees on that claim
hollow fire-gutted cedar shells
spiking up among the felled timber
"Goosequill snags" Barney called them
I never forgot the term
It was his only poetry. (40)

Goosequill snags. Barberchairs. Trower seldom tries to extend or interpret such metaphors. He simply savours them. "High wit," as when he writes "my eyes need no caulkboots," is rare (28).

"Grease for the Wheels of Winter" is a snag of unconnected metaphors with just a crinkle of logging vocabulary. Much of the poem's language, for example "boondocks" or "raingear" or "killed," will carry special meanings for West Coast loggers (although such possibilities disappear when the poem moves to a more distanced perspective at the end). The words unique to the woods seem restricted to single reference—the "crummy" for the truck (or vehicle) in which the loggers travel hardly echoes its punning sense of something worthless and falling apart; "spar-trees" do not suggest their origins in nautical terminology, although Trower's lunge at connecting them to backyard domesticity is part of the poem's freedom. The poem is a compendium of the ballad's exaggeration, the worker poet's documentary impulse and the banging verbal noisiness of Swanson.

The phrase "lying a mean lick" has perhaps the most potential in the poem. The *Shorter OED* suggests the dialect association of this term with a spurt of work, or particularly hard work, but the sense of idly talking to put in time, or more crudely, "shooting the shit," seems peculiar to the logging industry (McCulloch 80). "A mean lick" marks the poem's authenticity. Trower here is lying his own mean lick by wandering poetically from topic to topic, defying any obligation to niceties of verbal symmetry.

In the first two lines, he sees the landscape as a relief map of tree tops. But after line two he drops the metaphor. He turns to describe the "salted" distance: perhaps it is sprinkled with white flecks, or the first snow may preserve the distance, or hint at a false promise of riches. Whatever potential lies in this mean lick (of salt?), he immediately abandons it for "confetti" and the metaphor of a wedding. But a wedding may be inappropriate to the late fall setting: the metaphor disappears as unpredictably as it is introduced. Now he personifies the sky as "spooked," before turning to the metaphor of "woodwar," which could hardly be expected to relate to the simile of "abandoned elephants" or the imagery of backyard laundry mentioned earlier. When Trower ends the description of the land by moving from "maps" through "old house" to a "person," I am both baffled and somehow at home. "The white flutter," he explains stutteringly, returning to the vocabulary of the opening line, "will spread from ear to ear and nod this place calm like a mother— *What* is like a "mother"? And how do either "flutter" or "smile" "nod"? Are they to be imagined as heads?

Trower loves compounds, here as elsewhere: road-slashed, boondocks, woodwar, raingear, quittingtime, clothesline-pole spartrees. Compounds are exceptionally prominent in logging language, as if impatient and harried workers need to create new verbs of hurrying up and blurring (barber-chair from two nouns). The compound is the microcosmic form of the collapsing semantic and syntactical distinctions Grainger had in mind when he talked of a makeshift art of rough and ready. In this tendency, Trower follows closely Swanson and his logging poetry ancestors—and more distantly, Anglo-Saxon poetry (via Earle Birney) and Al Purdy, his most direct mentor. What happens in "Grease" is, I think, the mean lick of compounding and compounding again a collection of incomplete metaphors for the onset of winter in a logging landscape. The poem doesn't stand up to bookish standards of aesthetic unity and consistency. Precisely. Trower creates a logging poem through a bizarre collision of poetic possibilities, as brawling and crudely enthusiastic as the men chattering between bites of apple on their way to a winter's rest. Unity and consistency, the poem announces, are bullshit.

What, one might finally ask, has the poem to do with the metaphor of the machine proposed by the title? Joel Martineau answers: "Everything!" Oncoming winter describes the time of shutting down the logging operation, and a concern about a rapidly disappearing way of life. This winter has grease and wheels because it's the winter of mass environmental destruction brought on by the massive machinery of corporate logging (Trower 1994).

~

~

In BC, the species [arbutus] is fighting a losing battle with humankind over available coastal habitat. Recent wet winters have encouraged the growth of an insidious root rot. An invasive fungus is spreading by means of airborne spores, raising large cankers on arbutus stems and branches, which then die back, turning a burnt-looking black before fading to grey. Over the long term, arbutus could disappear from the northernmost parts of its range.
Andrew Scott "Revering the Robust Arbutus" 33

Caulk Boot Legacy

The brawling crudity of form and tumbling vocabulary, the essence of this legacy from Grainger through Swanson and Trower, culminates in the Northwest's biggest, most brilliantly makeshift logging novel. Why read Ken Kesey's *Sometimes a Great Notion* (1964)? Why read it regionally? First, although the novel is confined, in one sense, to a very restricted space, the Stamper family home and the Snag (the community's centre, for males at least), the sheer bravado and scope and range of the thing allows no chance for provincial blinkers to be fitted. Second, if there are many Northwests, and many place-stories are happening many times, then no single Pacific Northwest text has so many layered stories, so many voices overlapping in a not-quite-harmonized "round" (Kesey Collection 2-6). Third, Kesey rewrites the entrepreneurial romance, which like spirit quest and salmon migration is a regional defining narrative. Fourth, at every turn, Kesey places great emphasis on language, on learning the local names, both vocabulary and pronunciation, and on understanding what they reveal. Fifth, for all his bewildering "outburst of writing," he turns a passionate and attentive eye—as do almost all the writers discussed in this book—to details of flora, fauna, and climate. *What land is this?*, he keeps asking (120, 20; author's emphasis). And we can appreciate his passionate questioning of land and language by following him out of the archives. Sixth, most importantly, he doesn't take any of my other five claims too seriously. Or, his seriousness includes parody and self-mockery.

Ken Kesey's *Sometimes a Great Notion* tilts and slashes in so many directions that logging novel is hardly an adequate label. But for all his trib-

---

Our trees were among the tallest on the planet, so tall their tops couldn't be seen. Widowmakers he called them. Heartwood, the inside of a tree, was dead. Sapwood, the outside, was alive. To cut a tree down, he kept the saw in the same place. The tree wasn't going anywhere. Sooner or later, it fell. He looked for points of crooks or whorls of knots. He made an undercut. He talked about knaps, knars, stumps, and spars, and about all sorts of saws—bull, hula, muley, whip, and chain.

I didn't understand any of this, but I listened.

Linda Svendsen *Marine Life* 111

---

utaries and looping songs, Kesey's attention to the attempt (no, maybe it's a daring reluctance) of two half-brothers to learn their way from university bookishness to gyppo logging makes it an essential Pacific Northwest tale:

I'd begun to wonder if maybe what a man learns over twelve years in a world so different is like a foreign language that uses some of the words from our world but not enough to be familiar to us, not enough so we can talk. But when I see him watch that tree come down I think. There's that; just like any man I ever knew, he likes to see a tree felled. (178)

The viewpoint belongs to Hank Stamper, the brother who has stayed home, by the banks of the Wakonda Auga River, handlogging the Oregon mountainsides. "Him" is younger brother Leland (Lee), returned from Yale, a PhD degree in literature unfinished, to prove (with fretfully wavering conviction) that you can go home again.

For a university professor of English, trying to find the forms of logging in Northwest culture, this storyline has great appeal. Especially because Kesey's tolerance for "horseshit" is pretty high. Only the slightest shift in response to this passage will reveal that two "worlds so different" and two "foreign languages" confront one another at this edge of the forest. In the two paragraphs that precede this quotation, the terms "buck" (as verb), "scalers," "widow-makers," "dutchman" (it is also, elsewhere, the name of a creek)—assert their different sameness by appearing unglossed. Hank exults that Lee—as, he thinks, does any man— "likes to see a tree felled," a comforting bit of self-talk which validates his profession. Hank's conviction will make readers either nod assent, or squirm: the Northwest—urban and wilderness—often seems to be imagined by people who would wish never to see another tree felled anywhere. But for all of the brawling, reckless extractive culture of *Sometimes a Great Notion*, Kesey mulls the contradiction and irony, especially through burlesque, more thoroughly than the surfaces of a brawling extractive economy might first seem to allow. It's a notion confirmed by the learning, the predilection for a sophisticated metaphor of language and specialized vocabularies to which Hank's brainwaves so readily bounce.

The 1960s linger in the Pacific Northwest:

~

When Seymour Levin begins his new life teaching in Eastchester, Cascadia [Corvallis, Oregon], he must learn early where the Liberal Arts fits into the extractive natural resource economy. Professor Fairchild: "Ours is a land economy based on forestry—the Douglas fir and ponderosa pine for the most part; and agriculture. . . . We need foresters, farmers. . . . We need them—let's be frank—more than we need English majors. You can't fell a tree . . . with poetry." (Malamud 36)

Before he can make satisfying love in a new country, Levin needs to become a woodsman of the West: "his life had been lived largely without experience of very many trees, and among them he felt a little unacquainted." (182)

the Day-Glo colours just sit there rusting away in the drizzle and blackberry bushes alongside the Kool-Aid acid-test bus that apparently still smiles on a corner of Ken Kesey's dairy farm near Pleasant Hill, Oregon. As much as the Eisenhower-era Cold War mentality has a presence (no doubt, exaggerated) east of the Cascades, the nostalgia for sit-ins, teach-ins, and (paradoxically) doing-your-own-thing persist on the Pacific coast. A disposition no doubt reinforced, north of '49, by the disaffected youth and so-called draft dodgers who have contributed so significantly to journalism and the arts in Canada. For those of us who never quite dared to be hippies, *Sometimes a Great Notion* answers to our need for a kaleidoscopic, over-done, clamorous, cynical, and yet tenderly attentive regional encyclopedia. David James Duncan and Tom Robbins make their claims, too, although perhaps no writer in Canada does. George Bowering is more terse and selective, while Jack Hodgins, who celebrates excess, does so inexcessively.

Not very far beneath the myths of garden and drowsy Lotusland that cling to the coastal Northwest, zig-zag fault lines portend cataclysmic reconfiguring of the topography. Kesey's *Great Notion* is the Northwest's earthquake novel: its form shows the fissures and fractures of a stable novel not quite trusted. We apprehend fault lines while reading a novel of its varied typefaces, packed parentheses, and "sliding point of view" (Kesey Collection Box 2 typed note). The shifting forms register more strongly on a reader trying to follow the method of composition in the archives. In an earthquake novel, the chapters are neither titled nor numbered: in his notes, adding contradiction to confusion, Kesey calls them *parts*, associates his divisions with marking fluctuating levels of the river, and (especially given his use of song as title) also thinks of them as "movements" (Kesey Collection Box 2 holograph notes). In an early typescript version of Chapter Three, Kesey begins his compelling passage on the aesthetics of rivers and sloughs in placid documentary style:

The river has not always run this course. Along its twenty miles are numerous switchbacks and ox-bows, sloughs and backwaters that mark its old channel.

(Kesey Collection Box 1)

Scrawled over top of this beginning is a handwritten addition to be inserted between the two sentences: "You want to know something about rivers?" In the next typescript, this intervention is included, but again is amended by Kesey, placed in parentheses, with a typed insertion over the line, "friends a[nd] bours" (Kesey Collection Box 2). In th[e pub]lished version, the opening sentence and t[he] first addition become a separate paragraph, detached now from the longer paean to graceful willows and silver fingerlings:

As well as he knew that the Wakonda has not always run this course (Yeah . . . you want to know something about rivers, friends and neighbours?) (100)

So a declarative commonplace has become a drifting fragment, following from the epigraph on "Treacherous impermanence," but not permanently bound to it. And the register has shifted to a colloquial boast and then to a cajoling plea, almost aproaching the tone of a carnival hustler.

"Hear you tell it, this country use [sic] to all be eighty-degree slopes with earthquakes and geysers." (479)

A good deal more than point of view is sliding in this novel. Given handlogging in the saturated slopes of the Coastal Range, and shoring up the Stamper mansion that the river threatens every day to sweep away and out to sea, sliding is a prominent theme. The drizzle pervades, penetrates every notion. Sentences slide into ellipses; tenses slide into other time frames; chapters, and epigraphs, and syllables slide. Especially, stories and voices slide. Billboards slide into fairy tales and slide over the *Classic Comics* to slide under a family chronicle.

"What land is this?" Lee asks himself (Kesey

d neigh-
e pub-
he

: same question from a *are these creatures? Where is* italics are Kesey's, and asize but slide into the ithor's, own question- : answer are discovered in the locale and localisms of the Stampers' logging show. But the answer is also hinted—given the genius of the Lee/Hank counter-personalities—in the attention Kesey lavishes on the flora and fauna, especially on "flowers [and birds, surely, everywhere birds] common to the area, . . . not flowers bred in Holland and raised in California and flown in to be pampered in local nurseries" (92). Catalogues of these crowd almost every page: "the spider-wort and blue verrain, the trout lily and adder's tongue, the bleeding heart and pearly everlasting, and the carrion weed with its death-scented bloom" (140). Kesey does not pause after this list—even in this novel of paus-es, digressions, echoes, and overlaps—to mull over the texture of local metaphor, of the delightfully uncommon common names in this list. But one can imagine him doing so. And one suspects that the echoes exist (cer-tainly, yes, of snake and carrion) which one more fascinated reading of the novel will reveal. And why not, when Viv, with Lee's fin-gers light on her *throat* (my emphasis) hears the voices the flowers sound: "the drip of the bleeding heart, the rattle of firecracker weed, the hiss of adder's tongue" (252).

A marvellous example of such intently loving attention to the question "'where is this land?'"—which is also to ask "'what are these creatures?'"—grows from Lee's near totally irrelevant (to the narrative) description, now speaking in the first person, of Darlingtonia. I am not going to indulge in quoting the full paragraph that Kesey lavishes on these "chlorophyll beings from another planet," swamp plants of central Oregon and South popularly known as California pitcher plant, or Cobra plant (Underhill 1986 61). (Another adder's tongue?) But two analogies are espe-cially striking. "Imagine an elongated comma . . . or picture half-notes for vegetable musicians" (306). (To whom is this urging addressed? It may be directed to the narrating persona on page one.) Each of these answers Lee's questions with another element in the regional language: the "believe-it-or-not" (307) of a small meat-eating plant provides a pause—this is a pretty big comma—in the sen-tence of place, and again, it predicts a voice, a song perhaps "half humorous, half sinister."

Like Lee, Kesey is a notebook keeper, although the notes for *Notion* are often patched, in a big open and jostled hand, on eight-and-a-half-by-eleven sheets. One, the first on a sheet containing seven fragments, refers to Darlingtonia, the apparent germ from which spreads the extended description on pages 306 and 307. This brief, and isolat-ed passage, shows both the impatient process of composition and, in its metaphyical reflec-tion, how relevant the description I labelled near-irrelevant to the narrative may be:

Darlingtonias are patient—the little birds can't afford to be. Each is on his own. The darlingtonias sit with their roots joined in the water, one dies it is only the dropping of a leaf—but one little bird dies that is him.

(Kesey Collection Box 2)

The flower's meaning is extended (in the published novel, each detail is undercut), first by

Highballing

I sit thumbing through *Sometimes a Great Notion* for the sixth time this morning. I am looking for the highballer, but the novel keeps interrupting me with another surprising cross-reference to *Hamlet*, or the delicate sense of nuance in early morning bird-song (245), or the bravado of running prepositions and rimes together to tint the place: two doves "emerge together from the mist, of the mist, gray, graceful" (245). Or, to get back to woods words, what is a "stob"? (189).

And thumbing at the same time, again, through photocopies of some of Kesey's notes and typescripts, appreciating how much the actual literal writing process, the contact of ink with paper, is essential to the product. (Neither opening scene, nor its placement, simply *manifests* itself: Kesey thinks of an amputated leg, but wonders what it means; later, decides an arm would be better; still later chooses—"dast I?" he asks himself [Kesey Collection Box 2 holograph notes]—the memorably defiant upraised middle finger.)

Lee's admission that, even with his clever analogies, the reader is unlikely to be able to picture the plant, and then by his trying to talk—why not? this is about the regional voice?—into the "mouth" of the Darlingtonia. "'How's the life?'" (307). The one it has extinguished, or the one found?

~

If you spend your time writing a book about writing about place, this voyeur-ing into archives can be greatly encouraging. It's a constant reminder that the act of writing, and rewriting, is essentially a mode of thinking. You have to get this down. And once you do, you might be able to get something better down. So you realize that Kesey's novel, this 628 pages of Penguin paperback I am wearing out, is one out-take from this process. Hence, I am entitled, oddly, to rewrite his writing. Entitled to write about the writing that locates me, because Kesey writes about the writing that finds his place. Certainly the use of Dylan Thomas, Shakespeare, Faulkner (Kesey 227)— and the language of "dumbass loggers"— reminds us that a regional inflection is not an isolated, inward inflection. So, Doig's *Winter Brothers* makes such sense as a model. For me, it's rain-season brothers, and sisters, and grandmothers, and aunts. Important to me now, too, that *Sometimes a Great Notion* was Kesey's last great book—it's as if he did succeed in writing himself home. And then could pause and follow his family back into dairy farming.

But back to woodswords. It's a bit surprising to me, looking now at the photocopied archival pages, how few of Kesey's notes about logging and sawmill are self-conscious about logging lingo. The early field notes pick out a few images ("Lunch room: Benches, woodstove, walls papered with woman flesh" [Kesey Collection "Saw Mill"]) or, most often, begin to stretch and figure a metaphor ("Mill like a wild screaming out-of-its skull jazz band reaching for the climax." [Kesey Collection Box 2 holograph notes]). Much of the turning of logging language seems to be spontaneous. The marvellous twist, which turns what would in Britain be the local *snug*, into the Snag (the bar, with Viv in the back booth), is one such. The first written reference to snag? Probably this metaphysical jotting, on a page of one-liners titled "Things to add wherever possible" (Kesey Collection Box 2 holograph notes): "It isn't life against death, its man against death rotted snags like skeletons."

With the exception of "Dutchman," which is recorded in Kesey's handnotes without interpretation or gloss, the few other terms in the notes are already on the way to being interpreted. The term "highballer," for example, appears as metaphor—Highballer in Heaven—the phrase by which Joe attempts to save Leland by showing him how highballing is not highhanded. The phrase "that's the kind of talk Walker uses, Leland" is the analysis of language that occurs in the very earliest note. Joe's gloss—"A highballer, see, is a old loggin' term for a guy who did about twice as much as others" (300)—does not pause for the irony Kesey probably appreciates, that a highballing god may hurry to excess and take destructive and self-destructive risks. Like a highballing novel, I suspect.

~

Great Blue Heron File

Down the shore where sun drives
darkness through, a colder blue than sky
comes running in the tide's resolve.
And the heron moves, pauses, moves again
where shore and sky engage. Its moment hangs
like the earliest pleasure, heron's blue dark
on thin water there, and wings, like wings of the hurrying sky.

~Kenneth MacLean "Blue Heron's Sky"

Elegantly gray, the blue heron
. . .
. . . lands on the floating dock where the gulls cluster—

a tall prince come down from the castle to walk
proud and awkward, in the market square,
while squat villagers
break off their deals
and look askance.

~Denise Levertov "Heron II"

SALMON AND CEDAR. RAVEN AND COYOTE. Rain and laid-back. These images and motifs surface first when Pacific Northwest is mentioned. Compared to this formidable sextet, the great blue heron is but a hanging moment. The heron hardly has the region-specific associations of arbutus-madrone: I have visited the Blue Heron Gallery on Cape Cod, and I appreciate that the quintessentially Nebraskan poet Ted Kooser makes the "old blue heron" his alter ego, "with yellow eyes/and a grey neck tough as a snake" (n.p.). So, to linger long enough to ponder this endlessly pausing figure is to remember the limits of regional definition and the ridiculousness of exceptionalism: Ted Kooser and Wellfleet Massachusetts have very little, and maybe a great deal, to do with my subject.

The habitat of the great blue heron extends to most of North America and beyond. Sticking the great blue heron in the arbutus files, and encountering the Blue Heron Studio in Clayburn, BC, or Blue Heron Publishing in Portland, Oregon, is to circle back to the realization that "home is the whole earth, but it always wears the masks of particular places."

So, I was delighted to learn, listening to the radio in February 1997, that a very large, and uncharacteristic blue heron rookery can be found in that odd American appendage of Canada known as Point Roberts. And still more pleased to learn that, bioregions being what they are, the herons go border-crossing every day to feed on the eelgrass meadows at Roberts Bank on the Canadian side of the border. Those herons belong to a Pacific Northwest subspecies of the great blue heron, known to taxonomists as *Ardea herodias fannini* (Butler 5-7). Perhaps that the Northwest Coast Great Blue Heron is non-migratory, and that only in this particular place "has the great blue heron . . . been studied throughout the year" (Butler xiv), explains its potential as another icon of region. When Robert Butler, in his fine book mostly devoted to subspecies *fannini*, defines the crucial habitat "along the shores of the temperate rain forest" as "calm water, wide beaches with abundant fish, and mild weather" (16), he might be reinforcing the connections I have been testing in these pages. When Robert Sund, from his shack above the "fresh-water tidal marsh of the Skagit estuary" defines heron, his five terse lines compose a "study" throughout the year:

1.
Long spells of heron-watching,
Now that the swallows have gone.
2.
In April,
when the swallows return,
The old heron will have less to do.

(Sund 1992 n.p.)

On the title page of Sund's *Shack Medicine*, in which this poem is found, stands a heron, feet hidden in the white water of the page, with (at least as I interpret it) much to do. The poet's own spare brushstrokes in blue-gray return me somehow to the new Seattle Art Museum and its small gallery, which I have visited elsewhere in these pages, whose rotating exhibitions are devoted to "Early Modern Art of the Northwest." On 14 January 1994, the only two artists showing are Mark Tobey and Morris Graves. For all the regional importance, in my own mind, of Tobey's calligraphic Asian-inspired traceries (the regional palette, and book as "white writing") (PLATE 5), it is Graves on this day who seems to speak Northwest (PLATE 8). I push closer to the muted beige-grey-black of his colour schemes; even his green fades in a mix of muddy blue-brown—and in each of the paintings I notice a bird, a *shore* bird. When I return to the same gallery on 17 November 1995, I am able to view the grandly titled "The Great Blue Heron Yogi and the Rainbow Trout Yogi in Phenomenal Space and the Space of Consciousness" (1979 coll. Robert Yarber). In this triptych a fusion of hunter-heron and its prey; an interchanging of sea-land, too perhaps. I propose to myself that the great blue heron serves (in this encounter, at least) as the expression of the edge, unlike eagle or Steller's Jay.

Great blue heron is a sky creature and a tree-dweller, which we usually see standing solitary, independent, on an intertidal, or riparian edge, feeding. "[P]erhaps the heron was some kind of new buoy," worries the narrator of Malcolm Lowry's "The Forest Path to the Spring": maybe it marks the dangerous land, just hidden by the sea. "But then this tall buoy moved slightly," Lowry's narrator continues, "then stood motionless as before" (1961 238). Usually it seems enough just to watch: heron is the Zen-bird of contemplation. For Henry Lafleur, in John Keeble's *Broken Ground* (1987), heron is the "unchanged element," at once standing for the drowning of his daughter and healing:

The heron's long neck folded toward its body and unfolded again and swayed gracefully. It tipped its head to the side and froze, watching. Lafleur watched it. . . . He instructed himself in that: to watch, to be unafraid. (26)

~

You retreat beneath your cowl, spread wings, rise, drift upriver as silent as winter trees.

I follow you. You have caught me with your reticence. I will listen to whatever they say about you, what anyone who has seen you wishes to offer—and I will return to call across the river to you, to confirm or deny. If you will not speak I will have to consider making you up.

Barry Lopez
"The Search for the Heron"
River Notes 70

Carolyn Kizer's poem "The Great Blue Heron" does not use the verb *watch*, but the instructions of "eye" and courageous *seeing* are central to its development. An unshadowed shadow, heron is seen—as if in a Morris Graves's edge-scape—on "a canvas day." The figure collapses time and space as the memory—the poem is an elegy for the poet's mother—confuses place and occasion. The beiged hue, the tempting non-colour of canvas, reminds of the Northwest palette observed elsewhere in these files: the heron may be blue (in both senses), but the picture in the poem is "shadow," "dusty," "ashen," "a vapor,"—"like gray smoke," and the bird itself "spectral" (14-15). Many allusions to fire—fireworks? signals of danger?, a burned summer house?—promise a colour unarticulated. Kizer touches presumably on the possibility (see T.H. White's *The Book of Beasts*, for example) that heron is a model for the Phoenix.

In its four verse-paragraphs, the poem moves from uneasy observation (the heron's wings "tattered"), to metaphysical reflection (the speaker senses her own identification with heron) and fear, to discovery (through the speaker's mother) to some measured celebration, articulated in an emerging end-rhyme linking day, away, and play, of the heron as personal talisman, "denser than my repose." The heron's place is the poet-speaker's edge; it is found in the story of lonely "beach," once fifteen years earlier convivial "strand," become a "bare strip of shore." Day, dream, father, mother, heron, writing itself, "drift away" (Kizer 14-15). The story happens many times: great blue heron becomes spirit guide.

~

A snort. Or a chuckle. They might be Jack Hodgins's response to this reading of Kizer and heron. Inventing a world, writing his home place, has for Hodgins never been a simple matter of recording the peculiarities of local flora or speech patterns, though he does plenty of both. He goes out into the whole world, not so much to compare Ireland or Japan to Vancouver Island, but to realize the presence of other worlds in the local locale of his own novels. In *Innocent Cities*, we find a lot of Australia in Victoria. And we find a very dif-ferent version of great blue heron, which gives its name to the hotel that is the pretentious and fading centre of the pioneer community— and eventually the name of the bizarre flying machine whose flight is as awkward as the heron's is effortless. James Horncastle explains why his hotel must be named The Great Blue Heron:

Why was the hotel named for this great awkward bird? Simple. "You've seen him. Stands at the side of the water. Waits for his dinner to come to him." What else were any of them doing here, he challenged his listeners to tell him. Waiting for the next boom. "Waiting for gold to be discovered again somewhere so we can all become rich. Haven't you noticed? This city's how those foreigners get into the country." Many like himself had got their start during the Cariboo gold rush, and now they waited for the opportunity to take advantage of the next lot to come chasing after wealth. (34)

~

Intertidal File

Alice goes down to the shore, and to the tide pools among the rocks there. . . . She goes down there because it soothes her and pleases her, all this wealth of life in the intertidal zone. Small fishes, not much bigger than large exclamation points, swim back and forth in the shallow pools. Crabs relax in the warm water. Bits of seaweed sway graceful as hula dancers. Everywhere there are minute snails and chalky barnacles, fixed forever in one spot, condemned to spend their adult lives standing on their heads and kicking food into their mouths with their feet.

~Audrey Thomas *Intertidal Life*

It [diving near Point Whitney] was like being plunged into a culture medium, a womb. . . . Geoducks and anemones, like a lot of marine creatures, reproduce by spewing clouds of sperm into the water. I caught a mouthful of salt water, a teaspoon mouthful overflowing with seed.

~Sallie Tisdale *Stepping Westward*

Tide had gone out farther. . . . Driftwood scattered along the gravel slope mimicked every aspect of human life: here a side of beef, there a cannon, there a sea snake, an overturned canoe—a log so rotted out it was only a shell. Dragon faces, Medusa heads, circus performers with flung-out limbs, torpedoes.

~Jack Hodgins *The Macken Charm*

Whether the land had made
headway or the sea inroads,
it was a place of no compromise,
a harsh geometry of triangles,
steep mountain slopes disappearing
into cold green water.

~Gary Geddes *rivers inlet*

THIS BOOK BEGAN WITH CLAY CALVERT ON the edge of the continent, and Earle Birney's narrator muddling along a sea wall at the edge of city. In opening an intertidal file near the end of the accumulation, I return to such places of transition between sea and land. Places where you often see the great blue heron stand its haunting vigil. Places where freshwater smolts learn to become saltwater salmon. Places where the windfalls, and the logs escaped from their booms, come to rest and remind of another wealth of life.

The zone alternately covered and uncovered by the tides—twice daily—makes an ideal metaphor for a place in constant transition, a wonderland, as Audrey Thomas's Alice muses, of idle comfort and of acrobatic craziness. For me, looking for a place to stop, but not finish, the intertidal zone is a place of deposition, of layering, of a mix of communities, of crevices and hidden pools, of the occasional stranded visitor, of varying lines of debris, each of which might be read for clues to other worlds (PLATE 13).

Not that I would deposit here all the debris that fills two closets. Nor will I attempt to

~

I live in a house, with window curtains and a lawn, in British Columbia, which is as far away from Toronto as I could get without drowning. The unreality of the landscape there encourages me: the greeting card mountains, of the sunset-and-sloppy-message variety, the cottagy houses that look as if they were built by the Seven Dwarfs in the thirties, the giant slugs, so much larger than a slug needs to be. Even the rain is overdone, I can't take it seriously. I suppose these things are as real, and as oppressive, to the people who grew up there as this place is to me. But on good days it still feels like a vacation, an evasion.

Margaret Atwood *Cat's Eye* 14-15

unpack all the punning playfulness of *Intertidal Life*. But borrowing that novel's central metaphor, and remembering its form as commonplace book, may allow me to scatter near the book's end some of the driftwood that still provokes interpretation. Among the omissions in these files is the slippery elegant prose of Ethel Wilson. Wilson is the Jane Austen of Northwest writing, uncovering the tensions and motivations of social interaction. She might be said to best exemplify the Britishness of British Columbia writing. And in such Britishness, oddly enough, she also seems an anomaly. The West Coast toward which *The Innocent Traveller* travels—after an Arnoldian upbringing and cross-Canada train trip—is shaped, by Topaz's energetic naiveté, a relatively blank space where Raven and his progeny have no presence:

And the wind was blowing, too, among the great undiscovered pine trees in the yet unnamed place far away where some day Topaz Edgeworth would live and die. . . . This place was still silent and almost unknown. (36-37)

But even in its failure to acknowledge the millennia of naming which had spoken the place before a few newcomers would write that they and it were unnamed, *The Innocent Traveller* pivots on a crucial scene, during an interlude on Benbow (Bowen) Island, which has lineaments of a spirit quest in it. The "where" that Topaz reaches is a transition zone, an intersection not so much between tides, as between sea and sky, a water/land world, where her marvellously free spirit moves with the unpredictable smoothness of a water bug. A dancer on the edge. Although forested mountain meets sea, with nothing in between, it is *open* country:

> *Here she had come to live; and, drawing long breaths of the opulent air, she began to run about, and dance for joy, exclaiming, all through the open country (122).*

The Innocent Traveller floats between land and sky. It honours the world of the drawing-room—and the drawing-room novel—but viewed, with a child's eyes, from underneath the table. The prim novel of social manners wants to break into the open and go dancing, as it might if written by Audrey Thomas, or even Tom Robbins. The novel centres on Topaz Edgeworth (the surname celebrating the "nine thousand consecutive days of her apotheosis beside the Pacific Ocean" [273]), on the hundred years of her "uncertain, restless" life (274): she is at once, in curiously shifting tenses, looking forward to that long life and looking back over it.

The form is not quite biography, or family chronicle, or journey novel. Wilson flirts perhaps with covert autobiography. The fiction of her form is something of a depꞈ an archive—of stories, of fictions, of ways remembering, of what floats up from the bottom, or is visible after long careful staring through a magnifying medium. The voluble Aunt Topaz has a "special genius for repetition" (8). Simultaneously, the narrator is, and is not, Topaz: in the same sentence we will hear her judged, and will then sense the prose inflected, its decorum plundered by the exuberance of Topaz's own zest for surprise.

Attempting to follow Wilson's own technique and objectives through the drafts found in the Ethel Wilson Collection is also to be surprised by exuberant decorum. Most of the first drafts are written longhand in pencil. Wilson is a relatively light reviser. The greatest surprise lies in turning from published work, from a sentence which seems all poise and balance and crafted chiasmus, to find that instead of having been cast and recast and worried into its subversive balance, it appears in its final form in the first draft. Given this general absence of reworking, the revisions which are made (and still, of course, there are many) take on crucial significance.

"The metaphors are not mixed," Wilson intones in a prefatory "Author's Note" (presumably with tongue at least partly in cheek): "The drop of water, the bird, the water-glider, the dancer, the wind on the canal, and Topaz, are all different and all the same." This transition and integration especially prompts me to include Wilson in the intertidal file. Topaz

renzy and grace on land, on
. And her transformations
er to dancer are also trans-
he medium in which she
ightly.

So in Chapter Eleven, when we follow Topaz (and her eldest sister Annie, and Annie's daughter, Rachel) on their journey across Canada by train, we come to an account of how Topaz travels lightly, with little luggage, barely touching the water:

> Unencumbered by boots or boats they [water gliders] run, seldom wetting their feet and, one supposes, unaware of the dreadful deeps below them, in which other beings more heavily weighted are plunged, and swim or sink, caught in the mud or entangled by the débris of circumstance and human relations . (103)

In the first handwritten draft, Wilson has the crossed-through phrase "inches or feet" following "dreadful deeps" (Wilson Papers I-II). This playful but contradictory phrase is happily deleted without sacrificing any of the burlesque element. More significantly, the first draft has a comma following "weighted." That this more deliberate and studied punctuation is eliminated (consistent with Wilson's general preference for minimal and slightly bizarre punctuation) clearly keeps the sentence lightly rapidly moving in mimicry of its subject.

Chapter Seventeen, titled "The Innumerable Laughter," shifts to Benbow Island, an interlude touched by the movements of the sea. Topaz lies in bed: we read this description, first reproduced in the manuscript version, then in the published:

> The wind had died, but a slight motion of the salt sea remained, and with the motion a small continuing sound. (Wilson Collection 1-13: 24-25)

> The wind had died, but a slight wash of the salt sea remained, and with the wash against the shore only a small continuing sound, which grew more faint. (188)

Wilson has stretched this sentence, and added three more modifiers to intensify the build-up of this transformation scene—in the classroom I have called it the "spirit quest chapter." The use of "wash," instead of motion, is not only more specific, but more synaesthetic and onomatopoetic. It adds to the intertidalness of the scene, by reinforcing the to-and-froing of tidal water, and by suggesting a world washed with saltwater, all covered with it and hence transformed, as in a cleansing, or an artist's technique for blurring and softening outlines (PLATE 14).

~

Threshold and edge. Border and margin. Obviously these are not tropes exclusive to any particular region: they are the site of artistic activity itself. In ecology, and for Barry Lopez, the special version of edge is the ecotone, where two ecological systems interact and overlap, where the variety of species are greatest, and where the rate of adaptation accelerates. In the prose poem "Inlet People,"

Plate I: Lilita Rodman, *Arbutus on the edge*

Plate 2: Toni Onley, *Second Beach, Stanley Park, Vancouver, 23 June 1997*
The spotted water colour catches the immediacy of art made in the rain zone.

Plate 3: Paul C. Horiuchi, *Rain Forest* (1960)
Gouache and Sumi ink on paper. 95.9 cm x 59.4 cm

Plate 4: Jack Shadbolt, *Elegy for an Island* (1985)
Acrylic on canvas. 144.5 cm x 213.0 cm
PRINTED WITH THE PERMISSION OF DORIS SHADBOLT AND THE
VANCOUVER ART GALLERY, ACQUISITION FUND (86.49). PHOTO: JIM JARDINE

Plate 5: Mark Tobey, *White Night* (1942)
Tempera on cardboard mounted on masonite. 56.5 cm x 35.6 cm

PRINTED WITH THE PERMISSION OF THE SEATTLE ART MUSEUM, NORTHWEST ANNUAL PURCHASE FUND (62.78)
GIFT OF MRS. BERTHE PONCY JACOBSON

Plate 6: Mark Tobey, *Skid Road* (1948)
Tempera on paper. 62.6 cm x 47 cm

Plate 7: Barrie Jones, *Pacific Salmon Series: Summer I* (1981)

Plate 8: Morris Graves, *Sea, Fish, and Constellation* (1943)
Tempera on paper. 19" x 53.5"

Plate 9: Lawrence Paul Yuxweluptun, *Native Fishing* (1988)
Acrylic on canvas, 16" x 18"

Plate 10: Joseph M. Wilson (Salish), *Salmon* (1991)
Silkscreen print.

PRINTED WITH THE PERMISSION OF THE ISLAND ART PUBLISHERS AND THE ARTIST

Plate II: Nancy Pagh, *The Art of Canned Salmon* (2002)

Plate 12: Barbara Klunder, *Farm is a Four-Letter Word to a Fish* (1996)
Purse, 13", Pine Cones (from Clayoquot Sound), feathers, shell, silk, wire, hardware.
Photograph by Jeremy Jones. In the collection of Ted and Phyllis Reeves, Gabriola Island

Plate 13: Susan Heaslip, *Intertidal Life* (1999)

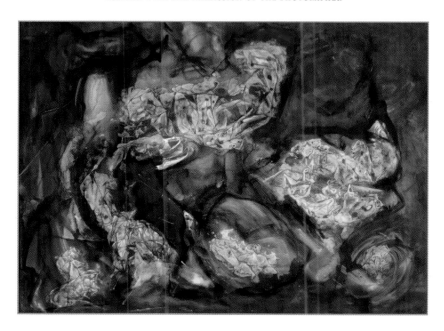

Plate 14: Kenneth Callahan, *The Tides* (1956)
Tempera on paper. 55.9 cm x 76.2 cm

Plate 15: Dale Chihuly, *Cadmium Yellow Seaform Set* (1990)
Photograph by Roger Schreiber

Plate 16: Emily Carr, *Arbutus Trees* (1907-08)
Watercolour on paper. 33.2 cm x 26.7 cm

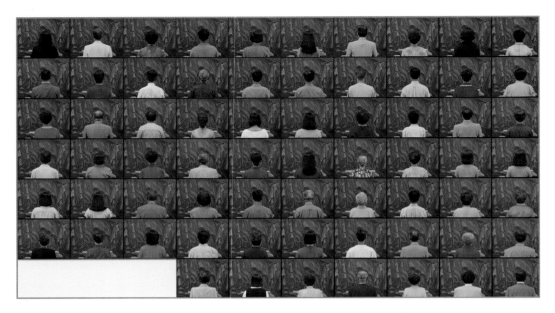

Plate 17: Jin-me Yoon, *A Group of Sixy-Seven* (1996)
138 cibachrome photographs on paper, each 40 x 50 cm (working dimensions)

PRINTED WITH THE PERMISSION OF THE ARTIST AND THE VANCOUVER ART GALLERY
ACQUISITION FUND (VAG 97.2A-GGGGGG). PHOTO: TREVOR MILLS

Plate 18: Jin-me Yoon, *A Group of Sixy-Seven* (1996)
Detail: One of 138 cibachrome photographs on paper, each 40 x 50 cm (working dimensions)

PRINTED WITH THE   OF THE ARTIST AND THE VANCOUVER ART GALLERY
ACQUISITION FUND (VAG 97.2A-GGGGGG). PHOTO: TREVOR MILLS

Plate 19: Lilita Rodman, *Madrone Undressing*

Florence McNeil tells the disconnected history of beach squatters, "belonging neither to sea or land holding on like lichen to the shore" (28). Kesey's *Sometimes a Great Notion*, set on a tidal river, jams the family between "vast green curtain of forest" and "steel-plated river" (123). Because we are on the "edge of one (or several)" empires, David Zieroth speculates, we don't even feel much "compulsion to generalize and define" our place (5). Kesey mused in his "Notion Notes": "You can't stop on land. The sea will get you" (Kesey Collection Box 2).

Annie Dillard chooses these crowded, frightening—albeit fecund—edges as setting for her ambitious historical novel *The Living* (1992). The story is as turbulent as Wilson's is restrained, as sombre as Wilson's is sly. Yet they seem to make sense together as variant women's histories of two communities close together: Vancouver and Whatcom (one of the four towns that came to constitute Bellingham).

Many readers in my acquaintance seem not to have warmed to Dillard's novel. Perhaps they are disappointed that so little of Tinker Creek runs through it. Perhaps it is the factual, understated reporting, especially of deaths, especially of grotesque deaths. But, for me, it's just that reporting, that sense of detail recorded as in "a Testament with pages stained red and yellow by pressed flowers, and two pies" (61), which memorably conveys a psychology of a period, the sensory environment (98), the clamouring disparity of characters, and the nicety of dimensions (96). Perhaps the understated reporting, and the abrupt transitions, seek to put a social message forward. When John Ireland finds the truth about Socialism and the expulsion of the Chinese, he thinks, oddly, about how "literature pained him." Maybe Ireland's reaction—concealing an assumption that social criticism is incompatible with high art—explains why Dillard uses so few metaphors, so little that registers as overtly literary *literature*.

The Living is a chronicle novel, following families and generations through the fractured boom and bust cycles of creating community; it covers the period from 1855 to 1897. But, paradoxically, these descriptive statements turn out not to be true. Dillard distrusts the pattern of patriarchal heroics leading to family—and agricultural, or industrial, or political—dynasty. Perhaps "the American way" (200) dictates an anti-chronicle. The honouring of ancestors, which she attributes to the Chinese, and to the Lummi Indians (both scorned by the majority history she depicts), has little place in this frantic ingenue society. (And that Dillard imagines this history is an excellent reason to read the novel.) *The Living* is in many ways a profoundly ironic title. Often, the story-line seems to track a sequence of unexpected, abrupt, and often horrifying deaths.

The Living is a big, capacious novel. Not

surprisingly, in one way or another it revisits much of the writing that has made this book. That the nature writers start writing fat historical novels, imagining the density of a racist culture, and a society impatient for progress might tell us something of where we are in the history of Northwest writing. Dillard alludes to the background of the spirit quest (51); she listens to lumber talk (67 94) and gives a meticulous account of how to fell a two-hundred-foot Douglas fir (17); the forest's benign spring is marked by the salal's "pink bells" (72); the "light rain" is remarkable only for being unremarkable—"rain they all worked through every winter without noticing it" (97); even the sunlight is "like fog" (102). The "twisting madrone trees, looking like flayed muscles" (371), give their name here to a whole island just off Whatcom.

In its documentary care, *The Living* seems to prefer its occasional metaphors in the more vernacular form of similes. By their being drawn, homegrown, from the texture and economy of the place itself, they show a regional self-confidence. Clare, in his "tan suit" (239), looks "like . . . a hops stake"; Grace Lee "seemed independent, but she clung like kelp to an oar" (239); when Eustace Homer and the Nooksack man Kulshan Jim work at two ends of the cross-cut saw loggers call the "misery whip," "[m]uscles moved all over their two backs like salmon in creeks" (94). The delight and texture of place-writing rests in such figures. The body as salmon;

madrone as body. This remarkable version of my title image turns me back to the edge. This tree on the edge is "flayed muscle," a startling reminder of the tormented beach on which this novel is set.

The novel opens, in fall 1855, with the Fishburn family, after a week's sailing up Puget Sound "along . . . unbroken forest" (3), landing in Bellingham Bay:

It was the rough edge of the world, where the trees came smack down to the stones. The shore looked to Ada as if the corner of the continent had got torn off right here, sometime near yesterday, and the dark trees kept on growing like nothing happened. (3-4)

Ada reflects that such a "plunging shore" (4) was not the sort of place where God had expected people to live. A vocabulary of violence and indifference—"rough edge," "smack," "torn," "nothing"—clings to the "narrow strip of pebbles" (4) on which the Fishburns had "washed up" (18) like some dying sea creatures, whatever occasional scenes of ecstatic light ensue. The edge attracts "settlers with a taste for the sublime" (22), an aesthetic that sometimes takes the form of "fifteen colors of clouds over the water and fifteen colors of sky between them" (61). But Dillard writes into the terror of the sublime: she explores its root sense—beyond the *limen*, beyond the threshold, beyond consciousness and conscience.

The railroad brochures promote the destiny of the "Last frontier." Dillard tests the irony: when the frontier runs out, then the community gets to know the edge. It's a "buckling edge" (144) to a "crack in the continent" (213), with psychologies to match: John Ireland's passion for his new wife Pearl "subsided [after the birth of their son], as an earthquake subsides after rearranging the landscape" (233). The *living* here is knowing the "sea will get you": "the people you knew were above the surface one minute, and under it the next" (61).

Intertidal life, in Dillard's version, is life on a mud flats where the "scuttled" and "broken" "tend to accumulate" and return, like the carcass of the shark, which "exploded and stank," was towed out to sea, but washed in again, where crabs devoured it "in their clattering fashion, by squatting over it and lowering what looked like arms from their mouths and passing bites directly into what looked like stomachs" (168). This mechanical process, coming where it does in the novel, echoes the brutal automatism of Beal Obenchain, who binds Lee Chin to a piling on an abandoned wharf and allows the inevitable necessary tide to commit murder:

> Obenchain left the lighted lantern, so the Chinaman could study the water for the first three hours as it rose, until it tipped the lantern and washed it out. After he would perforce imagine the water, until it touched his feet. Then he would feel the water, and measure its rise against his skin. (155)

When Lee Chin's body is discovered, "crabs had [already] been at it" (162). One of the roots of the verb flayed is the Old Norse *fla*, to skin. In Dillard's ambitious and distressing intertidal zone edge and the bark-shedding madrone join in a vision of land forms created of immense stress which in turn violently remove the skin and muscle of Lee Chin. On the "world's rim, mineral and geological" (367), the "spooling of tides" and attendant planetary motions form a "brainless company" (367). When Obenchain's own body is found—a prelude to the mockingly hopeful ending—it is half underwater, and like the flayed muscle of the land, "bent," "twisted," "flung," "skewed," and "pocked" (378). The crabs are also at his flesh. Both victim and murderer, at the edge of their living, have become intertidal.

~

The Nitinaht name for arbutus/madrone is x̣u·ʔuk̓ʷaʔλapt which comes from the word for "change" and means literally "descendant from a changeable plant." The "Nitinaht people were scared to touch the tree, because, doing so might cause their luck to 'peel off' like the bark."

Nancy Turner et al. 1983 104

ut File

. . . follow directions
Not yet invented—north
By south, upright by easterly, northwest by nothing—

~David Wagoner "The Middle of Nowhere"

Forget the boundary of Canada and America at the 49th parallel;
the Northwest is united by landscape, not divided by latitude
lines. The regional icons—salmon and trees and mountains and
water—spring from the elements.

~Timothy Egan *The Good Rain*

The illegality of Erks' business was brought back into focus by the
border, the 49th parallel, the legal brow.

~John Keeble *Yellowfish*

Read what the worms write on the madrone leaf, and walk sideways.

~Ursula K. Le Guin *Always Coming Home*

WITH THE WRITERS GATHERING IN THIS BOOK, and with arbutus/madrone trees of varied forms, I have learned to be at home—often uneasily—in a region that crosses the *pacific* with the *north* and again with the *west*. The preposition *with*, which sounds, especially in the opening phrases, as if it's translated from the Kesh, I have chosen deliberately. It echoes Ursula Le Guin, in the persona of translator, explaining that "to learn *with* . . . implies that learning is not a transfer of something by someone to someone, but is a relationship. Moreover, the relationship is considered to be reciprocal" (291-92). To learn *with* implies reciprocal humility; crucial, I think, both to the tree-learning and to the conversations with future Aboriginal cultures that Le Guin imagines. I hope *with* shows respect for collaborations to come among the writers assembled in these pages, and among the readers who might be urged by my enthusiasm to turn, and turn again, to their work. But learning *with* also cautions that the affiliations I have cultivated by placing these specific writers in these particular files grows a sub-species of regionalism that may thrive in some conditions, but will be profoundly vulnerable in others.

Ursula Le Guin's *Always Coming Home* is a speculative compendium of the poems and songs and stories of a people who "might be going to have lived a long, long time from now"; it dares to translate "from a language that doesn't yet exist" (ix). And with Le Guin, we learn what prepositions might configure learning. This ample and perplexing attempt to look forward also gives me many ways to look back on the arbutus/madrone files.

Le Guin's title—its grammar of conviction and motion toward, its intuition that home is a direction (northwest by nowhere?) and a song in process—prompts me to turn to Malcolm Lowry for a companion text. Lowry is best known for *Under the Volcano*, but my regionalist inclinations always draw me to his long short story "The Forest Path to the Spring," and to his sometimes chaotic and fragmentary novel *October Ferry to Gabriola* (1970). I agree with George Bowering that *October Ferry* is "the apotheosis of BC fiction" (Bowering 1988 32). For all that it has little salmon, few ravens, and few woodswords, in its unfinished state, and in the tumble of its manuscripts, *October Ferry*

might stand as another fine example of the unending transaction of place that is every person's writing life, and every person's failure. Our stories—told and written many times—make places happen. It remembers that the word for madrone and arbutus in this future language will be anasayú. With Le Guin, we learn how madrone will map another speculative space, how important arbutus will be in a future culture.

"So we have to get the geography clearer in our heads" (Malcolm Lowry Collection 16-22). Lowry scribbles this prefatory note to what became Chapter Thirty-seven in the published version of the novel. Ironically, we, as readers, get the geography clearer by making up the story Lowry could not finish. We read, that is we *compose*, the possibility of Gabriola Island, in the story of a trip to the Island—just off the east coast of Vancouver Island—which is *never* completed. And hence the reminder in this book's subtitle of the paradox of place as read.

Always Coming Home might be set in what is now northern California—and so, at the southern limit of most configurations of a west that is still north. But twenty-first-century landforms have shifted, and maps of the "places known to the Kesh," on the "Western Ocean" but with a north and south Inland sea, look considerably like the Puget Sound/Georgia Basin topography on whose eastern and western edges Lowry's narrative clings.

Always coming home. Always ferrying to

Gabriola. And yet, however restless, these books, like Richard Hugo's poems, or Sherman Alexie's stories, must read down into the meanings of that particular plant's names, of that specific roadside sign. In Le Guin, as in the romantic tales of the Kesh, the time may be imprecise, but "place detail [is] vivid and exact" (100). Le Guin finds place not in an alphabet, but in a syntax (an ecology, a relationship) of exact details, details which well up for a writer who imagines a future, and who creates a future culture's language (and mythology and social organization). Le Guin's local knowledge is the inward complicated imagining of an island culture (so much richer than Ernest Callenbach's *Ecotopia*, to which it bears an obvious kinship). Lowry's local knowledge is of a different sort: densely and recklessly allusive, Lowry is afraid not to mention everything he has ever read, not only the *Aeneid* and *Titus Andronicus*, but seemingly every billboard and advertisement on the northern reaches of the highway from Victoria to

~

mem: Sunset is not the skyfilling regal palette of prairie home (purples, oranges, reds). Today is perhaps 95 per cent cloud cover, and here, on Jericho Beach, one can't really speak of sunset. The light source is hidden somewhere south and west of me, around the corner of Point Grey. Yet it seems as if there are twenty different layers, types, densities of cloud and each a different tint in the grey-purple spectrum. And then too, there's the misted intensity of the ice-blue horizon, the bars of mist down across it from top left to bottom right. And the four shifting highlights: that amazing chrome-green of Bowen Island, the bronzed green of the Stanley Park forest, the laser whites of the housings on the freighter at anchor, the white-gold of the downtown buildings (are they really all white, as they seem in the horizontal sun?). And everywhere the draping of those twenty textures of cloud.

6 December 1996

Nanaimo. He recognizes that these labels and bumper stickers and the clutter of newspaper headlines which interrupt his packed and already interrupted sentences, catch scraps of a local, unwritten epic. Lowry is the genius loci whose local colour goes far beyond the local colour: he hears and repeats, puns and muses, until the most ordinary bit of phrasing branches toward wisdom. In the breadth of their encyclopedic fictions, Lowry and Le Guin gravitate to many of the configurations of Northwest accumulated in these files. Ethan Llewelyn no sooner thinks of "huge logged-off areas" in overblown polysyllables— "The abomination of desolation sitting in a holy place" (217)—than he cautions himself: "It was too easy to judge the loggers." Le Guin's section titled "Where It Is" describes "the Valley" as a familiar tension between wet and dry, old volcanoes and rifts of earthquake, where trails, tracks, and footpaths "don't go straight" (55). Inevitably, around the mountains, "the fog comes moistening and blurring and rubbing things out" (54). In the beckoning and remembering of the Ocean Spray Inn, Lowry understands his intensely unfamiliar adopted home. On an October ferry, given a deliberately literalist reading, the ocean spray seems to be *in*—within. In atmosphere and outline, the West Coast story is written again in mist, and home is afloat.

Where the rain falls "with the sound of muted ghostly sleigh bells" (329) the myth of drugged and dreamy world compels. *October Ferry* drives and floats along the most desperately bleak and hopeless edge-place. An uncharacteristic fire imagery (for the Northwest, though not for Lowry) keeps flaring up. The desperateness of Llewelyn's search for a home is marked by the awareness that the Lowrys themselves faced eviction from their squatter's shack in Dollarton—that essential reclusiveness and imaginative freedom, on that rocky beach between high-tide line and low, which is imagined to belong to no one.

Except for the impact of fire and imminent eviction, much of the Lotos mythology holds good. *October Ferry* is a compendium of synonyms and analogues for Eden. This landscape seems "embowered," and the possibility of home beckons "down a vista of paralyzing grandeur" (174). Llewelyn/Lowry shifts almost desperately from paralyzing beauty to paralyzing fear. At once attentive and extravagant, Lowry's word "vista" conveys narrowness of mountainous and forested confines, and the long, long time of paralysis.

~

Tree Language

Le Guin, for all the utopianism of her vision, is more ecologically attuned: she mulls the way humans respond to their world outside of, or beyond, the codes of "prospect" and "ownership" that cling to Lowry's European notion of Eden. Three pages of *Almost Coming Home*, with the archly silent-movie title "Pandora, Worrying About What She is Doing, Finds a Way Into the Valley Through the Scrub Oak," ponder some form of tree language. Wilderness, Le Guin speculates, will still be "messy" and "mixed up" (254-56).

Describing it requires an anxiously precise knowing ("a slight convex curve to the leaf, which pillows up a bit between the veins that run slanting outward from the central vein" [254]) and a placid admission to a fundamental unknowing. "Analogies are easy," Pandora reflects, as she abandons the momentary temptation to try to count all the "scrub oaks on this ridge" (255-56). She is thinking, of course, about *writing*. About her own writing. And she makes this writer think about his writing—writing that thinks about environment, about humans in their environment, about how the environment might shape them. She doesn't write "scientifically," yet she acknowledges in science a precision of eye and patience of

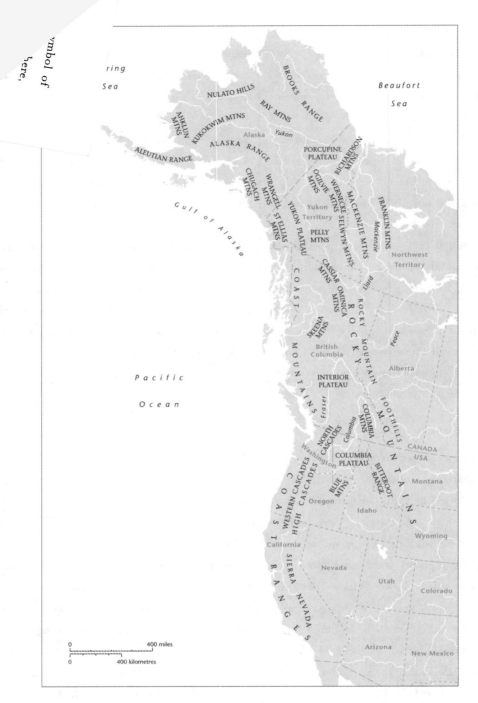

Fig. 13: *Mapping a Mountainscape*, Cartography by Eric Leinberger

PRINTED WITH THE PERMISSION OF THE ARTIST

measurements that other writers cannot reach. And then she turns this whole remarkable passage around to the process of reading. "The live oak, the humble evergreen, can certainly be made into a sermon, just as it can be into firewood. Read or burnt. *Sermo*, I read; I read scrub oak. But I don't and it isn't here to be read, or burnt" (256). The paradox is the heart of this book. I want to learn to read arbutus/madrone. I can read with Le Guin and Lowry, with Emily Carr and Ken Kesey. I have learned, and will learn with them. But, of course, as Le Guin reminds me, I don't, and arbutus is not here to be read.

Trying to think like a tree or a fish does, we have to admit we cannot feel what a cedar does, or see what a salmon sees. This contradiction, I would argue, criss-crosses Northwest writing, for when I say "argue" and repeat again the phrase "Northwest writing" I am foolishly organizing what is undoubtedly "imprecise, fortuitous, and full of risk" (Le Guin 256). The narrative of the spirit quest is inescapable. A person is compelled, often inexplicably, to take a solitary journey, often into forest or up mountain, where through extended fasting and prayer, and translated through a particular bird

~

I want to honestly try to focus on what might come next. To fill the gulf between the West of today and the West Ursula Le Guin foresees in *Always Coming Home*, for example. I mean, life with the Kesh would be, will be, great. But I'm fascinated by some of the mundane transformation questions. Nuts and bolts stuff. Like how we got rid of the IRS. And the Columbian River dams. And what killed enough of us off to keep the region inhabitable. Day-after-tomorrow prophecy.

Stephen J. Beard "An Interview with David James Duncan" 49

or animal or plant, he or she reaffirm individual being and earth are one. The jou neyer returns to human society, ready to accept a new responsibility. The story is writ large and small in *Always Coming Home*; it is guesswork and occasional hinge in *October Ferry*. What we end with, each time, is a paradoxical recognition: "This thing is nothing to do with us" (256).

Greek, Spanish, English, Latin, French— Lowry weaves his languages into his novel. Multiple languages intensify the defamiliarization so crucial to *October Ferry*. Le Guin, like Robert Bringhurst or Don Berry, like Seepeetza (Shirley Sterling) or Elizabeth Woody, recognizes that to read the Northwest you have continually to try to translate the original language indigenous to a particular locale. But in her writing down an indigenous language which does not yet exist, Le Guin profoundly questions this dream of an original language and frees each translator into ignorance. Where the word is unstable, and beyond meaning, a play of invention is more possible. The human animal finds the tree language beyond us. That is, we both can and cannot translate, even if we don't know Tillamook or Halkomelem.

that

...slated word might serve to remind
...t meaning, that intelligibility is an
...a function. . . . The untranslated
...piece of wood. Its use, its meaning,
...finite and limited, but concrete,
potential, and infinite. To start with, all the words we

say are untranslated words. (Le Guin 437-38)

Maybe all we have, suggests Ethan, speaking from a long tradition of fault-line eccentrics, is "'holy gibberish'" (Lowry 31).

~

Borderline

In this book about regional icons and sliding borders, three borderlines have been particularly prominent. One is the land-water boundary, where, as Sean Kane puts it, "exchanges happen, where things, good things and bad things, are given by the sea to the land" (204-205). And where the land becomes sea: a *rain* forest, a *mist*-story. The beach-boundary is the site of first contact between Aboriginal dwellers and European visitors. It is also, as we have seen, the form and metaphor of cultural exchange, of a trans-Pacific transaction where gifts are given by Asia to North America and by America to Asia. The other key boundary is that between Canada and the United States. An arbitrary line at once intangible and profoundly felt. Even, already, in this envoi, I recognize that the site of contact between Native Americans and new immigrant Americans was not, in the United States, the beach.

I have tried to respect these boundaries, and still to insist that in an ecological system a boundary is a membrane, permeable and necessarily so for the survival of species:

[A] living thing acquires its energy by means of exchanges across a boundary, so that the living thing remains distinct from its environment, yet interacts continuously with it. The lining surrounds the cell; bark surrounds the tree; skin surrounds the animal. (Kane 103)

This concept of domain, recognizably distinct yet interacting to survive, is especially attractive for describing a region whose marker is the arbutus/madrone, a tree with paper-thin bark, which seems sometimes to have no bark at all.

The Cascades mountain range begins in northern California and extends into southern British Columbia near Chilliwack. The Coast Mountains rise in North Vancouver and run north to Alaska. The string of active and inactive volcanoes—Shasta, Hood, St. Helen's, Rainier, Baker—extends to Mount Garibaldi in British Columbia. The coastal mountains are another crucial, if not much discussed, border in the region I have been reading (FIG. 14). In John Keeble's fiction of "land forms" the several mountain ranges form "a boundary between peoples, between the coast and the interior" (75). My reading has tested, and

sometimes ignored, the border between a community that calls the mountains to the east Cascades and has a Coast Range, and one that calls a different range the Coast Mountains (FIG 13). But this other border is as influential, in patterns of climate and trade, as the land-sea edge and the 49th parallel. I must acknowledge again that while George Bowering and Sherman Alexie and the Columbia need both interior and coast to make a Noı have developed some of that "physical sens blockage" on descending into the coastal region, and "scrunched" and "awkward[ly]" have not properly recognized "the high bright plateau country" which gives the Northwest its Wild West (Keeble 75).

~

Topographies

When I first saw the exhibition "Topographies: Aspects of Recent BC Art," at the Vancouver Art Gallery, 29 September 1996 to 5 January 1997, I came out muttering. Some of this is pretty borderline stuff, I thought. Not many of the works fit with my sense of British Columbia topography (cf. PLATE 16). But several images kept coming back to me, until, three days before the show closed, I went back for another look. I spent a long solitary morning looking again, thinking about the ways of "writing" the Northwest caught in that show, sensing that they gave a way of concluding this book.

The show's title, after all, literally evokes a writing of place, a detailed transcribing of the local. And I had been writing (all this book long) about writing about place. And the place-writing I most admire is the writing that makes me think again. So, I'd better think again.

On first viewing, I found a large canvas by Judith Currelly, "Land-marks: Tracks, Maps, Memories" (1994), the most wholly satisfying: three panels, three sepia rockscapes against which three inset images, in the same yellow-brown tones, of migrating cariboo, of antlers, and in the centre panel three shadowy humanoid figures. Its complicated framing of images within images within an overall image certainly could complicate a sense of borderlines, but the art in Currelly's work evoked for me the simplicity of petroglyphs or rock-paintings, and probably conformed to my expectation of a "primitive," mainly unpeopled landscape, whose patterns were to be contemplated from afar rather than its movement experienced close up.

I found other images, realistic images of place, each disrupting my plan for regional definition. Landon Mackenzie's large abstracts sharpened the attention. "Interior Lowlands" (1996) is very dark, but with bright colours here and there, as if Jean-Paul Riopelle had splashed and sprayed his way across the surface. But beneath that surface—sometimes readily legible, sometimes almost indecipherable—a mass archival material, and the presumably all drawn from [S]chewan, [actua]l series. [...stu]died the province, [but ...]er lived there.) Again, to impede any thought that topography in recent BC art would end at the BC border, I found "Cascadura Stories" (1994), by Melinda Mollineaux, five kraft-paper panels, each with text, a landscape photograph, and at the bottom a fragment of a map—representing some edges of Trinidad. And next, Arni Haraldsson's room-size photographic installation "Corporeal City," interrogating the civics and civic space of Chandigarh, India.

Discovering Saskatchewan explorers, Trinidadian snapshots, and Indian urban planning amid Pacific Northwest topographies muddles the definition of region, just as it calls into question the concept of a national culture. But any conclusion is only one further extension, I realized, of the binational region this book has been imagining, a Pacific Northwest whose stories incorporate the transnational and the bio-regional.

Frank Davey in the discussion period after his talk, 20 January 1997 at Green College, the University of British Columbia, says he doesn't see much potential in regionalism as a cultural force—for example, to maintain, or nurture, theatre, or galleries, or periodicals: "When it comes to choosing between a dinner out, and supporting a journal, people will opt for dinner." But surely this problem is more generally true—say for Greenpeace, or Native rights, or? . . . All charity, or volunteer work, is based on sacrifice and faces these challenges of choosing the necessity to persuade. The comment suggests again why romanticism, nostalgia, naiveté are central to the regionalist project—as elements that people will sacrifice for, even while being told by earnest intellectuals that this sensibility is 1. unthoughtful, and 2. powerless.

In "Topographies," the most effective reminders of writing environmental connection were Christos Dikeakos's fourteen colour prints of the distressed or just developing downtown waterfront lands in and near the site of the Expo '86 International Exposition in Vancouver. Each print was affixed beneath a plate of glass: at first you see the bright landscape of urban lifelessness; then single words and maps sand-blasted into the glass remind the viewer of what was once here: *waterfowl, crab, sole*. Because the spotlights are in the ceiling, their light hitting the glass at an angle, the words are shadowed onto the print behind, an echo, a trace of themselves. It's as if not only waterfowl, but the *word* waterfowl itself might disappear. Adjacent to the English-language terms, the same words and different in Hunqum'i'num and Squamish—words, and understandings, mostly invisible, save for here in this moment of viewing.

Still more borderline topographers emerged, or did not, in Rodney Graham's "Halcion Sleep" (1994): in a darkened room, on a large screen, a twenty-minute black-and-white video shows Graham in a drugged sleep in the back seat of his car, as he is driven late at night from Coquitlam to the Granville Street Bridge. Some of the always receding streetscape is seen out the car windows, but often the primary topography is the rain-covered rear window, with light glaring and dimming against it. A mobile water (non)colour.

Another multi-media installation and performance piece, is created by the impressive sound poet Judy Radul. Her space, titled "Active/Passive" (1996), has white walls and a black-stained false floor of plywood. Five television monitors are at the viewer's feet, one embedded so its screen is level with the floor. Another monitor is mounted on a wall bracket, with a telephone you can pick up in order to seemingly listen in on a partyline. Three speakers occasionally compete with varied tracks, sometimes speak the same speech. The monitors show mainly Vancouver street-scenes, although one or more are often blank blue (and passive). What connection among the bright streetscapes, the adolescent girl, and the pun on Active Pass, the dangerously narrow scenic passage between Galiano Island and Mayne Island through which the mainland-to-island ferry traffic must sail?

Oddly regional, in the context of these re-readings of place, I come to Rena Point Bolton's cedar basketry and Ron Hamilton's (Ki-Ke-In) "Ceremonial Screen" (1996), with the comfort of familiarity in First Nations ovoids and eyes. And yet, of course, this relief and comfort is short-lived as I acknowledge the absurdity: I can hardly admit to understanding Hamilton more than Radul's and Graham's videoed streets. And, as if to accentuate the new discomfort, at the left-hand side of Hamilton's wall-size work, three red handprints, trace of some raven smudging and smearing the ceremony of high art in this grandiose, classically monumental former Court House.

Most remarkable of all these definitions is the reincorporating of Emily Carr (the gallery's most marketable artist) in Jin-me Yoon's "A Group of Sixty-Seven" (1996), a collection of 138 cibachrome photographs in two panels (PLATE 17). One shows sixty-seven Korean Canadians staring at the camera, with Lawren Harris's "Maligne Lake, Jasper Park" (1924) in the background. The other panel shows the backs of the same sixty-seven staring toward Emily Carr's "Old Time Coastal Village" (c.1929-30) (PLATE 18). Two things strike me immediately and lastingly about this new entry for my Kuroshio File. Only three wear traditional Korean dress. Very few are smiling; almost all have their lips pursed (were they told to pose in this severe and reserved manner?). How much am I reading into the work when I note that although these are photographs, the backs and faces, like the landscapes, almost look to be painted? What does a face mean? Who fits in where? And how?

≈

Penumbra

I have just tried to "conclude" these Files, unsatisfactorily, with a discussion of the tangential forms of writing and reading we encounter in paint and woven threads, in video and Plexiglas. One other way to conclude is by taking two more texts (if single, companionable, words are texts), and pausing to read them as micro-versions, hypothetically compressed distillations of the Northwest story and poem.

My title glimpses in "arbutus" and "madrone" a unity of region: the Pacific Northwest is all the places where *arbutus menziesii* grows, or where its Mediterranean strangeness has ready significance as a regional symbol. And my title balances "arbutus" and "madrone" to acknowledge that in this region two "languages" in two national cultures complicate the regional unities. The slash that joins and separates "arbutus" and "madrone" stands particularly for the border between Canada and the United States, but it remembers many of the other borders that configure the region: the Cascades-Coast Mountains border that connects coast to interior, or the fractured fractal boundary where ocean meets land.

~

All of the characteristics of the "Northwest Style" are here [in the Jennings Sutor house]: concern for the setting and integration of landscaping, the open functional plan, the broad sheltering pitched roof [to shed rain], and the use of naturally finished woods. . . . [i]t was perhaps [Pietro] Belluschi's most significant achievement that he brought what started as an approach to designing a seashore cottage to a fully developed "style" applicable to any building type where wood construction is allowed."
George McMath, "A Regional Style Comes to the City" 476 498

Pondering the slash as a line of power, Gunnar Olsson speculates that the "'/' stands for the penumbra of a mutual relation." I find this a felicitous phrase for the misty dynamic I have been inventing. (A mistiness immediately countered by the frequent association of slash and burn with logging methods.) Olsson's further thoughts on the content of the slash are also valuable in explaining the absurd necessity of my book to myself: "What stands on one side of the line wants to merge with what stands on the other. But, here as elsewhere, the desire is defined by its impossibility" (92). Olsson continues, tending toward geography, where I have left him—in the place that happens like a story:

The slash tries to be a symbol of [an] excluded third which is neither either—or nor both—and but something entirely outside the realm of naming; the slash is not what it first might have seemed—a bridge between opposites—but the void of categorial [sic] limits itself. . . . [T]he slash perhaps can serve as the signifier of that constellation in which nothing takes place except the place. (92)

~

Arbutus/Madrone

Archibald Menzies, naturalist (and later surgeon) accompanying Captain Vancouver on his voyage to the Pacific Coast, went ashore, for the second time on this voyage, on 2 May 1792 at Port Discovery just south of Port Townsend. In Menzies's "voluminous journal" (McKelvey 27), now kept in the British Museum, we find the first written record of the arbutus/madrone:

> Besides a variety of Pines we here saw the Sycamore Maple—the American Aldar—a species of wild Crab & the Oriental Strawberry Tree [(named by the Saxon botanist Frederick Pursh in 1813) Arbutus Menziesii], this last grows to a small Tree & was at this time a peculiar ornament to the Forest by its large clusters of whitish flowers & ever green leaves, but its peculiar smooth bark of a reddish brown colour will at all times attract the Notice of the most superficial observer. (McKelvey 31)

Among the new species which he records on this occasion, arbutus merits the extended comment. Menzies repeats the word "peculiar," establishing in this first record associations of arbutus with the bizarre and mysterious. Writing back to Menzies two centuries later, I appreciate his repetition as beginning the troping of a regional marker. In its Latin derivation, peculiar means as one's own, a distinguishing characteristic: a small tree *peculiar* to the Pacific Northwest, peculiar in its aesthetic associations with *oriental* and *strawberry*.

The suffix *-ish* attached to colours tells something indeterminate, undecidable, something misted in this tree which forces its oddity on the most superficial observer.

By its tiny bell-shaped flowers, arbutus announces its affiliation with other members of the heath family that serve as regional markers—Kinnikinnick, and especially Salal. In the system of dependencies, its berries are "favourites with Pileated Woodpeckers, American Robins, Varied Thrushes, Cedar Waxwings and Band-tailed Pigeons" (Cannings and Cannings 148). The madrona tree often seems to be rooted in rock, leaning "out over the tidal water," adding its peculiarity to that uncertain land-water edge. How do they grow there?

The question keeps returning. When Ethan and Jacqueline are nearing Lowry's Gabriola, they feel a need to share their gin, and their conversation, with someone else. There ensues a conversation of odd tangents. Maybe deaf, perhaps slightly inebriated, the old man in the mackinaw speaks a sideways gibberish that must include, à propos of nothing, his spontaneous amazement at that tree on the edge: "'little mills on the coast, or in the interior, come to that, in Nanaimo . . . they even have arbutus growing, beautiful it is, on some of the rocks and the bluffs you see it, arbutus growing up to the Seymour Narrows . . .'" (327; author's ellipses). An unlikely combination of colours and textures, stands out on the edges, . . . sinuous, olive green, . . . ·let, and ash, . . . gleaming . . . rries" (Guterson 106).

. . . know what happened to madrone in the future, read Le Guin's *Always Coming Home*. There a live young madrone sits centre-stage in a sacred play. Madrone is a deity and a language: you can learn to speak the madrone (176). The Kesh would organize themselves into overlapping "Houses," "Lodges," "Societies," and "Arts." One of eight lodges is the Madrone Lodge. It is the lodge of the library, the archives, the keeping of history; it commissions writing. Madrone, the papery tree, gives a name to the book lodge: it holds on to books, but it also gets rid of them when they become too many:

Books are mortal. They die. A book is an act; it takes place in time, not just in space. It is not information, but relation. (334)

This humbling reminder of the transitoriness of the book I am writing returns me to definition. This book is relation. I have imagined it as accumulated files because I have found that any filing system's apparent ordering barely contains the ripples of unpredictable relations that exist within them. Inevitably, some items cannot be found, and others will not comfortably settle into any particular file. To collect some Northwest files is to acknowledge that the region is a set of shifting dependencies, partnerships, and conflicts. Here, Northwest might be the raven talking to arbutus, there the rain washing salmon's spectrum into a Japanese watercolour. On film, it's snow falling on cedars. Different filing systems would have created different Northwests. Chronology might suggest this sequence: Winter Ceremonies File, Mask File, Gold Rush File, Wobblies File, the Dam File, the Microsoft File. Settlement patterns might have provided a set of cultural files: the Finnish File, the Chinese American File, the Doukhobor File, the African American File, the Makah File. We might have also filed the region according to occupation, economic level, leisure activities.

Each possible structure reminds that, however fluid and shifting this set of files tries to be, it is one file that neglects many others. Like your region, mine is composed, as Don Gayton puts it, of "shreds of ancient mythology, half-remembered Disney movies, romantic yearnings, cultural assumptions, primal landscapes and genetic anachronisms. The final product . . . may not have much to do with the actual landscape itself" (62). I have made *files* just to resist a final product, the invariable place that nostalgia and the camera try to hang on to: I hope they help us think about region, like nature, "as a dynamic, instead of as a constant" (63).

Arbutus-madrone grew from my first jocular note as a possible title image into a haunting ambivalence. Its habitat is largely coastal, yet it has little presence in the rainforest that so often gives the region identity. In its preference for relatively arid sites, and its contorted asymmetry, it seems more Interior than coastal—an emblem, somehow, of the "visual disjunction" or "conceptual disparity" Ted Leeson encounters when he wants to compress the region (his is named "Oregon") into a "misty tract of Douglas fir and cedar" and still include the "harsh and brittle expanses of sage" (91). To Ethel Wilson, its bark "'is like copper in the sunshine'"; for Gary Snyder, madrona is common both to Lake City where he grew up, and the piece of land in the Sierra Nevada where he later settled (308 316); for Jack Hodgins's Logan Sumner, arbutus is erotic temptation,"newly exposed flesh . . .—smooth as Adelina's thigh" but with bark "papery" (1990 193), "curled parchment scrolls" (1990 189) waiting to be written on; it, or its very near relative, can be found in the fossil record ten million years ago (Anderson et al. 1997 21); the biggest arbutus in BC, at 5.33 metres in circumference, may be found in Colwood, Vancouver Island (Curtis B2); Madrona Valley Farm Country Inn is on Chu-An Drive, just off Vesuvius Bay Road on Saltspring Island; Howarth's treasured island of Madronna, place of escape and recuperation, is a dream-place deliberately unlocated; Goh Poh Seng wishes he "could emulate the arbutus,/slough off my thin skin as easily" (Seng 120). Arbutus conveys the dream of the Mediterranean, of orange and brown and undressed rather than blue and grey and slickered (PLATE 16). Of California and of California mythology pushed northward. Yet where a migrating California might be a blight, Briony Penn proposes a tactic of resistance for which she coins the term "'arbutage' (casting Arbutus seeds + sabotage; 'madronage' if you are in the United States—Madrone + sabotage)." In three pages of meticulous detail, she elaborates the technique: "I usually begin at the latest Arbutus Ridge/ Madrone Crest-type subdivision in the hope that one day there will actually be an Arbutus once again gracing the shattered slopes of rock and cement" (158-61).

The Kesh word for madrone, *Arbutus menziesii*, is anasayú (Le Guin 546). I don't know much Kesh but, trying to read Le Guin's glossary, I would guess it combines roots meaning *in/into/within* and *communicate/send a message*. In Kwakw'ala the word is x̱áx̱anale7ems: evidently the root words are x̱enx7id and x̱ánala, meaning (to) undress (Grubb 39 104). In Kwakw'ala, the arbutus files would be naked (PLATE 19). Arbutus/madrone is not information, but relation. It's about learning *with*. It's about understanding trees "in ways we cannot":

I felt as though my veins and nerves were grown into the ground, connected with tree roots. The faint red glimmer of a madrone trunk in the dusk of the rustle of last year's yellow leaves falling seemed as much as I needed out of life. . . . I had seldom felt so accompanied. (Wallace 76)

～

Afterfile: Mistory

THE EPIGRAPH FOR THE MISTORY FILE COMES from Kim Stafford's enormously suggestive "There Are No Names But Stories," in his *Places & Stories* (1987), a poem important enough to me that it always serves as both preface and envoi to courses I teach about Northwest writing. The book's cover photo, incidentally, shows the now windowless yet defiant riverbank house which inspired Ken Kesey's *Sometimes a Great Notion*. The sense of upstart indigenousness, the trope of instant attachment (and its uglier complement of smug complacency), appears in many forms in Northwest writing. It is burlesqued relentlessly in Hodgins's *The Invention of the World* (1977): no need to *build* a home, or *learn* a language, or *respect* a complex history—just *invent* a world. The op-ed page of the *Vancouver Sun* explained the tendency to newness by showing a map of Canada with British Columbia scissored out and set off by itself in the invented west. Lisa Hobbs Birnie's accompanying essay explained that "[i]n British Columbia, people tend to view history as something that happened last weekend. . . . What passions exist by and large attach to the physical—skiing, sailing, camping, gardening, making love and baring one's soul to whatever self-improvement cabal you find yourself in" (A19). In order to reinforce Birnie's take on a "distinct society," a bit of Canadian English that would be understood but scarcely comprehended across the border, the *Sun* chose to run side-by-side the *New York Times'* view of Seattle, which turns upstart to jumpstart: "I knew Seattle was not as laid-back as it liked to think. How could it be with so much caffeine pumping through its veins?" (Dowd A19) (FIG. 4)

~

In the opening piece of his *River Teeth: Stories and Writings* (1995), David James Duncan invents the genre of "river teeth" by noting that the "pitch-hardened masses where long-lost branches once joined the tree's trunk" (2) persist in rivers long after the rest of a fallen tree has decayed into "fertile muck":

There are . . . small parts of every human past that resist this natural cycle: there are hard, cross-grained whorls of memory that remain inexplicably lodged in us long after the straight-grained narrative material that housed them has washed away. (4)

This river-tree genre might now be discovered retroactively in Kim Stafford and Brenda Petersen, Stephen Hume, or Emily Carr.

Jonathan Raban's essay, "The Next Last Frontier" (1993), "makes a case" for the cultural and economic interdependence of Seattle and Spokane, and notes the coastward tilt. What I have called "Lower Mainland imperialism," George Bowering calls "Coast chauvinism." In *Bowering's BC* (1996), he observes that, coming from the South Okanagan Valley, "I always used to be amused by easterners who describe BC as a place where it rains a lot." He would remind anyone writing of the Pacific Northwest that "BC is larger than most countries in the world, and has a lot of regions" (4). *Bowering's BC*, by the way, integrates poets, storytellers and novelists, more extensively than any other *history* I know. Jan C. Dawson's "Landmarks of Home in the Pacific Northwest" (1996), which considers "the specialness of the region," also provides an extensive review of competing uses and ideologies of the metaphor of home. As for cautions about class bias, I recognize that even within my home city, I tend to tilt too far coastward. *East of Main: An Anthology of Poems from East Vancouver* (1989), edited by Calvin Wharton and Tom Wayman, opens with Pauline Rankin's "Blackberries," a poem whose enthusiasm for

the best portugese/italian/lesbian

feminist/radical/punk/working class
middle/class/coffeedrinking/pool
playing/foodshopping/district (18)

is one reminder of the many unincluded.

I discuss the mapping of Cascadia more extensively in "Island File." But the term predates contemporary marketing alliances, as we can see, for example, in the naming of state and college in Bernard Malamud's campus novel *A New Life* (1, 12). Malamud's Cascadia remembers the search for the "mythical Northwest passage" (101), and salutes the North in Northwest with a mock-sublime tribute attuned to the notion of mistory: "'North,' said Levin, with a throb in his throat. 'What profound mystery. You go north till there are no men. Imagine the silence, the cold, the insult to the human heart'" (19).

⁓

According to Statistics Canada, same-day car trips of Canadians across the international boundary (all crossings) peaked at 59.1 million in 1991, when the Canadian dollar was worth US $0.87. In 1995, same-day trips from the United States into British Columbia were 2.1 million (up 4.4 per cent), while from British Columbia to the US were off 1.1 per cent at 9.9 million (*Statistics Canada* 19). Many of these trips pass through Peace Arch Park, whose history I could only discover (before Matthew Sparke's article in *BC Studies*) in a Tourism BC press release by Joan Bellinger (1979). Sophisticated geographical surveys reveal that the majority of the boundary markers are inaccurately sited; according to Marian Botsford Fraser's *Walking the Line* (1989), the invisible border is not where it appears to be (43-44). During March 1998, the *Vancouver Sun* relished the anomalies and ironies of the imperfect boundary survey in a two-part series by Larry Pynn under the collective title "Crooked Border."

Most discussions of anti-Americanism in Canada play variations of the mouse-sleeping-with-an-elephant trope popularized by Pierre Trudeau. But in the mid-1990s, at least two commentaries have been considerably less certain of Canada's meek innocence: Michael Fellman's article "Sam I Am: Enough Yankee-bashing. It's Time We All Got in Touch with Our Inner American" in *Saturday Night* (1996), and J.L. Granatstein's *Yankee Go Home?: Canadians and Anti-Americanism* (1996). Throughout the book, I use the term *American* to refer to citizens and permanent residents of the United States. But I acknowledge that this usage may conceal a continentalist ideology: throughout *Bowering's BC*, for example, George Bowering consistently uses the more restrictive term "USAmerican." For a survey of burgeoning research on Canada in the US, see William Metcalfe's "'Modified Rapture': Recent Research on Canada in the United States."

American critics—for example, Frances W. Kaye's "The 49th Parallel and the 98th Meridian" (1981) and Carol Fairbanks's *Prairie Women: Images in American and Canadian Fiction* (1986)—brought to literary comparisons an interest in gender that contributed to a different recognizing of common mothers. Cross-border studies include Ramsay Cook, "Imagining a North American Garden: Some Parallels and Differences in Canadian and American Culture" (1984) and *Essays on Canadian Writing* (Summer 1981), a special issue on "Canadian-American Literary Relations," edited by Ildikó de Papp Carrington. The Borderlands Monograph Series includes the following titles: Lauren McKinsey and Victor Konrad, *Borderlands Reflections: The United States and Canada* (1989); Roger Gibbons, *Canada as a Borderlands Society* (1989); Seymour Martin Lipset, *North American Cultures: Values and Institutions in Canada and the United States* (1990); Clark Blaise, *The Border as Fiction* (1990); and Russell Brown, *The Borderlands and Borderlines in English Canada* (1990). Observing that "the cultural dissimilarities which exist between Canadians and Americans in the zone of the forty-ninth parallel are probably the least that can maintain national separation (439)," Stephen B. Jones outlines some differences engendered by the boundary: the Canadian preference for hedges and fences, the proportion of British-born, the Doukhobor presence, even the importance of Nelson as regional trading centre (where

Spokane might otherwise have served). Jones also points out the cross-border problems associated with forest-fire protection, dams, and the Trail smelter. For mention of the Seattle Chamber of Commerce's decision to meet in Vancouver, Canada, and other border-crossings, see Eileen V. Quigley's "Cascadia" (1990).

~

Many feminist critics link gender and environmental perspectives closely, while exposing the ideological assumptions of the trope mother earth. See, for example, Annette Kolodny *The Lay of the Land: Metaphor as Experience and History in American Life and Letters* (1975) and Susan Griffin *Women and Nature: The Roaring Inside Her* (1978). In *Ten Tough Trips* (1990), William Bevis quotes poet Richard Hugo's appropriate watchword on sentiment: "Bill Kittredge, my colleague . . . said once 'if you're not risking sentimentality you're not in the ball park'" (145). For his "soul-shaking" memory of the Meadowland Dairy wagon, see "Rose Vegetables" in David James Duncan's *River Teeth* (11-14).

~

Mist, both the lightly transforming and the densely obscuring, finds its way inevitably into Northwest mystery and detective novels. Among my favourites are Earl W. Emerson, Vince Kohler, L.R. (Bunny) Wright, and J.A.

Jance. Armchair detectives will also be interested in a more electronic experience. History professor John Lutz and doctoral student Ruth Sandevell have established a web site (www.uvic.ca/history-robinson/index.html) allowing investigators to determine for themselves who murdered William Robinson. Robinson was one of three black settlers killed on Saltspring Island in 1867-68; the documents allow searchers to question both the conviction of the native man Tshuanahusset, hanged for the murder, and the mythology of racial harmony which has adhered to stories of black settlement on the island.

Since Denise Levertov moved to Seattle, eagles, herons, and especially "white mist" (96) and "the mountain [Rainier?]" (97), often indistinguishable from "cloud" itself (7), rest everywhere in her poems. Her collection *Evening Train* (1992) opens with the poem "Settling," whose manifesto for "dig[ging] in" and learning "to live" here is to understand the currency of grey:

> *Grey is the price*
> *of neighboring with eagles, of knowing*
> *a mountain's vast presence, seen or unseen.* (3)

Clark Blaise is always a discerning commentator on border crossings, as readers of the short story series *A North American Education* (1973) will appreciate. His comment about Canadians seeking new identities comes from *The Border as Fiction*. My own monograph, in which I try to convey the layerings of a unique place just on the US side of the border, is *A Field Guide to "A Guide to Dungeness Spit"* (1997). George Faludy's *Notes from the Rainforest* (1988) ranges widely in its topics, and in its suggestive observations about the West Coast culture. Those wishing to follow up on the possibilities of slug space, slugs in ancient myth (non-existent), and forms of ickiness (infinite), might consult Eve Corbel's *The Little Greenish-Brown Book of Slugs* (1993). My version of the history, or more exactly the *legends*, of the Pig War comes from *British Columbia and the United States* (1942) by F.W. Howay, W.N. Sage, and H.F. Angus.

Arbutus menziesii has various names, and spellings, and pronunciations: arbutus, madrone, madroña, coast madroño, Pacific Madrone, and Strawberry Tree. To be consistent with a tree constantly transforming itself, we have allowed several of these variants to stand throughout the book.

~

Afterfile: Island

THE IDEA OF THE PACIFIC NORTHWEST AS international region may also gain force because few if any attempts to define a regional literature within the boundaries of political units have taken strong hold. Among essays, for example, that try to establish a level of coherence in British Columbia literature are Allan Pritchard's articles "West of the Great Divide: A View of the Literature of British Columbia" (1982); "West of the Great Divide: Man and Nature in the Literature of British Columbia" (1987); and "The Shapes of History in British Columbia Writing" (1992). George Woodcock's "The Wild Woman: Notes on West Coast Writing" (1987), and my "Dumb Talk: Echoes of the Indigenous Voice in the Literature of British Columbia" (1985) concentrate on the prominence of First Nations motifs. George Bowering's "Home Away: A Thematic Study of some British Columbia Novels" (1984) makes the most concerted claim for coherence, but with gobs of irony. W.H. New ranges most widely in his "A Piece of the Continent, A Part of the Main: Some Comments on BC Literature"

(1985), an essay whose title proclaims the paradox of islands crucial to New's understanding of British Columbia. For my own overview of these and other essays and anthologies, see "The Writing of British Columbia Writing" (1993-94), which notes a general reluctance to define. Incidentally, in the same anniversary issue of *BC Studies* (Winter 1993-94), Robin Fisher makes a parallel observation about the narratives of the province's history in "Matter for Reflection: *BC Studies* and British Columbia History."

A similar notion is taken up by Justine Brown, who argues the connection between utopianism and the sense of British Columbia as *nowhere*, in "Nowherelands: Utopian Communities in BC Fiction" (1996) and *All Possible Worlds: Utopian Experiments in British Columbia* (1995). (For a post-structuralist consideration of West Coast utopias see *Collapse* Number 5 [July 2000] edited by Grant Arnold.) The same hesitation to see unifying elements seems evident in Oregon and Washington. The impressive Oregon Literature Series from Oregon State University Press, under the general editorship of George Venn, is the most available and recent case in point: inclusiveness of form, theme, and quality far outweighs any thesis. See Glen A. Love, ed., *The World Begins Here: An Anthology of Oregon Short Fiction* (1993); Stephen Dow Beckham, ed., *Many Faces: An Anthology of Oregon Autobiography* (1993); Gordon B. Dodds, ed., *Varieties of Hope: An Anthology of Oregon Prose* (1993); Ingrid Wendt and Primus St. John, eds., *Oregon Poetry* (1993); Suzi Jones and Jarold Ramsey, eds., *The Stories We Tell: An Anthology of Oregon Folk Literature* (1994); and Shannon Applegate and Terence O'Donnell, eds., *Talking on Paper: An Anthology of Oregon Letters and Diaries* (1994).

≈

Cole Harris in "Moving Amid the Mountains, 1870-1930" (1983), argues that distance and rugged terrain also create a culture and economy of inland "islands," of communities shaped by difficulty of access: "Means of transportation easily imposed on gentler, more proximate lands penetrated the wilderness at enormous cost" (3). Islands and mountains multiply the amount of "edge," *The Last Wild Edge* as Susan Zwinger's 1999 book has it. Impinging glaciers, she marvels, in cascading prose, "end up down here, sending the swirling, milky turquoise of ground-up peaks into the dark channels. Such is this wild interface, termed the hypermaritime, where sea becomes land and land becomes sea" (60).

Edge-people such as Zwinger, who "pre-

fer [their] ocean beaches vertical" (162), read geological time and change exultantly. Tim Bowling reads both salmon and orgasm as earthquake. In his poem "Love in an Earthquake," from the book of the same title, Jarold Ramsey finds in "the big Seattle earthquake" his love's "dangerous joy" and "earthquake freedom" (1).

≈

For introductory studies and an annotated bibliography of Northwest writing, mainly in the United States, see especially Edwin R. Bingham and Glen Love, *Northwest Perspectives: Essays on the Culture of the Pacific Northwest* (1979). See also, Harold P. Simonson, "Pacific Northwest Literature—Its Coming of Age" (1980).

Cross-border comparisons are a natural and inevitable structure for studying North American regional cultures (including not only high art, but also folklore and geography, economics and politics). In literary study, the cross-border approach took new impetus from "Crossing Frontiers," the memorably successful conference held in Banff in 1978. The proceedings were published as *Crossing Frontiers: Papers in Canadian and American Western Literature*, edited by Dick Harrison (1979). The conference marked the passing of the most recent period of strong cultural nationalism in Canada and in Canadian Studies.

In the 1980s, numerous cross-border studies of literature appeared. See, for example, Stanley Fogel, *A Tale of Two Countries:*

Contemporary Fiction in English Canada and the United States (1984); James Doyle, *North of America: Images of Canada in the Literature of the United States, 1775-1900* (1983); Sherrill Grace, "Wastelands and Badlands: The Legacies of Pynchon and Kroetsch" (1981); Frances W. Kaye, "The 49th Parallel and the 98th Meridian: Some Lines for Thought" (1981); Carol Fairbanks and Sara Brooks Sundberg, *Farm Women on the Prairie Frontier: A Sourcebook for Canada and the United States* (1983); Ramsay Cook, "Imagining a North American Garden: Some Parallels and Differences in Canadian and American Culture" (1984). Particularly relevant to my study are James Doyle's "The Post-Ultimate Frontier: American Authors in the Canadian West, 1885-1900," which considers an American view of British Columbia in a brief discussion of Hamlin Garland's *The Trail of the Goldseekers* (1899), and Russell M. Brown's "Crossing Borders," on the literary uses of the Canadian-American border.

Robert Kroetsch's "The Canadian Writer and the American Literary Tradition" (1971) anticipated these studies, and his example influenced many of them. A particularly unusual (because Ontario is seldom seen as region) combination of regional definition and cross-border perspective is D.M.R. Bentley's "Preface" to *Canadian Poetry* (Spring-Summer 1986). Bentley argues against the "East-West dialectic" in Canada. The impor-tance of the "South-North axis" is most sig-nificant for Ontario poetry in the flow from New York of "more-or-less heterodox reli-gious ideas that are usually subsumed under such blanket terms as mysticism, hermeticism, or simply, the occult" (n.p.).

Among cross-border studies, however, the literature of the Pacific Northwest is seldom treated. A limited exception to this rule is Bruce Greenfield's examination of the ideology of place, "The Rhetoric of British and American Narratives of Exploration" (1985). He contrasts Samuel Hearne's function as "go-between for radically different European and Amerindian cultures" to Meriweather Lewis's "identification of self and nature . . . as a basis of a claim to control the land" (64). Ludwig Deringer, published his *Habilitationsschrift* on American and Canadian literature of the region, titled *Das Bild des Pazifischen Nordwestens von den Anfängen bis zur Gegenwart* (1996). His "model text pairs" include George Vancouver *A Voyage of Discovery* (1792) and John Hoskins *A Narrative of the Second Voyage of the "Columbia"* (1790-93); Morley Roberts *The Western Avernus: or Toil and Travel in Further North America* (1887-1896), and Theodore Winthrop *The Canoe and the Saddle of Klalam and Klickitat* (1862); Martin Grainger *Woodsmen of the West* (1908) and James Stevens *Big Jim Turner* (1945). See also Deringer's "The Pacific Northwest in American and Canadian Literature Since 1776: The Present State of

Scholarship" (1989). Thomas Griffith's "The Pacific Northwest" (1976) examines the idea of a regional culture for a more general audience.

~

The ghost of Geoffrey Chaucer is apparent in the social satire of both Birney and Davis. Birney, of course, was a Chaucer scholar; see Earle Birney's *Essays on Chaucerian Irony* (1985). Birney's frequent satirizing of the nationalistic poetaster has its most obvious parallel in the pamphlet Davis wrote, with James Stevens, titled *Status Rerum: A Manifesto, Upon the Present Condition of Northwest Literature Containing Several Near-Libelous Utterances, Upon Persons in the Public Eye* (1927). Glen A. Love's "Stemming the Avalanche of Tripe: Or, How H.L. Mencken and Friends Reformed Northwest Literature" (1981) explains the literary-political background for Davis's blast.

~

Echoing in Kim Stafford's thoughts about place as event is Walter J. Ong's *Orality and Literacy: The Technologizing of the Word* (1982), that shows the depth of the limitation in perception by making a convincing case that a typographic culture thinks in a way fundamentally different from an oral culture. See also Bob Hodge's "Aboriginal Myths and Australian Culture" (1986). Among the many other works which might be listed here, David Wagoner's *Who Shall Be the Sun? Poems Based on the Lore, Legends, and Myths of Northwest Coast and Plateau Indians* (1978) is particu-

larly important for its varied rewritings of Native forms. See his outline of the relevant ethnopoetics in Nicholas O'Connell's *At the Field's End: Interviews with Twenty Pacific Northwest Writers* (1987). For my thoughts on Fred Wah's transcreations of pictograms and their possible connections to ethnopoetics, see "Dumb Talk" (1985 44-47).

~

For a sampling of the persistence of notions of regional self-satisfaction, see *British Columbia: Visions of the Promised Land* (1986) edited by Brenda Lea White. A sign of rising interest in the common region was the symposium "On Brotherly Terms: Canadian-American Relations West of the Rockies" held at the University of Washington, 12-14 September 1996. There, the Canadian willingness to reassess the dominant dependency-imperialist explanation of cross-border relations found in Michael Fellman's "Sam I am: Enough Yankee Bashing. It's Time We All Got in Touch with Our Inner American" (1996) was presented as a lecture. An excellent overview of the Cascadia initiative, its history and connections, is Alan F.J. Artibise's "Cascadian Adventures: Shared Visions, Strategic Alliances, and Ingrained Barriers in a Transborder Region" (unpublished paper presented to Symposium "On Brotherly Terms" University of Washington 13 September 1996). Various websites are available. Try http://tnews.com:80/text/mccloskey. html.Cascadia Planet.

Describing Cascadia as "the greatest forestland in the world" (211), David Simpson makes the case for the Pacific Northwest as the inevitable site for realizing the bioregionalist "movement" through the political process of localization. Simpson's "The Bioregional Basis for Certification: Why Cascadia?" is one of many relevant pieces in Alan Drengson and Duncan Taylor's *Ecoforestry* (1997). In *Guardians of the Land: Indigenous People and the Health of the Earth* (1992), Alan Thein Durning reminds us that cultural diversity equals biological megadiversity (16), given the painful paradox that the world's indigenous cultures, largely removed to inaccessible and remote regions of refuge, are stewards of genetic diversity. For a corrective to the dreams and hopes implicit in these works, see Ellen Stroud's argument that the Pacific Northwest mythology of ecological conscience is acquired by hiding the filth in and among "communities of color": "Troubled Waters in Ecotopia: Environmental Racism in Portland, Oregon" (1999).

Behind my comments on maps in Marlatt and Keeble lies J.B. Harley's "Maps, knowledge and power" in Dennis Cosgrove and Stephen Daniels's, *The Iconograph of Landscape: Essays on the Symbolic Representation, Design and Use of Past Environments* (1988).

I have used the most recent edition of *Steveston* (2001), which includes a new supplementary poem. See also *Steveston* (1974) and a revised edition (1984), both with the photographs of Robert Minden. Marlatt's *Salvage* (1991) also revisits the Steveston riverscape with a more sustained and explicit dedication to "finding a way to write her [woman as woman] in. . . . her and the words all/uvial" (25). W.H. New proposed the reading of the accumulating syllables in the name of *Steveston* itself. Maclean's evocative triptych of Rocky Mountain stories about fly-fishing, logging and the forest service—*A River Runs Through It*—seems to echo frequently in Keeble's tracing of Northwest rivers.

The canning industry in the late nineteenth and early twentieth centuries relied primarily on Chinese labour. Japanese men were mainly fishers, while the women worked on the canning line. First Nations women (called "Klootchmen") did the most menial jobs and were supervised by Chinese bosses (Newell 70 71 100 113 163; Stacey 1986 2-6; Blyth 40-51 123).

For possible perspectives on trans-Pacific migration of forms, see Kenneth Rexroth "The Influence of Classical Japanese Poetry on Modern American Poetry" (273). Several ideas on tourism toward the end of the file are very freely adapted from lectures by James Clifford, in a course titled "The Ethnography of Modernity," International Summer Institute for Semiotic and Structural Studies, University of British Columbia, 2-26 August 1988.

Among the migrating names for region, with their shifting boundaries, Snyder's Ish River is the only one whose rather awkward sounding listens a little for storying and naming of the peoples with the longest history of trying to live on the north Pacific slope. A marvellously compact and elegant reminder of Salish and Squamish naming, which happens to be about the island just outside the Vancouver harbour, best known as Bowen, is found in Robert Bringhurst, "Fast Drumming Ground" (1994).

The old name, the Squamish name, for this overshadowed island is X̱wlil'xhwm [Fast Drumming Ground]: a stony protruberance of meaning cloaked in a forest of evergreen consonants which I think is worth learning to pronounce (3). . . . [This name] isn't enough, by itself, even to make us think very much about the people who used to live here and the way they used to live. But I prefer it. It reminds me of something I know I need to know (11).

John Keeble plays with the paradoxical *being* of places that are only verbal constructs in his novel *Broken Ground* (1987): "He didn't believe that location was ever immaterial. Location was always material. What was location if not material? 'Location is my material,' he said" (102).

～

Afterfile: Raven

THE FIRST EPIGRAPH INTRODUCES RAVEN IN the "Star-Child" story. The full story may be found in Jay Miller and Vi Hilbert, "Lushootseed Animal People: Meditation and Transformation from Myth to History" (J. Arnold 1996 136-56). As an emblem for translation, Raven, the Transformer, is, suitably, the bringer of light to the world, and an unpredictable tease: "Raven could turn himself into anything at any time" (Stewart 1979 57).

The fiction of the form in Joan Crate's *Pale as Read Ladies*, with virtual reflection in a bus window and moving landscape behind, might remind some readers of the superb pondering of self and landscape at the opening of Malcolm Lowry's *October Ferry to Gabriola* (1970):

And the light corruscated brilliantly from the windows in which the travelers saw themselves now on the right hand en-islanded in azure amid the scarlet and gold of mirrored maples, by these now strangely embowered upon the left hand among the islands of the Gulf of Georgia. (3)

A valuable study of Emily Carr as cultural construction is Stephanie Kirkwood Walker's *This Woman in Particular* (1996). On the retroactive linking of Carr and ecology, see, for example, pages 8 and 99, and Chapter Five titled "Deep Nature" (109-44). On the analysis of Carr's "D'Sonoqua" and the spirit quest, see Catherine Sheldrick Ross's discussion of the same pattern in "Female Rites of Passage: *Klee Wyck*, *Surfacing* and *The Diviners*" (1978). For more perspective on the poetics of the spirit quest, see Jerome Rothenberg and Dennis Tedlock.

Ravens and rain, salmon and madrone, camas and otters exchange places and names in *Dancing on the Rim of the World: An Anthology of Contemporary Northwest Native American Writing* (1990). Andrea Lerner's selection and bibliography provides effective amplification of the "translating" in this file, and its "Preface," incidentally, amplifies the concept of "rim" and personal redefinitions of regional boundaries, "using geography, linguistic clues, or our instincts," found elsewhere in this book.

The suggestions for differing principles of word formation in Native languages come from Mary R. Haas. Other perspectives and patterns are found in the work of Karl Kroeber and Dell Hymes. Further shaping my reflections on the imperative and responsibility and tactics of translation are such foundational pieces as Arnold Krupat's "Post-Structuralism and Oral Literature" (1987), and Dennis Tedlock's "On the Translation of Style in Oral Narrative" (1983), and "Toward an Oral Poetics" (1977). As Tedlock reminds us in the latter essay, translation, interpretation, representation have somehow to remember *performance*: "A tape of a live performance has an annoying way of reminding one that stories are *situated* in the real world rather than being isolated objects immediately available to impersonal analytical treatment" (509).

~

Don Berry's *Trask* (1960) is a novel that deftly carries over into print the rhythms of the ritual telling. Listening intently to the talk of the ocean waves, and of the grasses in the meadow which made them, Berry falls into the "almost-chant of the Chinook storyteller" (140), giving and asking for validation with the refrain "'This is what the people say'" (141). But translating patterns too easily ignores the "alphabet block" that Jo Whitehorse Cochran (Lakota/Norwegian) encoutners in a poem titled "Halfbreed Girl in the City School":

they want   to take our tongues
so we forget   how to talk   to each other
      you swallow the rock
      that was your tongue
      you swallow the song
      that was your voice
      you swallow   you swallow
      in the silence

                    (Lerner 41-42)

~

I borrow the phrase "ecological imagination" from Jarold Ramsey's fine essay, "'The Hunter Who Had an Elk for a Guardian Spirit,' and the Ecological Imagination" (1983). Ramsey set out the defining features of Native American myth-narrative in "The Wife Who Goes Out Like a Man, Comes Back as a Hero: The Art of Two Oregon Indian Narratives." A recurring central idea in the ecological imagination is the conviction that the rhythms and sounds within a particular geography shape its language. "As I understand it from my Okanagan ancestors," Jeanette Armstrong writes, "language was given to us by the land we live within" (175); her essay "Land Speaking" is her compelling elaboration of this understanding. For recent challenges to the notion of embedded ecological practice in Aboriginal cultures, see Shepard Krech, *The Ecological Indian: Myth and History* (1999), and Rod Preece, *Animals and Nature: Cultural Myths, Cultural Realities* (1999).

~

Some of my thoughts about Phyllis Webb's poem were shaped by Anne-Marie Fleming, a student in English 426 (Fall 1983), who wrote a poem-essay on "Free Translations" entitled "Nurturing Ambiguity." Also freely translating ambiguities are George Bowering's novel *Burning Water* (1980) and Susan Musgrave's *Kiskatinaw Songs* (1977); bill bissett's chanting performances, accompanied by a rattle, neatly combine a child's iconoclastic play and the shaman's secret, sacred songs.

≈

Although Raven has had a particularly long residence in Northwest coast literature and art, its cultural significance extends well beyond one region. In Leonard Lutwack's *Birds in Literature* (1994), for example, the references to Raven emphasize, of course, Edgar Allen Poe, but scarcely touch the Pacific Northwest. For but one sampler of Raven's inter-regional presence, in Alberta, Nova Scotia, and Ithaca, see Don McKay's essay "Baler Twine: Thoughts on Ravens, Home, and Nature Poetry": "At least that one area of tempera-ment—Droll Zone—is shared with ravens, whereas other wild species, even bears, strike us as requiring a stretch of some distance, and perhaps even metamorphosis, before com-munication is possible. . . . [R]avens, like otters, seem to venture three-fifths of the way into anthropomorphosis on their own: per-haps this is why, whenever I see one, I feel absurdly gregarious, and often find myself croaking back." (128-29). Less gregarious than "groping," Colleen J. McElroy, writing "To the Crow Perched on Chief Sealth's Fingertips," hears Raven as the voice of Harlem, of the "awful histor[ies]" of many Harlems perhaps:

And why does, Raven, harbinger of doom,
Pretend to jump to Jim Crow tunes—spindly-
Legged Rastus hiding knowledge behind a face
So thin, bones seem trapped on the outside.

(1998 55-57)

≈

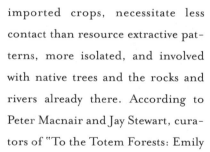

In conversation, my colleague Charles Menzies reinforced my sense of regional differences in the necessity of translating First Nations cul-tures by suggesting that agricultural settlement patterns, with their expansive emphasis on imported crops, necessitate less contact than resource extractive pat-terns, more isolated, and involved with native trees and the rocks and rivers already there. According to Peter Macnair and Jay Stewart, cura-tors of "To the Totem Forests: Emily Carr and Contemporaries" Vancouver Art Gallery 3 December 1999-23 April 2000, Carr's identification of a "graciously femi-nine" D'Sonoqua is mistaken: the inside house post which is her model is a male ancestor of the G̲usgima̲w family, wearing a Sisiyⱡ head-dress (32-33). This reminder of the slipperiness of translation is playfully extended in Ashok Mathur's "Orate Or" (1993), a parody of "oral story" featuring a Brahmin trickster called Ravan. Mathur reminds that we can only take forms of translation seriously by not taking them too seriously. A climate of whimsical transformation is created, for example, by Carl Chew's rugs, or "Cowpets," part of the building-wide artwork, "Raven Brings Light to this House of Stories" in the Kenneth S. Allen Library at the University of Washington. Readers who cannot visit the library might get some sense of this surprising collective translation at http://staffweb.lib.Washington.edu/ InformationServices/raven.

Susan Zwinger reminds us, somewhat ominously, that the local symbol is global: "The raven and I are two of the few species who spread ourselves all over the globe. Ravens survive well in the cold, see well in the dark, tolerate heat, and increase in numbers rapidly at the expense of other species" (23). Globally significant, yet crucial to local ecology: "I watch the raven do something absolutely stunning. . . . She is caching seeds! Raven logic *translated* into forests" (22; my emphasis).

Afterfile: Rain

ACCORDING TO JAMES LIPTON'S *An Exaltation of Larks* (1991), "collective noun" is a misnomer: he prefers *term of venery* (5). Since Lipton's book lists no collective term for rain, we might as well accept Stafford's *glory* as authoritative, or perhaps Helen Meilleur's more predictable *A Pour of Rain* (1980). I would put in my own claim for a version of David Guterson—a *travel* of rain.

Again, my notes on rain drift toward the sentimental, ignoring acid rain, and still bigger issues of watershed maintenance. Evidently, viewed from a more hard-headed perspective, the utopian rainforest mythology reinforced in these notes may be global capitalism's screen for not dealing with social and environmental injustices. A particularly disturbing reminder of a related mythology is the suggestion that low clouds foster a racially pure, that is white, society: this ridiculous link was proposed in a pamphlet by Erwin Weber titled "In the Zone of Filtered Sunshine: Why the Pacific Northwest is Destined to Dominate the Commercial World" (192). Matthew Sparke discussed Weber and Cascadian ideology at the symposium "On Brotherly Terms" (University of Washington 12-14 September 1996), and elaborates his thinking on cross-border politics in a very thorough *BC Studies* article (2000).

The idea of the Interstate 5 as river is central to poet Dian Million's "The Highway." Salmon were "a rain of silver," and rain, in "great sweeping hands/of spray," joins Sitka and Oregon, riverscapes where "the salmon don't come . . ./anymore" (Lerner ed. 129-35). Journalist Peter Chattaway uses rain to explain the expanding movie industry: "The abiding presence of precipitation, it is said, is one of the reasons Vancouver has attracted producers of so many dark and moody TV shows." Lowry reminds us that living in the rain is living in the sea: "'The rain itself is water from the sea, raised to heaven by the sun, transformed into clouds and falling again into the sea'" (1961 239).

On a different note, I must salute the rain-city acronym of Seattle's PONCHO, identifying Patrons of Northwest Culture and Health Organizations, although the garment is seldom seen in the Northwest, and regional terms for rainwear, other than perhaps bumbershoots, seem surprisingly rare.

~

Afterfile: Kuroshio

AMERICAN REDRESS LEGISLATION WAS SIGNED into law by President Reagan 10 August 1988. Two of the many laments over Canada's protracted delay were a *Globe and Mail* editorial, "An Example to Shame Us" on 8 August 1988, and the Canadian Press article "US law sets precedent, Miki says" in the *Vancouver Sun* on 11 August 1988.

The complicated history/mythology of Pacific voyaging and West Coast discovery is enriched by Samuel Bawlf's theory of a "clandestine exploration" by Sir Francis Drake in 1579 (Hume, Bawlf). Transpacific discourse is configured by Bruce Cummings as the distinctive rhetoric "rimspeak." I recommend Eva-Marie Kröller's emphatic discussion of rimspeak in, and concerning, Vancouver: her essay "Regionalism and the Pacific Rim" (1999) examines journalism, architecture, and bureaucracy.

~

All readings of *Obasan* must at least touch on the theme and poetics of silence. Gary Wills and King-kok Cheung give sustained consid-

eration to this aspect of the novel. According with my reflections on the effect of *Obasan* in the classroom, Chinmoy Banerjee argues that even if we take the novel to be polyphonic and postmodern, "it is never in any doubt about truth and falsehood or justice and injustice" (102). Of particular relevance to my argument is his careful examination of the connection between the dispossession of the Native population of British Columbia and the racist dispersal of Japanese Canadians. Paralleling potential polyphonies in *Obasan*, Jinqi Ling offers a reading of *No-No Boy* as (muted) political dissent, and interestingly links the narrative silences with the silence of the novel's initial reception, and Okada's apparent silencing after the novel's appearance. On the moral issues in Okada, and the shifting role of Christianity in the Japanese immigrant community, see Dorothy Ritsuko McDonald's "After Imprisonment: Ichiro's Search for Redemption in *No-No Boy*" (1979).

The term No-No Boy originates in responses to two questions on questionnaires originally prepared by the US Army for male

Nisei of draft age: "#27: Are you willing to serve in the armed forces of the United States on combat duty, wherever ordered?" "#28: Will you swear unqualified allegiance to the United States of America and faithfully defend the United States from any or all attack by foreign or domestic forces, and foreswear any form of allegiance or obedience to the Japanese emperor, to any other foreign government, power or organization?" For this information, and other context, see Bill Hosokawa's *Nisei: The Quiet Americans* (363-65). Lawson Fusao Inada provides extended reflections on the multiple paradoxes of the no-no position in "Of Place and Displacement: The Range of Japanese-American Literature" (254-65). For a much more optimistic reading of the novel's resolution than mine, see Elaine Kim, *Asian American Literature* (4-55).

~

This is not the place to attempt any representative bibliography of the rapidly expanding field of Asian American studies. Some sense of the range of the studies that give context to the dynamism of Kuroshio are Walter Hesford's "Thousand Pieces of Gold: Competing Fictions in the Representation of Chinese-American Experience" (1996); Timothy Stanley's "Schooling, White Supremacy, and the Formation of a Chinese Merchant Public in British Columbia" (1995); and Geoffrey Kain's *Ideas of Home:*

Literature of Asian Migration (1997), which extends to Britain, as well as to the US and Canada. Glenn Deer edited a special issue of *Canadian Literature* (Winter 1999) on "Asian Canadian Writing," an exhilaratingly open and tentative collection of articles, interviews, poems, and reviews that put my few comments in context—and in question.

On the power of the mother figure in Japanese culture, see "Mother Society" in Daniel I. Okimoto's *American in Disguise* (1971), and "The Eternal Mother" in Ian Buruma's *A Japanese Mirror: Heroes and Villains of Japanese Culture* (1984). Thomas Ferraro's *Ethnic Passages: Literary Immigrants in Twentieth-Century American* (1993) essentially defines the "immigrant novel" and shows its variations; interestingly, Kogawa is included, but otherwise no authors from the US Northwest.

~

Tom Koppel's *Kanaka* (1995) is light on analysis and context—more of an introduction, touching the genres of family and local history. Conceived as a set of anecdotes and character sketches, it is, nonetheless, a valuable documenting of a largely untold and invisible story of trans-Pacific migration. Beginning with Winee, the Hawaiian woman who visited the northwest coast as the personal servant of Frances Barkley, the wife of Captain Charles Barkley, in 1787, the book tells of the varied contribution of the Kanakas to whaling, fur-trading, the gold rush, and orcharding. A relatively large community of two dozen families lived on Saltspring Island in the 1890s. Concerning a luau in August 1994, which served as something of a "family reunion" for this community, we have the following account:

[Larry Bell] says a few words reminding everyone of the close familial ties between the Kanakas and the Indian peoples of the Northwest Coast. "We're all one people, all one blood." And he introduces visiting native dance groups. (135-36)

Jim Wong-Chu, president of the Asian Canadian Writers' Workshop, speaking at the BC Studies Conference, 12 November 1999, noted that his community, post-1967 (when introduction of a point system removed the last legal differentiations for immigrants from China), had to begin to "build a history." (I myself, he noted, came to Canada "illegally," as a "paper son.") Through Paul Yee's *Saltwater City* (1988) and others, he enthused, we found the power of publishing: when *books* appeared, the mainstream society accepted Asian Canadians.

The next, inevitable, step, Wong-Chu argued, was to extend history through literature and culture, a process perhaps, in the late 1990s, now in its second phase. His own first book of poems, *Chinatown Ghosts* (1986), was, he realized, the *first* book of poems by a Chinese Canadian about this community. Then, in editing *Many-Mouthed Birds*, he commented, "I

surprised myself: I found over a hundred writers. But they didn't know one another. The Asian Canadian Writers' Workshop serves to nurture this mutual knowing, to assist, when a book matures, to help find a publisher."

~

I have spoken of Kogawa's effect in the classroom. In the past few years that impact is extended by other politically powerful works. In English 110 in the Fall of 1997, three young Chinese Canadian women volunteered for the first time in our discussion group, each recognizing her own cultural silencing in Wayson Choy's *Jade Peony* (1995), a novel of growing up and family politics and racism in Vancouver's Chinatown. I might imagine a similar sense of identification in Peter Bacho's *Cebu* (1991). There, as in *No-No Boy*, we find little sense of a physical landscape, but a strong sense of the regions of class (Seattle's "lakefront mansions" are home to the uneasily staring "thin, pink people" [165]), and of the "something" in Filipino "culture, however diluted it was by life in America, that allowed wild swings in cruelty and compassion" (149). This awakening is signalled as well by such events as an exhibit at the Washington State History Museum (Tacoma) in late 1999-early 2000 titled "Across Oceans of Dreams: Filipino Pioneers in Washington." These writers might stand for those to which a whole book on Northwest Asian writers might be devoted: an excellent source of the range of material is the journal *Rice Paper*.

African American poet Colleen J. McElroy of Seattle calls attention to another dimension of this community in a poem titled "From *Homegrown: An Asian-American Anthology of Writers*":

> this picture holds names that are Asian
> but it is much like those I've seen
> on reservations or one my mother has
> of me near Selma with friends
> from my all-black high school. (*1990 57*)

~

For considerable detail on the cultural symbolism of the mother in Japan, the theme of "longing for mother," and some resistance to these traditions, see Kin'ya Tsuruta's *Mothers in Japanese Literature* (1997). But the essential reading would be *Mothertalk* (1997), that mediating of Mary Kiyoshi Kiyooka's life story through Matsuko Masatani, transcriber and translator, through Roy Kiyooka, recorder, through Daphne Marlatt, poet and editor. For an account of the complications of origins in this work see Susanna Egan and Gabriele Helms, "The Many Tongues of *Mothertalk*" (1999).

~

Kuroshio churns up quite a range of cross-currents. As early as 1925, A.M. Stephen was summarizing British Columbia poetry by its "tendency towards Oriental mysticism and a neo-pagan attitude toward life." Malcolm Lowry in "Forest Path to the Spring" (1961 234 236) reflects on uses of the Tao, which remind him of Chinese Hats, one of the common names for the snail, *Calyptraea fastigiata*. In *City of Words* (1971), Tony Tanner discusses the "Eastern" and Buddhist dimensions of Ken Kesey, especially the idea of the "Obliterated Self" (385-86). Poet Sam Hamill, whose comments on shadow work (work done for no pay) connect to Tom Wayman's arguments for a tradition of work poetry, is a practitioner of Zen, immersed in the history of the poetry of China and Japan. Like Robert Sund, whose reflections on Chinese poetry may be found in the "Introduction" to *Shack Medicine*, he inscribes the cultural narrative that makes Asian poetic forms the cause—and effect—of poetry in the Pacific Northwest. The range of connections is suggested by the anthology *The Forbidden Stitch: An Asian American Women's Anthology* edited by Shirley Geok-lin Lim, Mayumi Tsutakawa, and Margarita Donnelly and Roy Miki's bibliographical and theoretical work on Asian American writing in *Broken Entries* (1998). Phyllis Greenwood's haunting visual/textual response to the Fraser River, *An Interrupted Panorama*, uses four narratives to organize it: one is Japanese printmaker Hiroshige's *53 Stations on the Tokaido Road*, a means of incorporating both an essential aesthetic, and a history of the removal of Japanese Canadians from their home river in 1942.

A sustained, and complicated, writing of the problematics of "chink" is Fred Wah's "biotext" *Diamond Grill* (1996). In an e-mail interview with Ashok Mathur (January 1997), Wah reflects on the book's concluding with "a noisy hyphen." "What a large question 'inbetweenness' is . . . Its [the hyphen's] coalitional and mediating potentiality offers real engagement, not as a centre but as a provocateur of flux, floating, fleeting" (Wah 2000 103).

A very shrewd student of inbetweenness, Marilyn Iwama, tried to help when I asked about the meaning of Kenji's name. She explained that

After a couple of conversations, a group of native Japanese speakers have agreed on three possible kanji or characters for the first syllable, ken: 1) health, 2) clever, 3) to serve. The second syllable, ji, would, in any case be represented by the kanji "ni", meaning two, i.e. this ending is commonly given to a second son. The implications of the naming would be that the parents hope their son will either be healthy, clever, or of service to some group, probably family and society.

The primary meaning, presumably, would be the expectation "to serve": it's the crucial aspiration, and agony, of Okada's novel.

⁓

The photograph on page 71 (FIG. 7) of interees playing the great American game shows one version of the benign face wartime propaganda gave to the bleakness of forced exile.

⁓

What causes advection fog, wonders Susan Zwinger in *The Last Wild Edge*. She finds an answer in the Japan Current:

The ocean here is complexly layered; one of the contributors is the Japanese ocean current, called the Kuroshio, which brings warm water pouring over the cold upwelling ocean.

Suddenly the blue-gray infinite, sloshing monotone of the ocean takes on a new character: one of multiple, complex chords rising from endless chaos to create a beautiful order. (96)

Literally, and physically, it seems the story of mist orginates in the upwelling lushness of Kuroshio.

⁓

Afterfile: Salal

NEGLECT OF SALAL EXTENDS TO THE *Random House College Dictionary* (rev. 1975), which *does* define, for example, both camas and salmonberry. Trees, animals, and big birds are more likely than a shrub to focus a study of regional habitat, and a good deal more mythology clings to heather than to this unheatherlike heather. Nevertheless, I have begun to imagine a whole book devoted to salal, a cultural history, perhaps—something on the model of Hilary Stewart's *Cedar* (1984) or, better, Alexandra Murphy's *Graced by Pines: The Ponderosa Pine in the American West* (1994), which after three pages on origins, etymologies, and popular names for Ponderosa pines, notes that discovery begins where the names leave off. In the research diaries my students have been compiling, they have been demonstrating, for example, the book that might be written about skunk cabbage, which Hodgins, in the rhetoric of melodrama, likens to "gaudy yellow lanterns" (*Macken* 154).

Salal can stand for repeated articulations of a gaudy (overwhelming and impenetrable) green. Scouler's early desription (McKelvey 286), which provides my epigraph, leaps to abundance. In Don Berry's *Trask* the undergrowth of salal, manzanita, and briar is "head deep" (142), "reaching a height of twelve feet" (106); in a fern forest Trask felt "much as if he were immersed in an ocean; a never-ending sea of green, finely worked and reticulated into patterns of no meaning" (296).

Such books, I would argue, have a function in the science of ecology and in ecological education. Studying multiple names and learning the flora-narratives is an education in connection, in the awareness that nothing happens in isolation. So, to take the micro-example of salal: to learn the word "ground cone" to designate the herb that hides under salal and feeds on its roots is also to learn that language makes connections through a visual similarity of the bracts to an upright Douglas Fir cone (Kathleen Smith et al. 45). The special theme of these mixed salal greens might be *teaching*. Anne Rayner taught me much of what I know about salal and cutting greenery. Some of her thoughts can be found in her PhD dissertation. In 1999, Anna Ziegler prepared a research diary that dared to think of salal as a poem. As of April 2002 the web address for this project is www.geocities.com/gather-ingsalal. Proposing "salal writing" reconfigures the region and moves us out of the book to look—and look still more closely—and to touch and taste. It challenges the student of literature toward an eco-centric conception. But the idea of writing must also move us back into the book, into the human articulation, into the necessity of language and story. Maybe it hasn't got there yet, but literature can imagine how salal thinks.

∽

Afterfile:Sasqua[...]

RICHARD M. DORSON, IN *American Folklore and the Historian* (1971), offers informed caution to any literary critic who uses the term folklore—and certainly most writers on H.L. Davis do. His chapter on "The Identification of Folklore in American Literature" (186-203) provides criteria for establishing that a particular work of literature "incorporate[s] folk materials" (87), and his postscript fumes that the typical critic venturing to use the term "folk" "has never done any field work, has read no field collections, and knows nothing of type or motif indexes." *Mea culpa*. The most informed essay on Davis's folk materials is by Jan Harold Brunvand, although Brunvand only establishes two specific folk sources, one the "fiddle tune" behind the title, and otherwise speaks of analogies and general features.

Folklore extends to every facet of life. Some of my own favourite places to read Northwest folklore are in the collection of apple crate labels in the museum in Wenatchee, the salmon-tin labels in the Fairhaven Pharmacy (see "Salmon File" and PLATE 11), and the headstones in the Roslyn Cemeteries, Upper Kittitas County, Washington.

Sasquatch's website may make its first appearance in fiction in Eden Robinson's *Monkey Beach* (2000). Robinson titles the third of four parts in this choppy edge-novel "In Search of the Elusive Sasquatch," using Bigfoot, and his/her global presences as Yeti, the Abominable Snowman, and B'gwus (317), to open both the horror and laughter of growing up in Haisla territory.

Barre Toelken's textbook *The Dynamics of Folklore* (1979) is invaluable for the beginner and rich in nuance. His chapter titled "Folklore and Connotation" is especially useful for its reminder that in addition to overt verbal signals, such as neologisms or dialect variants, less evident variations in the connotations of words may carry great weight in establishing the "shared sense of 'we'" within a local community (201). Toelken's sense of the absence of giant "demigods" (e.g., Paul Bunyan) in the Pacific Northwest may make an opening for Bigfoot. Carolyn S. Brown's *The Tall Tale in American Folklore and Literature* (1987) provides a general classification of the types of

...ntion to discuss
, performer, per-
,ion never takes on
,e of my ideas about
,sider/insider, listen-
,is chapter originate in
5).

~

Some of the related ideas on the literary function of gossip in Hodgins come from Patrick Buckridge "Gossip and History in the Novels of Brian Penton and Thomas Keneally" (1990). Other ideas on the destabilizing subversiveness of "Oh, we're just gossiping" come from Joan N. Radner and Susan S. Lanser's "The Feminist Voice: Strategies of Coding in Folklore and Literature" (1987). Of course, any reference to gossip must pay homage to the "standard" established by Patricia Meyer Spacks's *Gossip* (1985). Undoubtedly, Jack Hodgins's parodies of folk institutions and ceremonies, from tsunamis to loggers' sports, create fissures to reveal what is excluded—a powerful female, and female views of world and power. Hodgins's cast of women might carry the reader back to Tristram Potter Coffin's *The Female Hero in Folklore and Legend* (1975), which suggests how the woman in patriarchal forms works "obliquely" (3).

Frank Davey's article on *Invention of the World* in *Present Tense* (1985) argues essentially that Hodgins must undo myth so that Maggie, for example, can be freed from patriarchy. Hence, gossip is recognized as a form for seeking alternatives, an unofficial language. In attempting to get the people right, Hodgins shows his predilection for free indirect discourse, a tendency he might be defending when he tells Hancock: "The people I'm writing about tell me how to write their stories" (63). More recently, Hodgins links western Australia and western Canada by their taste for oral narratives in "Down the red dirt road. . . ." (1990): "I suspect that the yarn, the tale, the rich humorous novel may be . . . the natural literary form for writers . . . who are either nursed or haunted by all that lies west of the Great Dividing Range" (3-4). Hodgins's earlier views on region, as discussed in an "Interview" with Gordon Morash in *Pacific Northwest Review of Books*, continue to resonate; the title of this lamentably short-lived magazine is one other evidence of the hardiness of the term Pacific Northwest for cross-border reference.

~

Sasquatch and friends, I feel, demand an affection for both language and the oddball. The same might be said of viewing woodpecker beside a bowl of fruit. With his usual bumptious enthusiasm, Tom Robbins, in *Still Life with Woodpecker*, splices the Hawaiian language, and indeed its attendant folklore, into a sign-system with a good deal more oral energy than concern for accurate representation: "Hawaiian was a language," he exults, "that could name a fish 'humuhumunuk unukua-pua'a' and a bird 'o-o,' and never mind that the bird was larger than the fish" (41). Robbins might be the post-1960s inheritor of the genre of the "windy" (presumably derived from long-winded) that is so crucial to H.L. Davis.

Bigfoot is only the most prominent of the West Coast versions of monsters. I have written elsewhere of the Dungeness monster (1997). "Wild man" legends fill the forest; one glimpse of their variety may be found in Jack Boudreau's *Crazy Man's Creek* (1998). Jay Connolly's novel *Dancewater Blues* (1990) centres on the quest for Naitaka (also known as Ogopogo), the "'great peaceful fish'" (173), and the inevitability of finding "yourself face-to-face with some-thing that did not exist" (10), a being as elu-sive and compelling as "the mysterious dance of the lake itself" (216). Ogopogo's legend is honoured by a sea-horse on the coat of arms of Kelowna (Watters 404).

In an unpublished paper written for one of my courses, Glen Thielman noted that "Sasquatch is . . . placed somewhere between Native myth and Western speculation, just as the North West itself must negotiate its iden-tity from between the forming and ruling cul-tures of our region." Thielman introduced me to some of the copious research and spec-ulation about Bigfoot, and her/his many worldwide companions. One of my epigraphs refers, indirectly, to a conference which resulted in the book *Manlike Monsters on Trial* (1980), edited by Marjorie M. Halpin and Michael M. Ames. Of the many pieces avail-able, notably within the pages of *Northwest Anthropological Research Notes*, I found particular pleasure in reading Richard Beeson "The Improbable Primate and Modern Myth" (1979), both for his entertaining skepticism, and his commentary on the psychological and cultural necessity of Sasquatch. It seems to me that the pervasiveness of the wild man phenomenon only marks more clearly the cultural sig-nificance of the local variant—in this case, for example, as Thielman's observation recognizes that the Salish name, however transliterated, persists.

"The word 'sasquatch' is an anglicization of the word *sés'qec*, [Pyle represents the Salish term as *saskehavas*] which occurs in the Mainland dialects of the Halkomelem lan-guage" (74). From this beginning, Wayne Suttles, in "On the Cultural Track of the Sasquatch," *Coast Salish Essays* (1987), assembles a fabulous ethnolinguistic portrait, in eleven languages, of the multiple identities, attrib-utes, and stories of Sasquatch and friends, male and female. Suttles is essential reading for anyone interested in Sasquatch, and any-one tempted to simplify the stories, or homogenize Coast Salish languages and tradi-tions on both sides of the present-day border.

The best book-length "Sasquatch File," complete with glimpses of Bigfoot's literary appearances, is Robert Pyle's *Where Bigfoot Walks* (1995). Where I file general folkloric material under Sasquatch, and reflect only obliquely on the cultus creature, Pyle peers deeply into essential "Sasquatchness" (121). Anyone looking for Bigfoot should go there. And perhaps also to a murder mystery that seemingly burlesques most of the regional motifs in this book, Vince Kohler's *Rainy North Woods* (1990); the whimsical thriller collapses the search for the murderer with the search for Sasquatch, the elusive *genius loci*: "'No, it really is Bigfoot,' said Frank playfully, foliage reflecting in his glasses. 'Can't you smell him? Can't you sense his presence everywhere? In the clouds, in the green and gray trees, in the matted, rain-soaked earth?'" (137).

~

Negotiating a coastal "landscape of grayness" (86), the mountain man Trask follows the long spirit quest so foundational to Northwest fiction, eventually realizing that "'[t]he gods and the land are the same, and the people are part of both'" (97). Don Berry's *Trask: The Coast of Oregon, 1848 . . .* (1960) fixes the oralness of paradoxically personal and impersonal forces of forest and mountain by using more Chinook than any other Northwest novelist. Trask moves from the strength of mastery to the strength of *being*, until in singing the novel's conclusion he becomes more elusive, by becoming more surely the running spirit of the forest.

~

Skookum, meaning strong, is perhaps the term from Chinook jargon that occurs most frequently in contemporary English. According to Charles Lillard in *A Voice Great Within Us* (1998), skookum may have once meant, or derived from, the word for Sasquatch (71-72). John Keeble's skookum novel *Yellowfish,* whose "emanation[s] of landscape" inspire the Island File, figures a "spiritual traffic" of "interior mountains", "coast tribes", and Chinese immigrants in the spell of the Sasquatch legend (Newberry 12).

~

Afterfile: Salmon

THE MOST ABUNDANT SPECIES SPAWNING in the Goldstream River is the Chum. Some Coho and Chinook also use the stream, as well as Steelhead and Cutthroat trout. The Goldstream is one of many sites of the Federal-Provincial Salmonid Enhancement Program, intended to increase the spawning capacity of streams. See "Spawning Salmon at Goldstream Park" (1978). Steelhead is an anadromous trout, but since it belongs to a salmon genus (*Salmo gairdneri*), and is often confused with salmon, Hugo's sense of colour can stand here. Richard Hugo's muted and tumbling fish and river poems—and many other touching on Northwest art, landscapes and culture—are best sampled in *Making Certain It Goes On: The Collected Poems of Richard Hugo* (1984).

~

In addition to the chapter "Salmon" (180-198), Timothy Egan's *The Good Rain* (1990) opens up thirteen other regional topics, including the spiritual significance of wolves and orcas (sea-wolves), and the orchards and wineries of the Yakima Valley. As the quotations from Egan suggest, his maps of the Northwest are not sliced off neatly at the Canadian boundary, and one chapter tries to understand the Victorian legacy of Victoria, BC. For an eloquent introduction to the radically different sense of "map" in West Coast writings and culture, see Hugh Brody, *Maps and Dreams* (1981). My concept of a community taking care of itself is paraphrased from Barry Lopez, discussing the importance of story, at the Vancouver Writers Festival, 19 October 1994. Lopez's *River Notes* (1979) and *Field Notes* (1994) are books whose value is far greater than the attention I have given them here. William Rueckert's "Barry Lopez and the Search for a Dignified and Honorable Relationship with Nature" (1994) is one appreciative account of Lopez's salmon narrative I can recommend.

~

Bertrand Sinclair's *Poor Man's Rock* (1920) deserves to be re-printed; until that happens, it is rather hard to find, even in libraries. I have written an outline of Sinclair's career, "Bertrand William Sinclair" for the *Dictionary of Literary Biography* (1990). Some of Sinclair's papers are fortunately preserved in Special Collections at the University of British Columbia Library. For a sense of their details and tantalizing gaps, see Richard Lane "Archive Simulations: Reading the Bertrand Sinclair Collection" (1993). For the River People of Craig Lesley's *River Song* (1989) salmon is what "[holds] things together" (180). For its eloquent singing of salmon as a *sharing* of place, the novel should be added to my shortlist of greatest Northwest salmon novels. Charles G.D. Roberts's salmon biography (autobiography) may be found in several collections including *The Last Barrier and Other Stories* (1958).

David Wagoner's witty guidebook-poems to salmon streams and many other Northwest sites can be read in his *Collected Poems 1956-1976*. Most of his poems re-imagining Native American song-stories were published as *Who Shall Be The Sun? Poems Based on the Lore, Legends and Myths of Northwest Coast and Plateau Indians*. Wagoner is the long-time editor of *Poetry Northwest*, the modest but influential quarterly whose pages often introduce us to the best of the region's poetry.

∼

After I presented some of these thoughts at the University of Northern British Columbia, one listener asked why I hadn't included First Nations stories. This is legitimate criticism, though absence unintended, because the account of the salmon ceremony and the (implied) connection between the salmon's ascent fasting and the spirit quest tried to write the inevitable, continuing, contemporary presence of salmon *told* (performed in oral literature and mask).

One response to my remarks came from a man who had had several experiences of teaching *Mist on the River* to First Nations students in the Skeena area. He said that they did not find the novel problematic, either as ethnocentric or sentimental. Or, he felt, the sentimental might be recognized and acknowledged, but also accepted, even honoured, as an essential of story. I suppose my comments do not object to the sentiment so much as the formulaic, the too-neatness of plot and sentence—that is, they don't recognize, as do, say, Wiebe or King or Riddington, the trickster presence or an alternate cadence, diction, pronunciation.

∼

For all its spiritual and ecological connotations, the climactic quest in *The River Why*, charged with sexual analogy, is a reminder of how often salmon fishing and salmon migration are automatically read as male. Maggie Vardoe, dedicated to fly-fishing, is the quite singular female angler-hero in Ethel Wilson's *Swamp Angel* (1954). Wilson's more poignant view of the male fishing adventure may be detected in "Lilly's Story," where the swarming Springs at the mouth of the Courtenay River provide Lilly less thrill than some undefined fear:

> He had rowed out into the estuary, and then Lilly had taken the oars, so that he could fish. She had seen dimly under the slaty sky of dawn the great forms of the salmon breaking the surface of the slaty sea. How cold it was at dawn. How hard she pulled on the oars against the slapping waves. And she remembered how the indolence of Major Butler had changed to a keenness; and how at last a fish had struck and the reel had screamed and the line had run out, and Lilly, cursed at and rowing hard, had worked until at last Major Butler landed the fighting forty-pounder and turned to Lilly proud and beaming, ill-temper forgotten, demanding praise. (1952, 160-61)

≈

Gordy Tweit took English 492 on a guided historical tour of Fairhaven. At the end of the tour, he invited us to the basement of the pharmacy, where not only is much of one hundred years of discarded pharmaceutical equipment preserved, and those hundreds of salmon cans (PLATE 11), but also an extensive, if cluttered, collection of local documents, school yearbooks, photo albums, posters, and the like.

≈

Readers interested in intelligent and imaginative writing about salmon, and about the epistemology of rivers, will want to read further in David Rains Wallace's *The Klamath Knot* (1983). This evolutionary reading of salmon—"The

anadromous way of life is an ingenious way of balancing the poverty of river life against the abundant but competitive life of oceans" (55)— is also a reminder of versions of the Northwest reaching into the northwests of California. Adopting a salmon-eye's point of view takes many forms in Northwest writing. One typical, extended, and sensitive example is John C. Ryan's report on the *State of the Northwest* for the Northwest Environmental Watch in 1994. Each section is prefaced by a salmon's perspective, as the salmon is a citizen of the varied environments: "forest denizen, desert creature, mountain climber, farm animal, and even city dweller" (7). In his essay "Valley of Giants, Mounts of Gods" in *Song for the Blue Ocean* (1997), Carl Safina refers to synthesized interdependent "ancient salmon forests" and notes the unique connection of salmon to the Northwest as symbol, culture, and continuing economy.

≈

As I compiled this File in July 1997, newspapers daily tried to manufacture a "salmon war," a discomforting reminder of the national animosities (however exaggerated by the press) which interfere, along with the dams, pulp mills, and clearcuts, in the transnational migration of the Salmon People. One useful source of background to the complexities of preserving the varied stocks is Joseph Cone and Sandy Ridlington eds. *The Northwest Salmon Crisis* (1996).

The cross-border politics of salmon are

so changeable, vexed, and urgent that I cannot hope to provide any summary here, and any summary I could make would be quickly outdated (unlike some of the novels and poems I have discussed). Some overview is provided in Donald Alper's essay "Transboundary Environmental Relations in British Columbia and the Pacific Northwest" (1997) and Allen Springer's "The Pacific Salmon Controversy: Law, Diplomacy, Equity and Fish" (1997). For an interesting counterpoint to the Woodswords File, we might have thought more about fish-words: see, for example, "Salmon Fishing Terms in British Columbia" by Barbara Harris and Joseph F. Kess (1975). The best essay on salmon language—and on language as salmon—is Tom Jay's "The Salmon of the Heart." Feeding on a *Glossary of Salmon Terms* while in search of the "wisdom of the salmon," Jay recognizes that "the image is knotted in us like a nerve" (121). In Jay's view, *play*, full of the joy of ambivalence and coincidence, is crucial to understanding "a *resource's* true nature" (116). Jay, incidentally, notes that Eric Partridge in *Origins: A Short Etymological Dictionary of Modern English* does speculate that *redd* derives from the colour red (as well as from to ready or arrange). Jay's piece is essential reading for anyone interested in the ecology of salmon.

More recent books continue to spread the salmon story. L. Freeman House in *Totem*

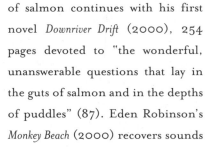

Salmon (1999) wonders and wonders at the salmon ceremony, the reach for apt metaphors, and the choosing of different routes home. Tim Bowling's life-long writing of salmon continues with his first novel *Downriver Drift* (2000), 254 pages devoted to "the wonderful, unanswerable questions that lay in the guts of salmon and in the depths of puddles" (87). Eden Robinson's *Monkey Beach* (2000) recovers sounds and songs "that don't exist in English" (193), including recipes for smoking salmon (148-49) and for salmonberry stew (76-77). bill bissett also approaches the sounds that don't exist in English in his four-line poem on the salmon titled "watching broadcast   nus":

i see th salmon talks will
　　　resume on Monday

well thank god   at leest th
　　salmon ar talking

　　　　　　　　　(1999 5)

Another valuable companion piece is the superb collection celebrating—and lamenting—the salmon, ancient and contemporary, on both sides of the Pacific, titled *First Fish First People* edited by Judith Roche and Meg McHutchison (1998). Among the intricately varied pieces is Lee Maracle (Métis/Coastal Salish) writing the salmon's autobiography: "I play between the mouth of the stream that emptied into the sea and here. I will need the thousand miles of space to flex and build the muscle it will take to make my final journey home. For the next four years I will focus on playing, gamboling, leaping waves, riding currents, familiarizing myself with the very nature of water, all in readiness for my last great splash" (172).

Kevin Roberts and Roderick Haig-Brown are other writers who should be part of a salmon file. M. Travis Lane gives an overview of some of Roberts's "practical knowledge" of fishing in "'Emotion First! Understanding Later!' The Poetry of Kevin Roberts" (1986). To complement my passing reference to Ethel Wilson, readers might look at two anthologies of women and fishing, both edited by Holly Morris and published by Seattle's Seal Press: *A Different Angle: Fly Fishing Stories by Women* (1995)

and *Uncommon Waters: Women Write about Fishing* (1991). Mark Browning discusses these, and Haig-Brown, and many of the books in this chapter in *Haunted By Waters: Fly Fishing in North American Literature* (1998). Glen Love crosses the border to celebrate Haig-Brown's contribution in "Roderick Haig-Brown: Angling and the Craft of Nature Writing in North America" (1998). Love also outlines how Northwesterners find definition by their defining of rivers in "Reading Pacific Northwest Rivers" (1993).

~

Afterfile: Woodswords

PETER TROWER'S COMMENT COMPARING log-
ging and poetry is quoted by Patrick Lane in his
"Introduction" to Trower's *Between the Sky and the
Splinters* (1974). In addition to Rupert
Schieder's "Introduction" to the New
Canadian Library edition of *Woodsmen of the West*,
important background on Grainger's remark-
able contributions to the forest industry in
British Columbia may be found in Rupert
Schieder's "Woodsman of the West: Martin
Allerdale Grainger" (1967); Carole Gerson's
"Martin Allerdale Grainger" (1990); and in
Janet Katharine Booth's "The Life and Times
of Martin Grainger" (1985). James Stevens's
Big Jim Turner (1948) is a border-crossing hobo
exemplar of the necessary link of logging and
poetry, though his "'sweet lines'" (254) seldom
use the workers' vocabulary. I have allowed logging and fishing to stand for the many patterns
of work in the Pacific Northwest. Some glimpse
of the writing of tree planting, fruit picking,
teaching, carpentry, and other forms of work,
by both Canadian and American, male and
female, writers, may be found in *Left Bank #4:
Gotta Earn a Living* (1993). Particularly valuable

are interviews with David James Duncan and
Gary Snyder on their conceptions of work. For
other West Coast literary versions of work language, consider Helen Potrebenko's *Taxi!*
(1975), the poetry of the cannery workers' dis-
gust in Michael Turner's *Company Town* (1991),
the metaphors turned out of a longshoremen's
lingo in Joseph Ferone's *BoomBoom* (1998), and
the bakery workers' specialized language in
Grant Buday's *White Lung* (1999).

Misao Dean's article "The Construction of
Masculinity in Martin Allerdale Grainger's
Woodsmen of the West" (1996) offers a feminist
reading of Grainger that intriguingly shades
from critique of the novel's gender bias to hint
at some feminist sensibility hiding in the novel.
Hilda McKenzie extends Dean's analysis by
showing how unthinkingly the novel's community is defined by its exclusions—not only of
women, but of the lower classes, non-British
immigrant workers, and Aboriginal peoples.
Arguing that the "white" history of the Pacific
Northwest is the record of "a place to be plundered," Glenda J. Pearson looks for a regional
literature that goes beyond description to

"intellectual statement," finding promise in H.L. Davis, and realization in Ivan Doig and Ken Kesey; see her "Regional Literature and "This House of Sky" (1979). Barnet Singer's "Outsider versus Insider: Malamud's and Kesey's Pacific Northwest" (1975-76) is an early regional approach to Kesey's *Notion* using Malamud's *A New Life*, and Kesey's more famous *One Flew Over the Cuckoo's Nest* as touchstones.

~

An outline of the narrative pattern and stock characters of the genre I call entrepreneurial romance can be found, although he does not label it such, in the opening chapter of Douglas Fetherling's *The Gold Crusades: A Social History of the Gold Rushes 1849-1929* (1988). Romance begets romance, and the novelist becomes advisor on the way to quick riches: someone named Army Adams, citing a case of "Northwest Fever," writes to Bertrand Sinclair on 10 March 1914, with ample allusions to the novels, asking "where a person could buy a relinquishment at a moderate price with the possibility of the land increasing in value?" (B.W. Sinclair Papers, Folder 1-1).

The Woodswords File develops the notion that we can approach regional literatures through regionalisms that adhere to economic patterns. As an alternative to topographical and climatic tropes, focus on the language of work, in an industry peculiar to a particular combination of geology and climate, implies an unself-conscious, and often restrained, authenticity in observing nature not available to the non-working observer. This emphasis seems especially suggestive in a country still very dependent on primary extractive industries. Just sticking with the West Coast version of logging language, one can quickly come up with a vocabulary recorded in print sources of 9,000 to 10,000 terms. Logging jargon is a rich, revealing study in its own right: as with any other separate language, learning woodswords uncovers new understandings: that the ubiquitous donkey (engine) appears to have been named because the original was *less* than one horsepower, or that "gandy dancer," the movement traced by a worker driving spikes into ties, may allude, however indirectly, to India. Moreover, it's surprising to find that such an extensive dialect has developed in an economy where workers are separated by long distances. This language is largely what sociolinguists label "expressive" or "purpose-free" (Meissner): it seems to be a bunkhouse language (which would suit Grainger's woodsmen), an afterwork language, a bull-shitting language. All of which should give it a great appeal to writers. On the West Coast, logging dialect seems to be the closest we have to an indigenous language in English. For a few years it penetrated the popular vocabulary in the names of ski runs at Blackcomb Mountain but, sadly, some marketing guru hearing "globalism" and "snowboard demographics" has caused most of these to be dropped.

I expected a stronger Scandinavian connection, since it is said that Scandinavians (largely Swedish and Finnish) grew from 10 per cent of the logging work force (at turn of century) to nearly 50 per cent of workers in the logging camps of the 1930s. Except for "snoose" (half-Danish), there seems to be almost no influence of words from Swedish. The term "Swede" occurs, however, fairly frequently (if not always positively). "Swede" is a pipe used as an extra handle on a wrench to improve leverage; "swede car" was a hand-pushed cart for dumping fill along railroad grades; "swede saw" (also "swede fiddle") was a cross-cut saw; "swede hooks" and "swede level" also occur. But whereas First Nations terms, especially hybrid words from Chinook jargon, extensively penetrated logging language, Swedish and Finnish did not. Why? Perhaps because the Scandinavians were eager to assimilate, and hid their own language; probably, too, because the Scandinavians who logged were not loggers in Scandinavia, but mainly farmers; perhaps because on the West Coast so many were second-stage immigrants, migrating from the Great Lakes provinces and states, not directly from Scandinavia.

British Columbia's history of confrontational labour relations, and its distinction as the most unionized province in Canada, makes it a natural centre of what we have come to know as work poetry. In the United States, this distinction within the nation-state is probably less tenable. Tom Wayman, in anthologies, articles, and as a prime mover in the Vancouver Industrial Writers' Union, has been the most important figure in defining this sub-genre in Canadian literature. See, for example, his anthologies *Going for Coffee: An Anthology of Contemporary North American Working Poems* (1987), *Paperwork: Contemporary Poems from the Job* (1991), and the collection of essays, *Inside Job: Essays on the New Work Writing* (1983). In British Columbia, logging poetry is its most visible strain, and, because of logging's distinctive argot, potentially its most interesting. On British Columbia's union politics, see, for example, Donald E. Blake *Two Political Works: Parties and Voting in British Columbia* (1985).

In his posthumous book, *A Voice Great Within Us* (1998), Charles Lillard salutes Walter McCulloch, of the Oregon State College School of Forestry, as the originator of the term *woodswords*; Lillard makes much of Swanson as an inheritor and extender of Chinook, and in his chapter entitled "West Talk" (109-15), focuses almost entirely on the "work-talk" of the logger.

A sense of the range of meanings used by Swanson in the jungle metaphor is found in *Woods Words*: "Jungle—a. a thicket. b. a hobo's hangout. c. a skidroad (town variety). d. a name for the logging camps and woods. e. the tall uncut timber in the back country" (McCulloch 100).

~

The best academic overview of the "folk poetry of Northwest loggers" is Robert E. Walls's

"Logger Poetry and the Expression of Worldview" (1987). Walls sets logging poetry within the typologies of folk poetry, occupational poetry, and cowboy poetry; categorizes the primary themes of logging poetry; and the key features of the culture's world view. Walls also cites several logger poets, mainly American; points to journals such as *Loggers World* and *American Timberman and Trucker*, where logging poetry is published; and lists a wide range of sources for study of the subject. His bibliography of Washington folklore includes a supplement by Jens Lund, listing recordings of relevant material.

~

Some of Swanson's verse has been set to music and recorded, evidence of his status as an originator, at least among British Columbia's logger balladeers, a group which includes, besides his brother, writers such as George McGinnis, Bill Charters, and no doubt scores unpublished. The recording by the *Tame Apes* reinforces various contemporary attempts to integrate the folk culture of British Columbia's first industry into its contemporary urban culture. The most important figure in this effort is Phil Thomas, whose research and singing keep alive many working songs of British Columbia (or, in Washington State, Jens Lund). Thomas's songs also formed part of the musical "Highball!" produced by Touchstone Theatre in Vancouver in 1980; most of the logging ballads in that production were written by Barry Hall.

~

All of us participate in groups with their own specialized vocabularies: nurses, fighter pilots, prison inmates, loggers, English professors, and soccer coaches. We all know how, though it's usually unconscious, to "talk shop." Shop talk satisfies two obvious needs: to foster a sense of cohesiveness and shared commitment, and to make it possible to communicate complex concepts economically. It seems that groups in crisis, in very dangerous occupations, are inclined to create particularly rich and extensive jargons. For a review of how sociolinguists have defined *speech communities*, see Charles Austin Braithwaite "Toward a Conceptualization of 'Speech Community,'" *Papers from the Minnesota Regional Conference on Language and Linguistics* (1984-85). In the broader shop talk of regional vocabulary, I have noted the honour of getting "skid road" right. I have not yet learned to use "skookum" and "salt chuck" as unselfconsciously as many residents of longer standing. Interestingly, the designation of the occupation itself is a regionalism: "Remember that *lumberjack* is a positive, masculine term in some parts of the United States, but among Northwest *loggers*, the term is used in derision" (Toelken 201).

Although the linguist's term "speech community" fits nicely with the group I write of in this file, specifics of linguistic variation (for example, pronunciation) or communication rules are often difficult to assess in print.

Hence, the criterion of "shared meaning" seems most relevant: in discussing logging speech (as, indeed, in discriminating Northwest regionalisms), we are most often in the domain of shared cultural meaning.

The ideas about specialist vocabularies I take from Thomas E. Murray's "The Language of Naval Fighter Pilots" (1986). The use of logging vocabulary in literature is a talking *about* work, rather than talk *in* or *at* work, so that the writer, even Swanson presumably, is writing in order to describe something of the culture and experience of logging to someone outside the profession. Hence, the specialized vocabulary will be selectively employed.

∾

In part, the emphasis on logging language here is to counter the arboreal mysticism in the Pacific Northwest. I do not doubt the ecological and mythical importance of (growing) trees, but I must also acknowledge the people who cut these trees. People who live in wood houses shouldn't throw flames. Movements toward a community-based eco-forestry show the most promise for a workable compromise between "harvest" and "preservation," as in Michael M'Gonigle and Fred Gale's presentation at the *BC Studies* Conference 3 May 1997 in Nanaimo, British Columbia. Jan C. Dawson, pointing to Sallie Tisdale's remark that logger and tree-hugger *share* an "improper depth of emotion"

about trees, suggests that "ambivalence toward the forest" is "the defining feature of the Pacific Northwest landscape" (17). The best commentary on these complex paradoxes is Richard White's "'Are You an Environmentalist or Do You Work for a Living?': Work and Nature" (1995).

Oddly enough, my emphasis on logging language means this file has little detail about actual *trees*, either arbutus/madrone, or any other. I cannot provide a full bibliography of key species, but I might mention again Hilary Stewart's *Cedar*, a celebration of the stunningly diverse uses to which the Northwest's totem species has been put. And the different but equally remarkable book on the marker species for the drier inland Northwest, Alexandra Murphy's linked essays on the ponderosa pine, *Graced by Pines* (1994). She describes the debate on logging jobs versus trees within the Native American community that resonates with the wood politics of coastal regions:

To call the debate an environmental issue is to see only its narrowest aspect. At its heart, it is a cultural issue, a confrontation between old and new, between traditional and progressive tribal members, not only over the appropriate use of the forest, but also over the appropriate way for Navajo people to inhabit the earth. (52)

∾

According to Jeffrey Ochsner, among all the

state pavilions at the Chicago World Exposition, 1893, only Washington's was consistently described in accounts of the fair—for its wooden building materials, all produced in the state: "Timber wealth was seen as the entire basis of the design" (177 n 41). I suggest the crucial book for the wider context of forests and writing in the European tradition is Robert Pogue Harrison's elegant *Forests: The Shadow of Civilization* (1992). For an accessible, varied approach to forest ecology, centred in "Cascadia," I would recommend *Ecoforestry: The Art and Science of Sustainable Forest Use*, edited by Alan Rike Drengson and Duncan MacDonald Taylor (1997).

∼

"Sliding" is also a prominent metaphor in conceptualizing plate tectonics. In using the metaphor, Kesey questions, "How can I work it so I am telling, as an author, about one character, then turn the narration over to him for a while and have him through [sic] a new light on another character" (Box 2 typed notes, 5-6 of 17). The Ken Kesey Collection includes many unnumbered and untitled notes, as well as holograph notes. It is often difficult to identify the sources more precisely than by box number. In preparing to write *Sometimes a Great Notion*, Kesey reminds himself to read, or re-read, or consult *Under Milkwood* (see 227). For all its gloom, the novel vibrates with the memory of Dylan Thomas's child-country, his love of compounds, and the Dylanesque feeling of

such key phrases as "this bounteous land was *saturated* with moist and terrible dying" (24). In slugspace, green held me moist and dying.

∼

The distribution of *Darlingtonia californica*, from the southwest corner of Oregon and northern California inland to the Sierra Nevada, bounds a more confined 'Northwest' than many considered in this book. The beauty-concealing violence of the insectivorous California Pitcher plant fits the wider paradox of Kesey's notion. Both the plant's habitat—in bogs and seepages—and its method of feeding—drowning insects in a pool of fluid—links it to the riverine psychology of the novel. My principal source for information on this plant is Frank Lang's "Nature Notes," available at www.fs.fed.us/r6/siskiyou/langnote.htm.

The knowledge of rivers is the primary Northwestern epistemology, as the orthographic semiotic switchbacks of David Duncan's *The River Why* and the recombinant backwaters of Daphne Marlatt's *Steveston* remind us. Interstate 5, which carries the region's traffic north and south, should be understood, writes Kim Stafford, as a river: rivers, after all (and even, in Oregon law, he notes), were highways.

The river made a lot of sense, and a pioneer could make sense, too, by figuring out the river. Salmon came up the river, logs came down . . . The river was everywhere—not a place, but a way of happening. (1986 149)

∼

Afterfile: Great Blue Heron

KOOSER ALSO DEVELOPS THE ANALOGY OF writer and great blue heron in a second poem from *Weather Central*, titled "Etude." Robert Butler's *The Great Blue Heron* (1997), although in many senses addressed to an audience of specialists, is sensitively written and quite stunningly illustrated. His account of the Point Roberts rookery and its feeding at Roberts Bank (74) is part of a larger argument for environmental stewardship. Updated summaries of his reports that the population of this crucial indicator species is declining at an annual rate of three and a half per cent may be found on the Environment Canada web page: www.ecoinfo.org/env_ind/ region/herons/heron.htm. References to heron in Leonard Lutwack's *Birds in Literature* (1994) include examples from Yeats, Robinson Jeffers, W.H. Hudson, and Atwood's *Surfacing* (where a heron is killed by dastardly "Americans"). Tim Bowling's poem "Great Blue Heron" might be seen to incorporate all of these references, and a density of mythic geographic and metaphorical associations as well. Bowling's heron, like so many,

stands waiting—for the apocalypse. I find the penultimate stanza—where Bowling lifts great blue heron into the mistory—especially evocative:

> now flies through a light drizzle,
> an umbrella with a broken spine
> swept against the darkening sky,
> a failed sketch for Kitty Hawk
> slowly erased from the page (1997 36)

Reading around the Morris Graves paintings in the Seattle Art Museum, I also discovered that in 1942 Graves was (briefly) interned as a pacifist conscientious objector, that in 1939 he built on twenty acres of Fidalgo Island (just west of the artists' colony of La Conner) a one-room cottage called The Rock, that in the same period he became increasingly devoted to Zen Buddhism, and that his objections to the war were magnified by his great love for Japan and his unease that many Asian American friends were under suspicion. Such associations attached themselves, that day, to the conviction that the great blue heron had to have a presence in this book. So, staring out the window while struggling to compose the next sentence, I scribbled this note:

The light branches of the Western Hemlock [is it?] are quite mobile; even in the slight breeze they wave from side to side and dip and rise all at once. Once in awhile, though, they gyrate wildly: you know, then, that the Steller's Jay is somewhere within, bounding frantically, impatiently from branch to branch. The jay is the opposite of the complacent, contemplative heron: the fault-line bird, always staying above the fractures. Whistler: 25 June 1999.

≈

In his retelling of parts of the creation story in Squamish country, Robert Bringhurst notes that various sites in what is now Howe Sound originated creatures crucial to the literary ecology—then and now. The island often called Gambier is where the Xhais brothers created the heron we now recognize in a different and more ominous sense as an indicator species:

Crossing to Cha'lkwnach, one of the south-facing bays on Gambier island, they met an old man fishing with a two-pronged spear. That is to say, he appeared to be fishing, but he was not really spearing his fish. He was rubbing the head of his spear against the bodies of the fish, then wiping the slime off the spear with moss and putting the moss and fish slime into his basket, letting the fish themselves swim off.

One of the brothers produced a barbed point and fixed it to the old man's spear, then speared a fish and held it up in front of the old man's eyes.

"Grandfather, this is the proper way to fish," said the brothers.

"Don't tell me what to do," the old man answered. "I prefer the slime."

"That is not how it ought to be, Grandfather," they said.

The brothers broke his spear in two and stuck the two halves to his legs. They stretched his neck, glued feathers to his hands, and fastened the spearpoint to his face, in place of his nose. Then they clapped their hands, and the old man rose unsteadily into the air. The brothers called him the Great Blue Heron. (1994a 8)

≈

Afterfile: Intertidal

SEVERAL OF THE DESCRIPTIONS OF THE intertidal zone I take from Rick Harbo's *Guide to the Western Seashore* (1988), a compact little book that provides an introduction, with colour photos, to the snails, limpets, barnacles, and sea crabs that thrive, even under duress, in Audrey Thomas's novel.

It should not be surprising that the most ample cultural history of the beach is written by Northwesterners, Lena Lenček and Gideon Bosker of Portland. Explaining the motivation of the book, Lenček writes in the "Foreword" to *The Beach* (1998): "The beaches of the Oregon Coast flash as many faces as a masked ball" (xvii). As "a site of transformations, the beach reclaims us from the strait jackets of routine and repression," (xx) they note, but the edginess of the Northwest is several times evident: in the "'drowned topography' of Puget Sound"; the beaches are "narrow, often rocky" (16), congenial to "strolling, riding, and scavenging," but not to swimming (xvi). This book is an affectionate, readable, and informative chronology, where the reader will find how tides work and how sand is formed.

Again, two of my favourite women essayists offer crucial understandings of the intertidal zone. Sallie Tisdale describes her perspective, throughout *Stepping Westward* (1991), as being "at the end of the line, shoved up against the ocean with no place else to go" (16). The penultimate chapter of Hazel Heckman's *Island in the Sound* (1967), "Time and Tide," contemplates the chitons, limpets, and mussels and the cliché of the beach as "a place for renewal" (272). A "universe controlled by the ebb and flow of tides" creates the "sensation that time is not passing or is passing [as in childhood] at a slug's pace" (270-71); thus Heckman uncovers the neat pun in that single word, *slugspace,* that, Shannon Timmers once told me, could substitute for all my possible words about the region. Malcolm Lowry's "Forest Path to the Spring" makes sustained use of these intertidal associations, especially in Section 3.

～

Other work by Ethel Wilson is more exclusively British Columbian than *The Innocent*

Traveller. Swamp Angel (1954), in particular, assembles several passages, virtually self-contained, of landscape description. And the story of Maggie Vardoe become Maggie Lloyd, leaving Vancouver and an oppressive marriage to travel to a remote lake in the Interior, echoes the spirit-quest pattern and, less certainly, the return portion of the salmon narrative. Heather Murray looks closely at the stylistic features of this novel as they contribute to an "inter-dependency of language and land" (241), both Wilson's message and Murray's focus.

~

"Edge" is a frequently recurring word in Steveston, a word Marlatt plays on to imagine a community on the delta of the Fraser River, on land being at once built up and eroded by the freshwater current meeting the saltwater tides. For Marlatt being "always on the edge of" is a method of composition, or deposition: the edge of words is the marginal shift in signifier that makes a massive shift in signified: the edge, for example, between "sedge" and "dredge" (29-30). I don't know enough about either rhizomes or fractals to be sure how and where they fit the shapes of edges. But I am tempted by the description of rhizome as a key to ecological thinking in Deleuze and Guattari's *On the Line* (1983): "A rhizome doesn't begin and doesn't end, but is always in the middle, between things, interbeing . . . the tree imposes the verb 'to be' but the rhizome

is woven together with conjunctions: and . . . and . . . and" (57). And following an article in *Science 85*, I imagine the Northwest as the accumulated forms and lines of materials which crack under high stress, "structures as diverse as rivers, mountain ranges and coastlines all take shape in a mixture of randomness and order called a fractal [i.e. "a fraction raised to a fractional power"]" (9).

For one reading of possible fractals in a crucially influential Northwest text, see Gordon E. Slethaug's "The Buried Stream: Stochastic Narration and 'A River Runs Through It'" (1997). Noting that "nature's love of fractal shapes is a deep one," Leonard Sander presents this simplified definition: "A fractal is an object with a sprawling, tenuous pattern. As the pattern is magnified it reveals repetitive levels of detail, so that similar structure exists on all scales" (94).

One of the wonkiest bits of island-edge art-making in Pacific Northwest history must be the project of Robert Smithson to create the *Island of Broken Glass* by placing "100 tons of tinted glass onto the small Miami Islet, a rocky island about 50 yards long" (Flam 197). Although the project was never realized—the British Columbia government withdrew Smithson's lease—it did result in conversations recorded in Vancouver with Dennis Wheeler, rich in the most audacious and perplexing theorizing of coast and edge. Here is just one small excerpt, which follows Smithson's reciting dictionary definitions of *shore*:

The support is liquid, also: [through] the weight action on the shore, it tends to get shoreless and it's the line between the water and the glass [which] becomes variable. There's the sharp cutting edge . . . it's very uncertain. The shore there is uncertain . . . once you start thinking about the possibility of finding that edge, you could arrive at something. What, I don't know. (Flam 226)

Support is liquid and the line between water and glass also variable in the studio of one of the Northwest's most popular artists, Dale Chihuly. Intertidal colours and ocean-edge forms have been central to his vision for three decades (PLATE 15).

~

In her thinking about the possibility of the edge, poet Sharon Bryan, contemplating the puzzle of "Deception Pass," comes to understand, in the fog, "how overlapping islands/ seemed to be uninterrupted coastline." Land meets water, but which is which? "[I]mpossible/to tell from the map or the cross-hatched land-/scape when we were afloat and when/on solid ground" (51-52). Of course, the *cascade*, which gives its varying name to the region, is a natural phenomenon dependent on water meeting land's edge: "Trask mused idly on the notion that the stream simply drifted to the edge of the cliff and toppled over . . . if he was a stream, he'd just go straight for the edge, by God" (Don Berry 109).

~

Intertidal organisms on the west coast of Vancouver Island: Susan Heaslip's photo of intertidal organisms on the west coast of Vancouver Island (PLATE 13) hints at the teeming linked stories of California mussels (*Mytilus califonianus*), the giant green anenome (*Anthopleura xanthogrammica*), the purple sea urchin (*Strongylocentrotous purpuratus*), the black leather chiton (*Katharina tunicata*), limpets, coralline red algae (*Lithothamnion*)—grazed on by chitons and limpets—and abalone *Haliotis*.

~

Afterfile: mental:
peor

THAT LOCAL KNOWLEDGE, EVEN NOSTALGIA, need not be inconsistent with nation-building is intriguingly argued in Paola Filippucci's "Landscape, locality and nation: The case of Bassano" (1997). Examining landscape management in the northeast Italian town of Bassano, Filippucci claims that "[t]he 'local' is taken as a refraction of a broader context, it stands for a specificity that is not antithetical to generality but integral to it. . . . an image of nested 'we's'" (56). From a distance, Italy may seem small enough, and Italian enough, to have a homogeneous nationality, but travelling in Italy actually reinforces my faith in region as a way of seeing. Italy has, after all, been a nation-state only for about as long as Canada, and regional affiliations are very strong. A tourist, at least, is constantly reminded of the local: Tuscan cooking, Chianti wines, bean soup, Fiorentine steak, and the light and colour of each estate's olive oil. Which is to say, of course, that tourists display a marketer's dream vulnerability. The local knowledge present in Italy, and missing in North America, is the immense sense of

human history, surrounding, pervading—even if unthought about.

A richly varied book on place and its uprooting only came to my attention too late to be given full attention: Lucy R. Lippard's *The Lure of the Local* (1997). Its comments on Christos Dikeakos, discussed in this File, and her featuring of Kim Stafford's poem "There are no Names but Stories" are just two of many reasons to pay attention to the ways Lippard pays attention.

⁓

In *The Location of Culture* (1994), Homi Bhabha suggests that *border* and *boundary* may be such dominant tropes because of our being on the uncertain edge of an old and new century. I hope this borderline work participates in the more transnational and "translational sense of the hybridity of imagined communities" (5) which Bhabha identifies. But transnational and translational is a long way to go. I realized this challenge when I heard Dionne Brand, reading at the Belkin Gallery in September 1997, reframe a question I regard as fundan a burlesque tone, she dismissed e "who ask stupid questions like 'where re you from?'". To ask this question in a racialized context is to assume that if you are a person of colour, or your accent or dress is different, you must be from elsewhere. I wonder if the question could also be voiced with an "ecological" inflection, asking about connections—about all the forms of life we depend on, and that depend on us. If so, "where are you from?" might be spoken as an invitation and a beginning of friendship.

~

Topographies make borders. Answering the question "Where is the Pacific Northwest?" the website "Pacific Northwest Native Wildlife Gardening" leans to the edge: "For the purposes of this site, the Pacific Northwest is the ecological region bounded from north to south by Cook Inlet, Alaska to Eugene Oregon, and from east to west by the ridge of the Cascade and Coast mountain ranges to the Pacific Ocean" (www.tardigrade.org/natives). Correcting maps and charts which "suppos[ed] nothing but sea between *Japan* and *California*," Lemuel Gulliver located a narrow, precariously mountainous Brobdingnag in "the North-west Parts of *America*":

The kingdom is a peninsula, terminated to the north-east by a ridge of mountains thirty miles high, which are altogether impassable by reason of the volcanoes upon the tops. Neither do the most learned know what sort of mortals inhabit beyond these mountains, or whether they be inhabited at all. On the three other sides it is bounded by the ocean. There is not one seaport in the whole kingdom, and those parts of the coasts into which the rivers issue are so full of pointed rocks, and the sea generally so rough, that there is no venturing with the smallest of their boats so that these people are wholly excluded from any commerce with the rest of the world. (Swift 89)

Insofar as this peninsula-kingdom still exists, the commerce of exchange rates has come to shape the imagined topography. Hodgins's Victoria looks nervously south to big money; Dillard's Bellingham looks hopefully north for more gold rushes. In sympathy with his Canadian neighbour's "looney" economy, the *Seattle Post-Intelligencer*'s food columnist even took to re-naming favourite recipes: Stanley Park Schnitzel, English Bay Enchiladas (Owen D3). I take the jocular extremes of these inventions as reminders that the traditions I am inventing here have limited patriotic function but some motivating potential: something of a word-dance into the roots of things, a step toward the complicated dance of words that makes us aware.

Unlike most countries, Canada, practically speaking, has only one international boundary. At its western end, the border has been more of a site of exchange than a barrier. Or, when a barrier, still a site of exchange, as in the thriving trade in smuggled liquor from 1920 to 1933 (Henry 112). Seattle and Vancouver function as one another's complementary "getaways," the comfortable exotics, situated on the east coast of a western inland sea, metropolitan capitals of commerce, but neither a political capital. Cascadia is the dream of a region based on endlessly vertically plunging streams of (now mostly polluted) green-white water, and the "two-nation vacation" is a marketer's rhyme for how to sell it (FIGS. 5 11). Whatever cross-border transactions are detected in the literature—from Craig Lesley to Roderick Haig-Brown, from Jack Hodgins to John Keeble, it may not be surprising that most of the flow of ideas in these pages is from south to north. Perhaps a Canadian, living so close to a cultural behemoth, would be more likely to have written this book looking south across the border than would an American looking north. Since this book recognizes much that is common to Canada and the United States, indeed may err toward the common, I hope US readers will learn the Canadian books included—and a Canadian language—and recognize in them the differences I have downplayed.

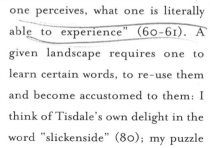

∼

I like the notions of home as a process, even a "form of resistance," in James Clifford's *Routes: Travel and Translation in the Late Twentieth Century* (1997 85). And connected to this notion, the concept of place name as a "figure of speech to evoke the nature of exploration," in Paul Carter's *The Road to Botany Bay: An Essay in Spatial History* (1987 14). But for all the attractive motility of these concepts, I embrace some

notion (following Gary Snyder) of mental determinism, at least to the articulated in Sallie Tisdale's *Steppi* "A given landscape permits and prohibits how one perceives, what one is literally able to experience" (60-61). A given landscape requires one to learn certain words, to re-use them and become accustomed to them: I think of Tisdale's own delight in the word "slickenside" (80); my puzzle at the phrase "flammulated owl" (100-101) in Alexandra Murphy's *Graced by Pines*; the need, still felt by a newcomer to the West Coast to learn any number of words in Chinook, such as skookum. Anne Rayner has taught me a good deal about Pacific Northwest flora. Here's what she has to say about arbutus (and Howarth's dream-place Madronna) in her thesis "Everything Becomes Island" (1995):

> In naming her island after the arbutus, Howarth identifies the condition of Gulf Island with the range of that species: since the islands constitute the northernmost part of the arbutus' range, the tree signifies the warm, dry climate associated not with Canada but with the coast south of the international border as far as northern California. The zone to which the arbutus belongs is known as "Cool Mediterranean": the arbutus thus connotes benign, comfortable natural places in both the old world and the new. The tree thus connotes pastoral. (163 n 69)

Arbutus menziesii itself might be thought of as a "southern: species whose range extends only a relatively slight distance north into Canada.

butus/madrone is but one of many curious (and persuasive) language variants. The famous Garry Oak (*Quercus garryana*) on Vancouver Island is the Oregon White Oak further south (Rupp 10). And Heckman reminds us that the service berries (*Amelanchier*) she harvests on Anderson Island are known to Canadians as Saskatoons (243).

Andrew Scott calls arbutus "an icon, a local lifeform that expresses perfectly the spirit of the land" (102). His chapter "The Arbutus" in *Secret Coastline* (2000) is a compact history of the naming, painting, ecology, and legends of arbutus. According to First Nations myth, Scott tells us, arbutus holds the whole world together: "if the arbutus should disappear . . . the planet would fly apart and be utterly destroyed" (105).

~

Leaving *Always Coming Home* to the end of the book was, in part, an honouring of its success in recognizing and renegotiating the traditional boundaries between fiction and science, between anthropological field notes and the novel. I had in mind Stephen Greenblatt's 1997 manifesto, celebrating Clifford Geertz for making the infinitely precious "literary work" and the powerful "anthropological (or historical) anecdote" "each other's thick description."

~

In the domain of translation, Chinook jargon,

a lingua franca that took the place of translator/ interpreter, was crucial to articulating the Northwest, and facilitating its economy. See Richard Brown's "Language and Exploration: The Role of the Chinook Jargon" (1994). A lighter compendium on the language, as I've several times noted, is Charles Lillard (with Terry Glavin) *A Voice Great Within Us: The Story of Chinook* (1998); H.L. Davis pays warm tribute to Chinook in *Honey in the Horn* (238 411).

Translation from a score of markedly different First Nations languages, I have argued, tempts almost every writer in the Northwest. The temptation is closely allied to the possibility of animals, birds, and stones talking: take, for example, the owl's "tree-consonants" and "wind-vowels" in Duncan's *The River Why* (240) and found in the same work's punning ecotopian poetic "The River Writes" (131). But even the most sensitive translation may hide the very borders it hopes to uncover. Anna Ziegler, intent student of salal and tides, told me as much on her final exam:

It was suggested in class many times that the narratives of the First Nations may be threaded through the entire body of Pacific Northwest narrative. But, Alexie challenges this. Perhaps, we (the off-reserve, primarily non-Native recent immigrants) only hope that the First Nations narratives have been absorbed and appreciated. Alexie's book suggests that the Native American reservation life experience is like being in a different world altogether. In Smoke Signals, *one of the girls, in the car that can only go in reverse, asks Victor and Thomas, who are leaving the reserve for the first time ever, if they have their passports. No, Victor tells them, they are only leaving the reserve, not the country. The girls shake their heads and laugh (at how different Victor and Thomas will find it . . .). So, indeed, life, as well as narrative and heroism, according to Alexie is hardly the same thing in these two worlds.*

As David Wagoner wrote on another occasion: "It felt like my final exam" (Ricou 1997 20).

～

Always Coming Home, despite its futurist disposition, implies some realized exceptionalism or separatism. The Kesh world seems so total, and so self-contained. (Tisdale, in seeming sympathy, remembers a petition for a fifty-first state, "The Wilderness State," made of Eastern Washington, western Montana, and part of Idaho [107]). Since the "On Brotherly Terms" conference (1996), I have been hearing the term Pacifica, to complement Cascadia, the most prominent label for an emergent marketing or environmental alliance. Examples of the grammar of Pacific Northwest exceptionalism may be found in several places, including in a review of *Honey in the Horn*, and a lead editorial in the *Northwest Literary Review*, "Marks of the Northwesterner": "There is something in the human animal, . . . which resents being standardized" (Anon 1935 2). Ken McGoogan finds that "[i]t is the Dawning of the Age of Cascadia" in *BC Bookworld* (1993), and Robert D. Kaplan

embraces the Cascadian concept in *An Empire Wilderness: Travels into America's Future* (1998). Terry Glavin responds trenchantly to Kaplan's book with a column in the *Globe and Mail* entitled "We've had enough of Cascadia" (1998). Michael Treleaven (1997) tries to imagine a regional social policy distinctive to the Northwest, but he seems most persuasive when outlining the differences in the Canadian and American systems. Something of a how-to book on drawing maps of the Cascadia bioregion is Doug Aberle's *Boundaries of Home: Mapping for Local Empowerment* (1993). One of the most sensitive and engaging essays on the "unity of this diverse bio-region" and his love of home is Alan Thein Durning's *This Place on Earth: Home and the Practice of Permanence* (1996).

～

Lowry's unarrived-at destination, Gabriola, is apparently a corruption of the Spanish word for seagull. He is a true squatter, in fluid affiliation with the hundreds of Northwesterners, in float homes and on stilts, who live quite literally on the edge, between high-tide and low-tide mark, a zone that might seem to be beyond ownership. For a sense of Lowry's affiliation with the home between, see Jill Wade's essay on the individual motivations and community affiliations of the Vancouverites who lived in "foreshore shacks and boathouses": "Home or Homelessness? Marginal Housing in Vancouver, 1886-1950" (1997).

Lowry's *Ferry* keeps a fairly steady eye on

Mount Baker, just across the border. His ultimate border-crossing story is "The Bravest Boat," in which a child's toy launched off Cape Flattery washes up in Stanley Park. Lowry's predilection for gibberish, which I cherish, links with the maverick spirit of Swanson and *Status Rerum*, of Amor de Cosmos, and Alan Twigg summarizing *Twigg's Directory of 1001 BC Writers* (1992): "Possibly authors, being independent-minded sorts, have tended to gravitate west to a freer-thinking, less institutionalized society" (Foreword)? "What is real," urges Richard White, writing of the Columbia River, "is the mixture." And then laments, "This is a river subdivided into separate spaces whose users speak to each other in a babel of discourses: law, religion, nature talk, economics, science, and more . . . The Columbia runs through the heart of the Northwest in ways we have never imagined" (1995 III 113). Maybe the imagination has it: gibberish is the language of mixture.

～

Sources File

"An Example to Shame Us" *The Globe and Mail* August 8 1999 A6.

"U.S. Law Sets Precedent, Miki says" *Vancouver Sun* August 11 1988 A6.

"Marks of the Northwesterner" *Northwest Literary Review* 1:3 (September/October 1935): 2-3.

Canada. Parliament. House of Commons. "Parliament 36. Session 1" *Official Report of Debates, House of Commons [Hansard]* 22 September 1988.

Aberle, Doug ed. *Boundaries of Home: Mapping for Local Empowerment* (Gabriola Island: New Society Publisher 1993).

Adams, John Coldwell *Sir Charles God Damn: The Life of Sir Charles G.D. Roberts* (Toronto: U Toronto P 1986).

Agee, James and Walker Evans *Let Us Now Praise Famous Men: Three Tenant Families* (1941; rpt. Boston: Houghton Mifflin 1960).

Akrigg, G.P.V. and Helen Akrigg *British Columbia Place Names* (Victoria: SonoNis P 1986).

Alexie, Sherman *The Man Who Loves Salmon* (Boise ID: Limberlost P 1998).

Alcorn, John *The Nature Novel from Hardy to Lawrence* (London: Macmillan 1978).

Allen, Barbara "Regional Studies in American Folklore Scholarship" *A Sense of Place: American Regional Cultures* (Lexington KT: UP of Kentucky 1990): 1-13.

Alper, Donald "Transboundary Environmental Relations in British Columbia and the Pacific Northwest." *The American Review of Canadian Studies* 27:3 (Autumn 1997): 359-83.

Anderson, M.K., Michael G. Barbour and Valerie Whitworth "A World of Balance and Plenty: Land, Plants, Animals, and Humans in a Pre-European California" *California History* 76: 2-3 (Summer-Fall 1997): 12-47.

Anonymous "Mathematics of a liquid squeeze play" *Science 85* (June 1985): 9.

Applegate, Shannon and Terence O'Donnell eds. *Talking on Paper: An Anthology of Oregon Letters and Diaries* Oregon Literature Series Vol 6 (Corvallis: Oregon State UP 1994).

Armitage, Susan H. and Deborah Gallacci Wilbert "Black Women in the Pacific Northwest: A Survey and Research Prospectus" in Karen J. Blair ed. *Women in Pacific Northwest History* (Seattle: U Washington P 1988): 136-151.

Armour, Leslie *The Idea of Canada and the Crisis of Community* (Ottawa: Steel Rail 1981).

Armstrong, Jeannette *Slash* (Penticton BC: Theytus Books 1985).

Armstrong, Jeannette "Land Speaking" in Simon J. Ortiz ed. *Speaking for the Generations: Native Writers on Writing* (Tucson: U Arizona P 1998): 174-194.

Armstrong, Jeannette "Words" *Telling It: Women and Language Across Cultures* (Vancouver: Press Gang 1990): 23-29.

Arnold, A. James ed. *Monsters, Tricksters, and Sacred Cows: Animal Tales and American Identities* (Charlottesville: U P of Virginia: 1996).

Arnold, Grant, ed. *Collapse 5 Rhetorics of Utopia: Early Modernism and the Canadian West Coast* (July 2000).

Arnold, Grant, Monika Kin Gagnon and Doreen Jensen *Topographies: Aspects of Recent BC Art* Catalogue of an exhibition held at the Vancouver Art Gallery September 29 1996-January 5 1997 (Vancouver: Douglas & McIntyre 1996).

Artibise, Alan F.J. "Cascadian Adventures: Shared Visions, Strategic Alliances, and Ingrained Barriers in a Transborder Region" Presentation to "On Brotherly Terms: Canadian-American Relations West of the Rockies" Symposium, U Washington, Seattle, 12-14 September 1996.

Atwood, Margaret *Cat's Eye* (1988; rpt. Toronto: Seal Books 1989).

Atwood, Margaret *The Journals of Susanna Moodie* (Toronto: Oxford UP, 1970).

Babcock, Barbara A. "Taking Liberties, Writing from the Margins and Doing it with a Difference" *Journal of American Folklore* 100 (1987): 390-411.

Bacho, Peter *Cebu* (Seattle: U Washington P 1991).

Bacho, Peter *Dark Blue Suit* (Seattle: U Washington P 1997).

Banerjee, Chinmoy "Polyphonic Form and Effective Aesthetic in *Obasan*" *Canadian Literature* 160 (Spring 1999): 101-119.

Barnes, Trevor and James S. Duncan eds. *Writing Worlds: Discourse, Texts and Metaphor in the Representation of Landscape* (London/New York: Routledge 1992).

Bawlf, Samuel "Secret Voyage to BC" *Vancouver Sun* 5 August 2000 B1-B6.

Beard, Stephen J. "'Imagine a Stack of Blocks': An Interview with David James Duncan" *Left Bank #4: Gotta Earn a Living* (Hillsboro OR: Blue Heron 1993): 45-53.

Beckam, Stephen Dow ed. *Many Faces: An Anthology of Oregon Autobiography* Oregon Literature Series Vol 2 (Corvallis: Oregon State UP 1993).

Beeson, Richard "The Improbable Primate and Modern Myth" *Northwest Anthropological Research Notes* 13:1 (Spring 1979): 91-110.

Bellerby, Greg L. "Foreword" *Mark Tobey* (Victoria: Art Gallery of Greater Victoria, 1983): n.p.

Bellinger, Joan "Arch Event to Salute Children and Peace" press release. 14 May 1979. (Victoria: Tourism British Columbia).

Bennett, Bruce "Concepts of 'the West' in Canadian and Australian Literary Studies" *Westerly* 29:2 (July 1984): 75-83.

Bentley, D.M.R. "Preface" *Canadian Poetry* 18 (Spring-Summer 1986): n.p.

Berry, Don *Trask: The Coast of Oregon, 1848 . . .* (1960; rpt. Sausalito CA: Comstock Editions 1984).

Berry, Wendell *A Continuous Harmony: Essays Cultural and Agricultural* (New York: Harcourt Brace Jovanovich 1972).

Bevis, William W. "Region, Power, Place" in Michael Kowalewski ed. *Reading the West: New Essays on the Literature of the American West* (Cambridge: Cambridge UP 1996): 21-43.

Bevis, William W. *Ten Tough Trips: Montana Writers and the West* (Seattle: U Washington P 1990).

Bhabha, Homi K. *The Location of Culture* (New York: Routledge 1994).

Bingham, Edwin R. and Glen Love eds. *Northwest Perspectives: Essays on the Culture of the Pacific Northwest* (Eugene: U Oregon P; Seattle: U Washington P 1979).

Birney, Earle *Essays on Chaucerian Irony* (Toronto: U Toronto P 1985).

Birney, Earle "November Walk near False Creek Mouth" *Ghost in the Wheels: Selected Poems* (Toronto: McClelland & Stewart 1977): 90.

Birnie, Lisa Hobbs "The West Coast: A Unique Land with a Powerful Sense of Newness" *Vancouver Sun* 10 August 1996: A19.

bissett, bill *canada gees mate for life* (Vancouver: Talonbooks 1985).

bissett, bill *scars on the seehors* (Burnaby BC: Talonbooks 1999).

Blaise, Clark *The Border as Fiction* Borderlands Monograph Series No.4 (Orono ME: Borderlands Project, 1990).

Blaise, Clark *A North American Education: A Book of Short Fiction* (1973; rpt. Don Mills ON: General 1974).

Blake, Donald E. *Two Political Worlds: Parties and Voting in British Columbia* (Vancouver: U British Columbia P 1985).

Blyth, Gladys Young *Salmon Canneries: British Columbia North Coast* (Lantzville: Ooolichan Books 1991).

Boas, Franz and Henry W. Tate *Tsimshian Mythology* (Washington: Smithsonian Institution 1916).

Bold, Alan *The Ballad* (London: Methuen 1979).

Booth, Janet Katharine "The Life and Times of Martin Grainger" (Bachelor of Arts Forestry Thesis, U British Columbia 1985).

Boudreau, Jack *Crazy Man's Creek* (Prince George: Caitlin P 1998).

Boulet, Robert *Toni Onley: A Silent Thunder* (Scarborough ON: Prentice Hall Canada 1981).

Bowering, George *Burning Water* (Don Mills ON: General 1980).

Bowering, George *Bowering's BC: A Swashbuckling History* (Toronto: Viking 1996).

Bowering, George "Home Away: A Thematic Study of Some British Columbia Novels" *Imaginary Hand: Essays by George Bowering* Writer as Critics Series, Vol. 1, Smaro Kamboureli gen.ed. (Edmonton: NeWest 1988): 23-41.

Bowering, George *Kerrisdale Elegies* (Toronto: Coach House P, 1984).

Bowering, George "Sheila Watson, Trickster" in John Moss ed. *Modern Times: A Critical Anthology* (Toronto NC Press 1982): 209-23.

Bowling, Tim *Downriver Drift* (Madeira Park BC: Harbour Publishing 2000).

Bowling, Tim *Dying Scarlet* (Gibsons BC: Nightwood Editions 1997).

Bowling, Tim *Low Water Slack* (Gibsons BC: Nightwood Editions 1995).

Braithwaite, Charles Austin "Toward a Conceptualization of 'Speech Community'" *Papers from the Minnesota Regional Conference on Language and Linguistics* (1984/1985): 13-29.

Bringhurst, Robert "Fast Drumming Ground" Richard Littlemore ed. *Howe Sounds: Fact, Fiction and Fantasy from the Writers of Bowen Island* (Bowen Island: Bowen Island Arts Council 1994): 3-11.

Bringhurst, Robert "Off the Road: Journeys in the Past, Present and Future of Canadian Literature" in Douglas Fetherling ed. *Best Canadian Essays 1989* (Saskatoon: Fifth House 1989): 185-194.

Bringhurst, Robert *The Black Canoe: Bill Reid and the Spirit of Haida Gwaii* (1991; rpt. Vancouver: Douglas & McIntyre 1995).

Bringhurst, Robert "Point-Counterpoint: The Polyhistorical Mind" *Journal of Canadian Studies* 29:2 (Summer 1994): 165-175.

Brody, Hugh *Maps and Dreams: Indians and the British Columbia Frontier* (Vancouver: Douglas & McIntyre 1981).

Brown, Carolyn *The Tall Tale in American Folklore and Literature* (Knoxville: U Tennessee P 1987).

Brown, J.D. "Long Distance to the Sixties: Postmark: Eugene, Oregon" *The New Pacific* No. 3 (Summer 1990): 61-67.

Brown, Justine S. *All Possible Worlds: Utopian Experiments in British Columbia* (Vancouver: Transmontanus/New Star Books 1995).

Brown, Justine S. "Nowherelands: Utopian Communities in BC Fiction" *BC Studies* 109 (Spring 1996): 5-28.

Brown, Richard Maxwell "Language and Exploration: The Role of the Chinook Jargon" Carlos Schwantes ed. *Encounters with a Distant Land: Exploration and the Great Northwest* (Moscow ID: U Idaho P 1994): 86-101.

Brown, Russell M. *The Borderlands and Borderlines in English Canada: The Written Line* (Orono ME: Borderlands Project 1990).

Brown, Russell M. "Crossing Borders" *Essays on Canadian Writing* 22 (Summer 1981): 154-168.

Browning, Mark *Haunted by Waters: Fly Fishing in North American Literature* (Athens: Ohio UP 1998).

Bruggman, Maximillien *Indians of the Northwest Coast* (1987; transl. Barbara Fritzmeier New York: Facts on File 1989).

Brunvand, Jan Harold "*Honey in the Horn* and 'Acres of Clams': The Regional Fiction of H.L. Davis" *Western American Literature* 2:2 (Summer 1967): 135-145.

Bryan, Sharon *Salt Air* (Middletown CT: Wesleyan UP 1983).

Buckridge, Patrick "Gossip and History in the Novels of Brian Penton and Thomas Keneally" *Australian Literary Studies* 14:4 (October 1990): 436-449.

Buday, Grant *White Lung* (Vancouver: Anvil P 1999).

Buruma Ian "The Eternal Mother" *A Japanese Mirror: Heroes and Villains of Japanese Culture* (London: Jonathan Cape 1984): 18-37.

Butler, Robert *The Great Blue Heron: A Natural History and Ecology of a Seashore Sentinel* (Vancouver: U British Columbia P 1997)

Callenbach, Ernest *Ecotopia: The Notebooks and Reports of William Weston* (Berkeley, CA: Banyan Tree Books 1975).

Cannings, Richard and Sydney Cannings *British Columbia: A Natural History* (Vancouver: Douglas & McIntyre 1996).

Carr, Emily *Klee Wyck* Centennial Edition (1941; rpt. Toronto: Clark Irwin 1971).

Carr, Emily *Hundreds and Thousands: The Journals of Emily Carr* (Toronto: Clarke Irwin 1966).

Carrington, Ildikó de Papp ed. "Canadian-American Literary Relations" *Essays on Canadian Writing* 22 (Summer 1981): 5-13.

Carter, Paul *The Road to Botany Bay: An Essay on Spatial History* (London: Faber & Faber 1987).

Carter, Robert E. *Becoming Bamboo: Western and Eastern Explorations of the Meaning of Life* (Montreal/Kingston: McGill-Queen's UP 1992).

Chan, Jeffery Paul and Marilyn Alquiloza "Asian-American Literary Traditions" *A Literary History of the American West*, sponsored by the Western Literature Association (Fort Worth: Texas Christian UP 1987): 1119-1138.

Chapman, Charles E. *A History of California: The Spanish Period* (1921; rpt. New York: Macmillan 1930).

Chattaway, Peter T. "Hope springs eternal on Squamish 'island'" *The Vancouver Courier* 19 December 1999 21, 30.

Cheney, Jim "Postmodern Environmental Ethics: Ethics as Bioregional Narrative" *Environmental Ethics* 11 (Summer 1989): 122-123.

Cheung, King-kok "Attentive Silence in Joy Kogawa's *Obasan*" *Listening to Silences: New Essays in Feminist Criticism* Elaine Hedges and Shelley Fisher Fishkin eds. (New York: Oxford UP 1994): 113-29.

Chin, Frank et al. eds. *Aiiieeeee!: An Anthology of Asian-American Writers* (Washington DC.: Howard UP 1974).

Choy, Wayson *Jade Peony* (Vancouver/Toronto: Douglas & McIntyre 1995).

Clifford, James *Routes: Travel and Translation in the Late Twentieth Century* (Cambridge: Harvard UP 1997).

Coffin, Tristram Potter *The Female Hero in Folklore and Legend* (New York: Seabury P 1975).

Cole, Christina "Daphne Marlatt as Penelope, Weaver of Words: A Feminist Reading of *Steveston*" *Open Letter* 6th Series No. 1 (Spring 1985): 5-19.

Cone, Joseph and Sandy Ridlington eds. *The Northwest Salmon Crisis* (Corvallis: Oregon State UP 1996).

Conklin, Ellis E. "Kesey's Great Notion" *Seattle Post-Intelligencer* 18 January 1990 C1.

Connolly, Jay *Dancewater Blues* (Lantzville: Oolichan 1990).

Cook, Ramsay "Imagining a North American Garden: Some Parallels and Differences in Canadian and American Culture" *Canadian Literature* 103 (Winter 1984):10-23.

Cooley, Dennis *The Vernacular Muse: The Eye and Ear in Contemporary Literature* (Winnipeg: Turnstone 1987).

Corbel, Eve comp. *The Little Greenish-Brown Book of Slugs* (Vancouver: Arsenal Pulp P 1993).

Cosgrove, Dennis and Stephen Daniels eds. *The Iconography of Landscape: Essays on the Symbolic Representation, Design and Use of Past Environments* (New York: Cambridge UP: 1988).

Crate, Joan *Pale as Real Ladies: Poems for Pauline Johnson* (Ilderton ON: Brick Books 1989).

Crockford, Ross "Wild Men of the Woods" *The Georgia Straight* 6-13 June 1996 13, 15-18.

Curtis, Malcolm "Giant arbutus stirs interest in BC Big Trees Registry" *Vancouver Sun* 8 January 2000 B2.

Davey, Frank "Disbelieving Story: A Reading of *The Invention of the World*" *Present Tense: A Critical Anthology* The Canadian Novel, Vol. 4, John Moss ed. (Toronto: NC Press 1985): 30-44.

Davis, H.L. *Collected Essays and Short Stories* (Moscow ID: U Idaho P 1986).

Davis, H.L. *Honey in the Horn* (1935; rpt. New York: Avon Books, 1962).

Davis, H.L. and James Stevens *Status Rerum: A Manifesto, Upon the Present Condition of Northwest Literature Containing Several Near-Libelous Utterances, Upon Persons in the Public Eye* (The Dalles, OR: privately printed 1927).

Dawson, Jan C. "Landmarks of Home in the Pacific Northwest" *ISLE* 2:2 (Winter 1996): 1-23.

Day, David *The Cowichan* (Madeira Park BC: Harbour Publishing 1975).

Dean, Misao "The Construction of Masculinity in Martin Allerdale Grainger's *Woodsmen of the West*" *Canadian Literature* 149 (Summer 1996): 74-87.

de Barros, Paul "In a Draw" *Roothog: Contemporary BC Writing* John Harris ed. (Prince George BC: Repository P 1981): 7-11.

Deer, Glenn ed. "Asian Canadian Writing" Special Issue *Canadian Literature* 163 (Winter 1999).

Deleuze, Gilles and Felix Guattari *On the Line* (New York: Semiotext(e) 1983).

Deringer, Ludwig *Das Bild des Pazifischen Nordwestens von den Anfängen bis zur Gegenwart* (Tübingen: Stauffenburg Verlag 1996).

Deringer, Ludwig "The Pacific Northwest in American and Canadian Literature Since 1776: The Present State of Scholarship" *Oregon Historical Quarterly* 90:3 (Fall 1989): 305-27.

Deringer, Ludwig "'Unfinished Business': National Identity and the American West." Roland Hagenbüchle and Josef Raab eds. *Negotiations of America's National Identity* Vol. 1 (Tübingen: Stauffenburg Verlag 2000): 504-25.

Deutsch, Herman J. "The Evolution of the International Boundary in the Inland Empire of the Pacific Northwest" *Pacific Northwest Quarterly* 51:2 (April 1960): 63-79.

Dickinson, Peter "'Orality in Literacy': Listening to Indigenous Writing" *The Canadian Journal of Native Studies* 14:2 (1994): 319-340.

Dillard, Annie *The Living* (New York: Harper Collins 1992).

Dodds, Gordon B. ed. *Varieties of Hope: An Anthology of Oregon Prose* Oregon Literature Series Vol. 3 (Corvallis: Oregon State UP 1993).

Doig, Ivan, *Winter Brothers: A Season at the Edge of America* (New York: Harcourt Brace Jovanovich 1980).

Dorson, Richard M. *American Folklore and the Historian* (Chicago: U Chicago P 1971).

Dowd, Maureen, "Everyone's Too Jumped up on Caffeine to be Laid-Back in Seattle" *Vancouver Sun* 10 August 1996: A19.

Doyle, James *North of America: Images of Canada in the Literature of the United States 1775-1900* (Downsview: ECW Press 1983).

Doyle, James "The Post-Ultimate Frontier: American Authors in the Canadian West, 1885-1900" *Essays on Canadian Writing* 22 (Summer 1981): 14-26.

Drengson, Alan Rike and Duncan MacDonald Taylor eds. *Ecoforestry: The Art and Science of Sustainable Forest Use* (Gabriola Island, BC: New Society Publishers 1997).

Duff, Wilson *Bird of Paradox: The Unpublished Writings of Wilson Duff* E.N. Anderson ed. (Surrey BC/Blaine WA: Hancock House 1996).

Duncan, David James *The Brothers K* (1992; rpt. New York: Bantam Books 1993).

Duncan, David James *River Teeth: Stories and Writings* (1995; rpt. New York: Bantam Books 1996).

➤ Duncan, David James *The River Why* (1983; rpt. Toronto/New York: Bantam Books 1984).

Durning, Alan Thein *Guardians of the Land: Indigenous People and the Health of the Earth* (n.p.: World Watch Institute 1992).

Durning, Alan Thein *This Place on Earth: Home and the Practice of Permanence* (Seattle: Sasquatch 1996).

Eadie, Tom *Dead Letters* (Stratford ON: Trout Lily P 1996).

Eadie, Tom "Salmon Spawn" *Quarry* 40: 1/2 (Winter/Spring 1991): 56.

Egan, Timothy *The Good Rain: Across Time and Terrain in the Pacific Northwest* (New York: Alfred A. Knopf 1990).

Egan, Susanna and Gabriele Helms "The Many Tongues of *Mothertalk*: Life Stories of Mary Kiyoshi Kiyooka" *Canadian Literature* 163 (Winter 1999): 47-77.

Emerson, Earl W. *The Rainy City* (New York: Avon 1985).

Evans, Hubert *Mist on the River* New Canadian Library Edition (1954; rpt. Toronto: McClelland & Stewart 1973).

Fairbanks, Carol and Sara Books *Farm Women on the Prairie Frontier: A Sourcebook for Canada and the United States* (Meuchen NJ: Scarecrow P 1983).

Fairbanks, Carol *Prairie Women: Images in American and Canadian Fiction* (New Haven: Yale UP 1986).

Faludy, George *Notes from the Rainforest* (Willowdale ON: Hounslow P 1988).

Fellman, Michael "Sam I Am: Enough Yankee Bashing. It's Time We All Got in Touch with Our Inner American" *Saturday Night* October 1996: 43-46.

Ferone, Joseph *BoomBoom* (Vancouver: Bitterroot P 1998).

Ferraro, Thomas *Ethnic Passages: Literary Immigrants in Twentieth-Century America* (Chicago/London: U Chicago P 1993).

Fetherling, Douglas *The Gold Crusades: A Social History of the Gold Rushes 1849-1929* (Toronto: Macmillan 1988).

Filippucci, Paola "Landscape, locality and nation: The case of Bassano" *Paragraph: A Journal of Modern Critical Theory* 20:1 (March 1997): 42-58.

Fish, Stanley *The Living Temple: George Herbert and Catechizing* (Berkeley: U California P 1978).

Fisher, Robin "Matter for Reflection: *BC Studies* and British Columbia History" *BC Studies* (Winter 1993-94): 59-77.

Flam, Jack ed. *Robert Smithson: The Collected Writings* (Berkeley: U California P 1996).

Fleming, Anne-Marie "Nurturing Ambiguity" Unpublished essay on "Free Translations" (University of British Columbia 1983).

Fogel, Stanley *A Tale of Two Countries: Contemporary Fiction in English Canada and the United States* (Toronto: ECW Press, 1984).

Fraser, Marian Botsford *Walking the Line: Travels Along the Canadian/American Border* (Vancouver: Douglas & McIntyre, 1989).

Fraser River: Sand Heads to Douglas Island, Marine Chart no. 3490 (Ottawa: Canadian Hydrographic Service 1987).

Furst, Peter T. "The Roots and Continuities of Shamanism" *artscanada* nos. 184-187 (December 1973/January 1974): 33-59.

Fussell, Paul *Wartime: Understanding and Behavior in the Second World War* (New York: Oxford UP 1989).

Garreau, Joel *The Nine Nations of North America* (Boston: Houghton Mifflin 1981).

Gastil, Raymond D. "The Pacific Northwest as a Cultural Region" *Pacific Northwest Quarterly* 64:1 (October 1973): 147-162.

Gayton, Don *Landscapes of the Interior: Re-Explorations of Nature and the Human Spirit* (Gabriola Island BC: New Society Publishers 1996).

Geddes, Gary *rivers inlet* (Vancouver: Talonbooks 1971).

Geddes, Gary ed. *Skookum Wawa: Writings of the Canadian Northwest* (Toronto: Oxford UP 1975).

Geertz, Clifford *Local Knowledge* (New York: Basic Books 1983).

Geertz, Clifford *The Interpretation of Cultures: Selected Essays* (New York: Basic Books 1973).

Gerson, Carole "Martin Allerdale Grainger" *Dictionary of Literary Biography* 92 (Detroit: Gale Research 1990): 124-126.

Gibbons, Roger *Canada as a Borderlands Society* (Orono ME: Borderlands Project 1989).

Glavin, Terry "We've had enough of Cascadia" *The Globe and Mail* 14 August 1998: A21.

Gottlieb, Erika "The Riddle of Concentric Worlds in *Obasan*" *Canadian Literature* 109 (Summer 1986): 34-53.

Grace, Sherrill "Wastelands and Badlands: The Legacies of Pynchon and Kroetsch" *Mosaic* 14:2 (Spring 1981): 20-34.

Grainger, M. Allerdale *Woodsmen of the West* (1908; rpt. Toronto: McClelland & Stewart 1964).

Granatstein, J.L. *Yankee go Home?: Canadians and Anti-Americanism* (Toronto: Harper Collins, 1996).

Greenblatt, Stephen "The Touch of the Real" *Representation* 59 (Summer 1997): 14-29.

Greenfield, Bruce "The Rhetoric of British and American Narratives of Exploration" *Dalhousie Review* 65 (Spring 1985): 56-65.

Greenwood, Phyllis *An Interrupted Panorama: An Installation Revealing Selected Views of the Fraser River* MFA Graduate Exhibition, Belkin Gallery, UBC, November 1997 (Vancouver: Phyllis Greenwood 1997).

Griffin, Susan *Women and Nature: The Roaring Inside Her* (New York: Harper 1978).

Griffith, Thomas "The Pacific Northwest" *The Atlantic Monthly* 237:4 (April 1976): 46-93.

Groot, C. and L. Margolis eds. *Pacific Salmon Life Histories* (Vancouver: U British Columbia P 1991).

Grubb, David McC. *A Practical Writing System and Short Dictionary of Kwakw'ala (Kwakiutl)* (Ottawa: National Museums of Canada 1977).

Guterson, David *Snow Falling on Cedars* (1994; rpt. New York: Vintage Books, 1995).

Haas, Mary R. "Boas, Sapir and Bloomfield" *American Indian Languages and American Linguistics* Wallace L. Chafe ed. (Liss, Belgium: Peter de Ridder 1976): 61.

Haig-Brown, Roderick L. *Return to the River: A Story of the Chinook Run* (1942: rpt. Toronto: Collins 1965).

Hall, Rodney *A Dream More Luminous than Love: The Yandilli Trilogy* (Sydney: Pan Macmillan 1994).

Halpin, Marjorie *Jack Shadbolt and the Coastal Indian Image* (Vancouver: U British Columbia P/UBC Museum of Anthropology 1986).

Halpin, Marjorie and Michael M. Ames eds. *Manlike Monsters on Trial: Early Records and Modern Evidence* (Vancouver: U British Columbia P 1980)

Hamill, Sam *A Poet's Work: The Other Side of Poetry* (Seattle: Broken Moon P 1990).

Hamill, Sam *Passport* (Seattle: Broken Moon P 1989).

Hancock, Geoff "Jack Hodgins" *Canadian Writers at Work: Interviews with Geoff Hancock* (Toronto: Oxford UP 1987): 51-78.

Handler, Richard "On Dialogue and Destructive Analysis: Problems in Narrating Nationalism and Ethnicity" *Journal of Anthropological Research* 41:2 (Summer 1985): 171-182.

Harbo, Rick M. *Guide to the Western Seashore: Introductory Marinelife Guide to the Pacific Coast* (Surrey BC/Blaine WA: Hancock House 1988).

Harris, Barbara and Joseph F. Kess "Salmon Fishing Terms in British Columbia" *Names* 23:2 (June 1975): 61-66.

Harris, Cole "Moving Amid the Mountains, 1870-1930" *BC Studies* 58 (Summer 1983): 3-39.

Harrison, Dick *Unnamed Country: The Struggle for a Canadian Prairie Fiction* (Edmonton: U Alberta P 1977).

Harrison, Dick ed. *Crossing Frontiers: Papers in American and Canadian Western Literature* (Edmonton: U Alberta P 1979).

Harrison, Robert Pogue *Forests: The Shadow of Civilization* (Chicago: U Chicago P 1992).

Heaney, Seamus *The Place of Writing* (Atlanta: Scholars P 1989).

Heckman, Hazel *Island in the Sound* (Seattle: U Washington P 1967).

Henry, Tom *Westcoasters: Boats that Built BC* (Madeira Park BC: Harbour Publishing 1998).

Hesford, Walter "Thousand Pieces of Gold: Competing Fictions in the Representation of Chinese-American Experience" *Western American Literature* 3:1 (Spring 1996): 49-62.

Hodge, Bob "Aboriginal Myths and Australian Culture" *Southern Review* 19 (Adelaide: November 1986): 277-90.

Hodgins, Jack "Down the red dirt road . . ." *The Weekend Australian* 9-10 (June 1990): 3-4.

Hodgins, Jack "'Interview' with Gordon Morash" *Pacific Northwest Review of Books* 1:4 (July/August 1978): 16-18.

Hodgins, Jack *The Invention of the World* (1977; rpt. Toronto: Signet 1978).

Hodgins, Jack *The Macken Charm* (Toronto: McClelland & Stewart 1995).

Hodgins, Jack *Innocent Cities* (Toronto: McClelland & Stewart 1990).

Hodgins, Jack *The Resurrection of Joseph Bourne* (Toronto: Macmillan 1979).

Hodgins, Jack ed. *The West Coast Experience* (Toronto: Macmillan 1976).

Holbrook, Stewart, Nard Jones & Roderick Haig-Brown *The Pacific Northwest* Anthony Netboy ed. (Garden City NY: Doubleday 1963).

Holbrook, Stewart H. *The Far Corner: A Personal View of the Pacific Northwest* (1952; rpt. Sausalito: Comstock Editions 1986).

Hosokawa, Bill *Nisei: The Quiet Americans* (New York: William Morrow 1969).

House, L. Freeman "Totem Salmon" in Van Andruss, Christopher Plant, Judith Plant and Eleanor Wright eds. *Home! A Bioregional Reader* (Philadelphia: New Society 1990).

House, L. Freeman *Totem Salmon: Life Lessons from Another Species* (Boston: Beacon P 1999).

Howarth, Jean *Treasure Island* (Toronto: Dorset, 1979).

Howay, F.W., W.N. Sage, and H.F. Angus *British Columbia and the United States: The North Pacific Slope from Fur Trade to Aviation* ed. H.F. Angus (Toronto: Ryerson 1942; New Haven: Yale UP 1942).

Hugo, Richard *Making Certain It Goes On: The Collected Poems of Richard Hugo* (New York: W.W. Norton 1984).

Hume, Stephen "'Compelling' discovery rewrites BC History" *Vancouver Sun* 5 August 2000 A1-A2.

Hunter, Robert *Warriors of the Rainbow: A Chronicle of the Greenpeace Movement* (New York: Holt Rinehart & Winston 1979).

Hutchison, Bruce *The Struggle for the Border* (Toronto: Longmans Green, 1955).

Hymes, Dell "Discovering Oral Performance and Measured Verse in American Indian Narrative" *New Literary History: A Journal of Theory and Interpretation* 8:3 (Spring 1977) (Baltimore: Johns Hopkins UP): 431-457.

Hymes, Dell "Some North Pacific Coast Poems: A Problem in Anthropological Philology" *"In Vain I Tried to Tell You": Essays in Native American Ethnopoetics* (Philadelphia: U Pennsylvania P 1981): 35-64.

Iglauer, Edith *Fishing with John* (Madeira Park BC: Harbour Publishing 1988).

Iko, Mimoko "The Gold Watch [Act I]" in Chin, Frank *et al* eds. *Aiiieeeee! An Anthology of Asian-American Writers* (Washington D.C.: Howard UP 1974): 88-114.

Inada, Lawson Fusao"Of Place and Displacement: The Range of Japanese-American Literature" *Three American Literatures: Essays in Chicano, Native American and Asian-American Literature for Teachers of American Literature* (New York: Modern Language Association of America 1982): 254-265.

Isenor, D.E., E.G. Stephens and D.E. Watson *Edge of Discovery: A History of the Campbell River District* (Campbell River BC: Ptarmigan P 1989).

Ives, Rich ed. *From Timberline to Tidepool: Contemporary Fiction from the Northwest* (Seattle: Owl Creek P 1986).

Iwama, Marilyn "If You Say So: Articulating Cultural Symbols of Tradition in the Japanese Canadian Community" *Canadian Literature* 140 (Spring 1994): 13-29.

Iwama, Marilyn "When Nissei Women Write: Transforming Japanese Canadian Identities 1887-1987" (PhD Thesis Vancouver: University of BC 1998).

Jance, J.A. *Trial by Fury* (New York: Avon 1986).

Jay, Tom "The Salmon of the Heart" in Finn Wilcox and Jeremiah Gorsline eds. *Working the Woods, Working the Sea* (Port Townsend WA: Empty Bowl 1986): 100-124.

Jencks, Charles A. *The Language of Post-Modern Architecture* (1977; rev. ed. New York: Rizzoli 1984).

Johnson, Emily Pauline (Tekahionwake) *Legends of Vancouver* (1913; rpt. Toronto: McClelland & Stewart 1931).

Jones, R.P. "Duwamish: Remembering Richard Hugo" *Left Bank* 1 (Winter 1991): 46-47.

Jones, Stephen B. "The Cordilleran Section of the Canada-United States Borderland" *The Geographical Journal* 89:5 (May 1937): 439-50.

Jones, Suzie and Jarold Ramsey eds. *The Stories We tell: An Anthology of Oregon Folk Literature* Oregon Literature Series, Vol. 5 (Corvallis: Oregon State UP 1994).

Kain, Geoffrey ed. *Ideas of Home: Literature of Asian Migration* (East Lansing: Michigan State UP 1997).

Kamboureli, Smaro "Fred Wah: A Poetry of Dialogue" *Line* 4 (Fall 1984): 44-62.

Kane, Sean *Wisdom of the Mythtellers* (Peterborough ON: Broadview P 1994).

Kaplan, Robert D. *An Empire Wilderness: Travels into America's Future* (New York: Random House 1998).

Kass, Ray *Morris Graves: Vision of the Inner Eye* (New York: George Braziller 1983).

Kaye, Frances W. "The 49th Parallel and the 98th Meridian: Some Lines for Thought" *Mosaic* 14:2 (Spring 1981): 165-75.

Kearns, Lionel *Convergences* (Toronto: Coach House P 1984).

Keeble, John *Broken Ground* (1987; rpt. New York: Harper Row 1989).

Keeble, John *Yellowfish* (1980; rpt. New York: Harper Row 1987).

Kesey, Ken Ken Elton Kesey Collection. Collection Number Ax279. Special Collections. University of Oregon Library. Eugene Oregon.

Kesey, Ken The Ken Kesey Papers. Special Collections Library, University of Oregon, Eugene, Oregon.

Kesey, Ken *Sometimes a Great Notion* (1964; rpt. London: Penguin Books 1988).

Kim, Elaine H. *Asian American Literature: An Introduction to the Writings and Their Social Context* (Philadelphia: Temple UP 1982).

Kingsbury, Martha *Northwest Traditions* (Seattle: Seattle Art Museum 1978).

Kirk, Ruth *The Olympic Rain Forest: An Ecological Web* with Jerry Franklin (Seattle: U Washington P 1992).

Kitano, Harry H.L. *Japanese-Americans: The Evolution of a Sub-Culture* (Eaglewood Cliffs, NJ: Prentice-Hall 1969).

Kittredge, William *Owning It All: Essays* (Saint Paul: Graywolf Publishers, 1987).

Kiyooka, Roy *Mothertalk: Life Stories of Mary Kiyoshi Kiyooka* ed. Daphne Marlatt (Edmonton: NeWest P 1997).

Kizer, Carolyn *Mermaids in the Basement* (Port Townsend: Copper Canyon P 1984).

Kodansha Encyclopedia of Japan Vol 4 (Tokyo: Kodansha 1983).

Kogawa, Joy *Obasan* (1981; rpt.Toronto: Penguin 1983).

Kohler, Vince *Rainy North Woods* (New York: Pocket Books 1990).

Kolodny, Annette *The Lay of the Land: Metaphor as Experience and History in American Life and Letters* (Chapel Hill: U of North Carolina P 1975).

Kooser, Ted *Weather Central* (Pittsburgh: U Pittsburgh P 1994).

Koppel, Tom *Kanaka: The Untold Story of Hawaiian Pioneers in British Columbia and the Pacific Northwest* (Vancouver/Toronto: Whitecap Books 1995).

Krech, Shepard *The Ecological Indian: Myth and History* (New York: Norton 1999).

Kroeber, Karl "Poem, Dream and the Consuming of Culture" in Brian Swann ed. *Smoothing the Ground: Essays on Native American Oral Literature* (Berkeley: U of California P 1983): 323-333.

Kroetsch, Robert "The Canadian Writer and the American Literary Tradition" *English Quarterly* 4 (Summer 1971): 45-49.

Kroetsch, Robert "The Grammar of Silence: Narrative Pattern in Ethnic Writing" *Canadian Literature* 106 (Fall 1985): 65-74.

Kroetsch, Robert *Seed Catalogue* (Winnipeg: Turnstone P 1977).

Kröller, Eva-Marie "Regionalism and the Pacific Rim: The Example of Vancouver" Lothar Hönnighausen ed. *Regional Images and Regional Realities* (Tübingen: Stauffenburg 1999): 271-282.

Kruckeberg, Arthur R. *Gardening with Native Plants of the Pacific Northwest* (Seattle: U Washington P 1982).

Kruckeberg, Arthur R. *The Natural History of Puget Sound Country* (Seattle: U Washington P 1991).

Krupat, Arnold "Post-Structuralism and Oral Literature" *Receiving the Word: Essays on Native American Literature* Brian Swann and Arnold Krupat eds. (Berkeley: U California P 1987): 113-128.

Lane, M. Travis "'Emotion First! Understanding Later!': The Poetry of Kevin Roberts" *Essays on Canadian Writing* 32 (Summer 1986): 27-40.

Lane, Patrick *Poems New and Selected* (Toronto: Oxford UP 1978).

Lane, Richard "Archive Simulations: Reading the Bertrand Sinclair Collection" *BC Studies* 97 (1993): 51-71.

Lane, Richard *Literature & Loss: Betrand William Sinclair's British Columbia* Open Archive Vol. 1 (London: London Network for Modern Fiction Studies 2000).

Le Guin, Ursula K. *Always Coming Home* (1985; rpt. Toronto: Bantam 1987).

Learned Societies "Learned Societies Conference" Brochure (Victoria: The University of Victoria 1990).

Lee, SKY *Disappearing Moon Cafe* (Vancouver: Douglas & McIntyre 1990).

Lee, SKY "Women In Touch Coming Home" *Telling It: Women and Language Across Cultures* (Vancouver: Press Gang 1990): 105-109.

Lee, SKY "Yelling It: Women and Anger Across Cultures" *Telling It: Women and Language Across Cultures* (Vancouver: Press Gang 1990): 177-189.

Leeson, Ted *The Habit of Rivers: Reflections on Trout Streams and Fly Fishing* (New York: Penguin 1994).

Lenček, Lena and Gideon Bosker *The Beach: The History of Paradise on Earth* (New York: Viking 1998).

Lerner, Andrea ed. *Dancing on the Rim of the World: An Anthology of Contemporary Northwest Native American Writing* (Tucson: Suntracks/U Arizona P 1990).

Lesley, Craig *River Song* (1989; rpt. New York: Dell 1990).

Levertov, Denise *Evening Train* (New York: New Directions Books, 1992).

Lillard, Charles with Terry Glavin *A Voice Great Within Us: The Story of Chinook* (Vancouver: Transmontanus/New Star Books 1998).

Lim, Shirley Geok-lin, Mayumi Tsutakawa and Margarita Donnelly eds. *The Forbidden Stitch* (Corvallis, OR: Calyx Books 1989).

Lim, Sing *West Coast Chinese Boy* (Montreal: Tundra Books 1979).

Ling, Jinqi "Race, Power and Cultural Politics in John Okada's *No-No Boy*"*American Literature* 67:2 (1995): 359-82.

Lippard, Lucy R. *The Lure of the Local: Senses of Place in a Multicentered Society* (New York: The New Press 1997).

Lipset, Seymour Martin *Continental Divide: The Values and Institutions of the United States and Canada* (New York: Routledge, 1990).

Lipset, Seymour Martin *North American Cultures: Values and Institutions in Canada and the United States* (Orono ME: Borderlands Project 1990).

Lipton, James *An Exaltation of Larks: The Ultimate Edition* (New York: Viking, 1991).

Lopez, Barry Holstun *Desert Notes: Reflections in the Eye of a Raven/River Notes: The Dance of Herons* (1976, 1979; rpt. New York: Avon Books, 1998).

Lopez, Barry Holstun *Field Notes* (New York: Alfred A. Knopf 1994).

Love, Glen A. and Edwin R. Bingham eds. *Northwest Perspectives* (Eugene: U Oregon P/Seattle: U Washington P 1979).

Love, Glen A. "Reading Pacific Northwest Rivers" François Piquet ed. *Le fleuve et ses metamorphoses* (Paris: Didier Erudition 1993): 479-483.

Love, Glen A. "Roderick Haig Brown: Angling and the Craft of Nature Writing in North America" *ISLE* 5:1 (Winter 1998): 1-11.

Love, Glen A. "Stemming the Avalanche of Tripe: Or, How H.L. Mencken and Friends Reformed Northwest Literature" *Thalia* 4:1 (Spring/Summer 1981): 46-53.

Love, Glen A. ed. *The World Begins Here: An Anthology of Oregon Short Fiction* Oregon Literature Series Vol 1 (Corvallis: Oregon State UP 1993).

Lowry, Malcolm *Hear Us O Lord from Heaven thy Dwelling Place* (1961; rpt. Vancouver: Douglas & McIntyre 1987).

Lowry, Malcolm *October Ferry to Gabriola* (New York: World Publishing Co. 1970).

Lutwack, Leonard *Birds in Literature* (Gainesville: UP of Florida 1994).

M'Gonigle, Michael and Fred Gale "Community Forestry: An Innovative Solution to Ongoing Struggles" *BC Studies Conference* (Nanaimo, British Columbia 3 May 1997).

MacLean, Kenneth *Blue Heron's Sky* (Mansfield, TX: Latitudes P 1990).

Maclean, Norman *A River Runs Through It* (Chicago: U Chicago P 1976).

Macnair, Peter and Jay Stewart *To the Totem Forests: Emily Carr and Contemporaries Interpret Coastal Villages* (Victoria: Art Gallery of Greater Victoria 1999).

Malamud, Bernard *A New Life* (1961; rpt. New York: Pocket Books 1973).

Maracle, Lee "Ramparts Hanging in the Air" *Telling It: Women and Language Across Cultures* (Vancouver: Press Gang 1990): 161-172.

Maracle, Lee *Ravensong* (Vancouver: Press Gang 1993).

Maracle, Lee *Sojourner's Truth & Other Stories* (Vancouver: Press Gang 1990).

Marlatt, Daphne *Ana Historic: A Novel* (Toronto: House of Anansi P 1997).

Marlatt, Daphne *Steveston* (1974; rpt. Vancouver: Ronsdale P 2001).

Marlatt, Daphne *Salvage* (Red Deer: Red Deer College P 1991).

Marlatt, Daphne ed. *Steveston Recollected: Japanese Canadian History* (Victoria: Provincial Archives of British Columbia 1975).

Martineau, Joel. "Fishing for Texts on the BC Coast" Unpublished paper. English 547A. U British Columbia 1995.

Masuda, Koh ed. *Kenkyusha's New Japanese-English Dictionary* (Tokyo: Kenkyusha 1974).

Mathur, Ashok "An Interview with Fred Wah on *Diamond Grill*" *Rice Paper* 3:2 (Spring 1997) 18-19.

Mathur, Ashok "Orate Or" *Open Letter* Ser. 8 Nos. 5-6 (Winter-Spring 1993): 142-45.

Maud, Ralph *A Guide to BC Indian Myth and Legend: A Short History of Myth-Collecting and a Survey of Published Texts* (Vancouver: Talonbooks 1982).

McConnaughey, Bayard H. and Evelyn McConnaughey *Pacific Coast* Audubon Society Nature Guide (New York: Alfred A. Knopf 1985).

McCulloch, Walter F. *Woods Words: A Comprehensive Dictionary of Loggers Terms* (n.p.: Oregon Historical Society & Champoeg P 1958).

McDonald, Dorothy Ritsuko "After Imprisonment: Ichiro's Search for Redemption in *No-No Boy*" *Melus* 6:3 (1979): 19-26.

McElroy, Colleen J. *Travelling Music* (Ashland OR: Story Line P 1998).

McElroy, Colleen J. *What Madness Brought Me Here: New and Selected Poems 1968-1988* (Hanover/London: Wesleyan UP 1990).

McGoogan, Ken "It is the Dawning of the Age of Cascadia" *BC Book World* (August 1993).

McKay, Don "Baler Twine: Thoughts on Ravens, Home, and Nature Poetry" *Studies in Canadian Literature* 18:1 (1993): 128-138.

McKelvey, Susan Delano *Botanical Exploration of the Trans-Mississippi West* (1956; rpt. Corvallis: Oregon State UP 1991).

McKenzie, Hilda "Remapping a Subject and Counter-Subject" Unpublished M.A. Graduating Essay. University of British Columbia. English Department. September 1998.

McKervill, Hugh W. *The Salmon People: the Story of Canada's West Coast Salmon Fishing Industry* (Sidney BC: Gray's Publ. Int'l 1967).

McKinsey, Lauren and Victor Konrad *Borderlands Reflections: The United States and Canada* (Orono ME: Borderlands Project 1989).

McMath, George "A Regional Style Comes to the City" Thomas Vaughan ed. *Space, Style and Structure: Building in Northwest America* vol. 2 (Portland OR: Oregon Historical Society 1974): 467-499.

McMillan, Alan D. *Native Peoples and Cultures of Canada: An Anthropological Overview* (Vancouver: Douglas and McIntyre 1988).

McNeil, Florence *A Company of Angels* (Victoria: Ekstasis Editons 1999).

Meilleur, Helen *A Pour of Rain: Stories from a Westcoast Fort* (Victoria: Sono Nis P 1980).

Merivale, Patricia "Framed Voices: The Polyphonic Elegies of Hébert and Kogawa" *Canadian Literature* 116 (Spring 1988): 68-82.

Metcalfe, William "'Modified Rapture': Recent Research on Canada in the United States" *International Journal of Canadian Studies* 1-2 (Spring/Fall 1990): 203-16.

Miki, Roy *Broken Entries: Race, Subjectivity, Writing* (Toronto: Mercury P 1998).

Miller, Jay and Vi Hilbert "Lushootseed Animal People: Mediation and Transformation from Myth to History" in James A. Arnold: 136-56.

Miller, J. Hillis "The Critic as Host" *Modern Criticism and Theory: A Reader* David Lodge ed. (London: Longman 1988): 278-285.

Molotsly, Irvin "Senate Votes to Compensate Japanese-American Internees" *The New York Times* 21 April 1988 A1.

Morash, Gordon "Jack Hodgins: An Interview" *Pacific Northwest Review of Books* 1:4 (July-August 1978): 16-18.

Morgan, Murray *Skid Road: An Informal Portrait of Seattle* (1951; rev.ed. New York: Ballantine Books 1971).

Morris, Holly ed. *A Different Angle: Fly Fishing Stories by Women* (Seattle: Seal P 1995).

Morris, Holly ed. *Uncommon Waters: Women Write about Fishing* (Seattle: Seal P 1991).

Morton, James *In the Sea of Sterile Mountains: The Chinese in British Columbia* (Vancouver: J.J. Douglas 1974).

Murphy, Alexandra *Graced By Pines: The Ponderosa Pine in the American West* (Missoula: Mountain P 1994).

Murray, Heather "Metaphor and Metonym, Language and Land in Ethel Wilson's *Swamp Angel*" *World Literature Written in English* 25:1 (1985): 241-252.

Murray, Thomas E. "The Language of Naval Fighter Pilots" *American Speech* 61:2 (Summer 1986): 121-129.

Musgrave, Susan *Kiskatinaw Songs* (Victoria BC: Paros P 1977).

New. W.H. "A Piece of the Continent, A Part of the Main: Some Comments on BC Literature" *BC Studies* (Autumn 1985): 3-28.

New, W.H. *Borderlands: How We Talk About Canada* (Vancouver: U British Columbia P 1998).

New, W.H. "Beyond Nationalism: On Regionalism" *World Literature Written in English* 23:1 (1984): 12-18.

New, W.H. *Land Sliding: Imagining Space, Presence, and Power in Canadian Writing* (Toronto: U Toronto P 1997).

Newell, Dianne ed. *The Development of the Pacific Salmon-Canning Industry* (Montreal and Kingston: McGill-Queen's UP 1989).

Newberry, Frederick "Dialogue with John Keeble" *Northwest Review* 20:2/3 (1982): 7-25.

Ochsner, Jeffrey Karl "In Search of Regional Expression: The Washington State Building at the World's Columbian Exposition, Chicago, 1893" *Pacific Northwest Quarterly* 86:4 (Fall 1995): 165-77.

O'Connell, Nicholas *At the Field's End: Interviews with Twenty Pacific Northwest Writers* (Seattle: Madrona 1987).

O'Connor, Mark "The Poetry of the North: Finding the Words" *Westerly* 31:1 (March 1986): 18-27.

Okada, John *No-No Boy* (1957; rpt. Seattle: U Washington P 1979).

Oke, T.R. and Graeme Wynn eds. *Vancouver and its Region* (Vancouver: U British Columbia P 1992).

Okimoto, Daniel I. *American in Disguise* (New York: Walker/Weatherkill 1971).

Olsson, Gunnar "Lines of Power" Trevor J. Barnes and James S. Duncan eds. *Writing Worlds: Discourse, Text and Metaphor in the Representation of Landscape* (London/New York: Routledge 1992): 86-96.

O'Neil, Peter " "Japanese-Canadians Get Apologies from Mulroney" *Vancouver Sun* 22 September 1988 A1, A2.

Ong, Walter J. *Orality and Literacy: The Technologizing of the Word* (London: Methuen 1982).

Ortiz, Simon J. ed. *Speaking for the Generations: Native Writers on Writing* (Tucson: U Arizona P 1998.

Owen, John "Earmark Stanley Park Schnitzel for your next dinner" *Seattle Post-Intelligencer* 19 January 2000: D3.

Partridge, Eric *Origins: A Short Etymological Dictionary of Modern English* 2nd ed. (New York: Macmillan 1959).

Pearson, Glenda J. "Regional Literature and 'This House of Sky'" *PNLA Quarterly* 43:3 (Spring 1979): 4-8.

Penn, Briony *A Year on the Wild Side* (Victoria BC.: Horsdal & Schubart 1999).

Peter, Susie Sampson "Star Child" in Miller and Hilbert: 141-155.

Peterson, Brenda *Living by Water: Essays on Life, Land and Spirit* (Anchorage/Seattle: Alaska Northwest Books 1990).

Phillips-Wolley, Clive "Autumn Salmon Run" *Transactions of The Royal Society of Canada* ser.3 vol.8 (September 1914) 179.

Pojar, Jim and Andy MacKinnon eds. *Plants of Coastal British Columbia, including Washington, Oregon and Alaska* (Edmonton: Lone Pine Publishing 1994).

Pollock, Sharon *The Komagata Maru Incident* (Toronto: Playwrights Canada 1978).

Potrebenko, Helen *Taxi!* (1975: rpt. Vancouver: New Star Books 1989).

Powell, Jay and Gloria Cranmer Webster "Geography, Ethnogeography, and the Perspective of the Kwakwaka'wakw" in Robert Galois *Kwakwaka'wakw Settlements, 1775-1920: A Geographical Analysis and Gazetteer* (Vancouver: U British Columbia P 1994): 4-11.

Preece, Rod *Animals and Nature: Cultural Myths, Cultural Realities* (Vancouver: U British Columbia P 1999).

Pritchard, Allan "West of the Great Divide: A View of the Literature of British Columbia" *Canadian Literature* 94 (Autumn 1982): 96-112.

Pritchard, Allan "West of the Great Divide: Man and Nature in the Literature of British Columbia" *Canadian Literature* 102 (Autumn 1987): 36-53.

Pritchard, Allan "The Shapes of History in British Columbia Writing" *BC Studies* 93 (Spring 1992): 48-69.

Pyle, Robert *Where Bigfoot Walks: Crossing the Dark Divide* (Boston: Houghton Mifflin 1995).

Pynn, Larry "Crooked Border" [two-part series] *Vancouver Sun*, 14 March 1998: A15, 16 March 1998: A8.

Quigley, Eileen V. "Cascadia" *The New Pacific: A Journal of the Pacific Northwest and Western Canada* 4 (Fall 1990): 3-6.

Raban, Jonathan "The Next Last Frontier" *Harpers* 287: 1719 (August 1993): 30-48.

Radner, Joan N. and Susan S. Lanser "The Feminist Voice: Strategies of Coding in Folklore and Literature" *Journal of American Folklore* 100 (1987): 412-425.

Ramsey, Jarold *Love in an Earthquake* (Seattle: U Washington P 1973).

Ramsey, Jarold "'The Hunter Who Had an Elk for a Guardian Spirit,' and the Ecological Imagination" in Brian Swann ed. *Smoothing the Ground: Essays on Native American Oral Literature* (Berkeley: U California P 1983): 309-22.

Ramsey, Jarold "The Wife Who Goes Out Like a Man, Comes Back as a Hero: The Art of Two Oregon Indian Narratives" *PMLA* 92 (1977): 9-18.

The Rand McNally Atlas of the Oceans (New York: Rand McNally 1977).

Rayner, Anne "Everything Becomes Island: Gulf Island Writing and the Construction of Region" PhD thesis. University of British Columbia 1995.

Reid, Bill and Robert Bringhurst *The Raven Steals the Light* (Vancouver: Douglas & McIntyre 1984).

Relke, Diana M.A. "'time is, the delta': Steveston in Historical and Ecological Context" *Canadian Poetry* 38 (Spring-Summer 1996): 29-48.

Rexroth, Kenneth "The Influence of Classical Japanese Poetry on Modern American Poetry" in *World Outside the Window: the Selected Essays of Kenneth Rexroth* Bradford Morrow ed. (New York: New Directions, 1987): 267-74.

Rice, Tom *Marine Shells of the Pacific Coast* (Tacoma WA: Erco 1973).

Richmond, W. Edson "Folk Speech" Richard M. Dorson ed. *Folklore and Folklife: An Introduction* (Chicago: U Chicago P 1972): 145-157.

Ricou, Laurie *A Field Guide to "A Guide to Dungeness Spit"* (Lantzville: Oolichan Books 1997).

Ricou, Laurie "Articulating Ectopia," *To See Ourselves: Ecology and Culture in Canada,* Canadian Issues Vol. 13 (Montreal: Association for Canadian Studies 1991): 51-62.

Ricou, Laurie "Bertrand William Sinclair" *Dictionary of Literary Biography* 92 *Canadian Writers 1890-1920* ed. W.H. New (New York: Gale Research 1990): 362-365.

Ricou, Laurie "Children of a Common Mother: Of Boundary Markers and Open Gates," *Zeitschrift der Gesellschaft für Kanada-Studien: Kanada-USA/USA-Kanada* 19/20 (1991): 151-62.

Ricou, Laurie "Crossing Borders in Literature of the Pacific Northwest," *Borderlands: Essays in Canadian-American Relations* (Toronto: ECW P 1991): 286-308.

Ricou, Laurie "Dumb Talk: Echoes of the Indigenous Voice in the Literature of British Columbia" *BC Studies* 65 (Spring 1985): 34-47.

Ricou, Laurie "Field Notes and Notes in a Field: Forms of the West in Robert Kroetsch and Tom Robbins" *Journal of Canadian Studies* 17 (1982).

Ricou, Laurie "No Writing At All Here: Review Notes on Writing Native," *Canadian Literature,* 124-25 (Spring-Summer 1990): 294-301 rpt. in *Native Writers and Canadian Writing,* ed. W.H. New (Vancouver: U British Columbia P 1990): 294-301.

Ricou, Laurie "The Pacific Northwest as a Cross-Border Region," "David Wagoner," in the Western Literature Association, *Updating the Literary West* (Fort Worth: Texax Christian UP 1997):262-67, 289-94.

Ricou, Laurie "Two Nations Own These Islands: Border and Region in Pacific-Northwest Writing," *Context North America: Canadian/US Literary Relations,* Camille R. La Bossière ed. (Ottawa: U of Ottawa P 1994): 49-62.

Ricou, Laurie "The Writing of British Columbia Writing" *BC Studies* (Winter 1993-94): 106-120.

Rigal-Cellard, Bernadette "*No-No Boy* de John Okada (1957): Les Japonais Nisei Après La Deuxiéme Guerre Mondiale et les Affaires de l'Américainisation" *Seminaires* 1985 (Talence: Centre des Recherches sur l'Amérique Anglophone 1986): 89-104.

Robbins, Tom *Another Roadside Attraction* (1971; rpt. New York: Ballantine Books 1972).

Robbins, Tom *Still Life with Woodpecker* (1980; rpt. New York: Bantam Books 1981).

Robbins, Tom "The Chink and the Clock People" in Rich Ives ed. *From Timberline to Tidepool: Contemporary Fiction from the Northwest* (Seattle: Owl Creek P 1986): 320-335.

Robbins, William G. "The Social Context of Forestry: The Pacific Northwest in the Twentieth Century" *Western Historical Quarterly* 16:7 (October 1985): 413-427.

Roberts, Charles G.D. *The Last Barrier and Other Stories* (Toronto: McClelland & Stewart 1970): 83-100.

Robinson, Eden *Monkey Beach* (Toronto: Alfred A Knopf 2000).

Roche, Judith and Meg Hutchison eds. *First Fish First People: Salmon Tales of the North Pacific Rim* (One Reel: Seattle: U Washington P/Vancouver: U British Columbia P 1998).

Roethke, Theodore *The Collected Poems of Theodore Roethke* (Garden City: Anchor P/Doubleday 1975).

Ross, Catherine Sheldrick "Female Rites of Passage: *Klee Wyck*, *Surfacing* and *The Diviners*," *Atlantis* 4: 1 (Fall 1978): 87-94.

Rothenberg, Jeremy and Dennis Tedlock "The Shaman as Proto-poet: An Anthology of Shamanic Texts and Commentary" *artscanada* nos. 184-187 (December 1973/January 1974): 172-81.

Rueckert, William H. "Barry Lopez and the Search for a Dignified and Honorable Relationship with Nature" in John Cooley ed. *Earthly Words: Essays on Contemporary American Nature and Environmental Writers* (Ann Arbor: U Michigan P 1994): 137-164.

Rupp, Rebecca, Jill Mason and Judy Eliason *Red Oaks & Black Birches: The Science & Lore of Trees* (Pownal VT: Storey Communications 1990).

Ryan, John C. *State of the Northwest* (Seattle: Northwest Environment Watch 1994).

St. John, Primus and Ingrid Wendt eds. *From Here We Speak: An Anthology of Oregon Poetry* Oregon Literature Series Vol. 4 (Corvallis, OR: Oregon State UP 1993).

St. Pierre, Paul *Breaking Smith's Quarter Horse* (Vancouver: Douglas & McIntyre 1984).

Safina, Carl *Song for the Blue Ocean: Encounters Along the World's Coasts and Beneath the Seas* (New York: Henry Holt 1997).

Sander, Leonard M. "Fractal Growth" *Scientific American* (January 1987): 94-128.

Schieder, Rupert "Woodsman of the West: Martin Allerdale Grainger" *Forest History* 11 (October 1967): 6-13.

Schwantes, Carlos A. *The Pacific Northwest: An Interpretive History* (Lincoln: U Nebraska P 1989).

Scott, Andrew "Revering the Robust Arbutus" *The Georgia Straight* 10-17 December 1998 33.

Scott, Andrew *Secret Coastline: Journeys and Discoveries Along B.C.'s Shores* (Vancouver: Whitecap Books 2000).

Seiberling, Dorothy "Mystic Painters of the Northwest" *Life* 35:13 (28 September 1953): 84-89.

Seng, Goh Poh *The Girl from Ermita and Selected Poems 1961-1998* (Gibsons BC: Nightwood Editions 1998).

Shadbolt, Doris *The Art of Emily Carr* (Toronto: Clarke, Irwin; Vancouver: Douglas & McIntyre 1979).

Simonson, Harold P. "Pacific Northwest Literature—Its Coming of Age" *Pacific Northwest Quarterly* 71:4 (October 1980): 147-151.

Sinclair, Bertrand. The Bertrand Sinclair Papers. Special Collections, University of British Columbia Library, Vancouver, Canada.

Sinclair, Bertrand *Poor Man's Rock* (Boston: Little, Brown 1920).

Sinclair, Bertrand *The Inverted Pyramid* (Boston: Little, Brown 1924).

Singer, Barnet "Outsider versus Insider: Malamud's and Kesey's Pacific Northwest" *South Dakota Review* 13:4 (Winter 1975-76): 127-144.

Slethaug, Gordon E. "The Buried Stream: Stochastic Narration and 'A River Runs Through It'" *English Studies in Canada* 23:3 (September 1997): 315-329.

Smart, Ninian "Foreword" in Robert E. Carter *Becoming Bamboo: Western and Eastern Explorations of the Meaning of Life* (Montreal/Kingston: McGill-Queens UP): ix-xiii.

Smith, Barbara Herrnstein "Contingencies of Value" Robert von Hallbeg ed. *Canons* (Chicago: U Chicago P 1984).

Smith, Kathleen M., Nancy J. Anderson, Katherine J. Beamish eds. *Nature West Coast: A Study of Plants, Insects, Birds, Mammals and Marine Life as seen in Lighthouse Park* Vancouver Natural History Society (Victoria: Sono Nis P 1988).

Smith, R. J. F. *The Control of Fish Migration* (Berlin: Springer-Verlag 1985): 62-208.

Snyder, Gary "Interview" *At the Field's End: Interviews with Twenty Pacific Northwest Writers* Nicholas O'Connell ed. (Seattle: Madrona 1989): 307-322.

Sorfleet, John Robert "Transcendentalist, Mystic, Evolutionary Idealist: Bliss Carman, 1886-1894" GeorgeWoodcock ed. *Colony and Confederation: Early Canadian Poets and Their Background* (Vancouver: U British Columbia P 1974): 189-210.

Spacks, Patricia Meyer *Gossip* (New York: Knopf 1985).

Sparke, Matthew "Excavating the Future in Cascadia: Geo-economics and the Imagined Geographies of a Cross-Border Region" *BC Studies* 127 (Autumn 2000): 5-44.

"Spawning Salmon at Goldstream Park" (Victoria: Province of British Columbia, Ministry of Recreation and Conservation 1978).

Spector, Robert "Refashioning the Northwest Apparel Industry" *The New Pacific* (Summer 1990): 51-59.

Spier, Leslie and Edward Sapir *Wishram Ethnography* U Washington Publications in Anthropology 3:3 (May 1930) (Seattle: U Washington P 1930).

Springer, Allen "The Pacific Salmon Controversy: Law, Diplomacy, Equity and Fish" *American Review of Canadian Studies* 27:3 (Autumn 1997): 385-408.

Stacey, Duncan *Steveston's Cannery Channel: A Social History of the Fishing Community* Document 4063K (Richmond BC: Planning Department 1986).

Stafford, Kim *Having Everything Right: Essays of Place* (Lewiston ID: Confluence P 1986).

Stafford, Kim *Places & Stories* (Pittsburgh: Carnegie Mellon UP 1987).

Stanley, Timothy "Schooling, White Supremacy, and the Formation of a Chinese Merchant Public in British Columbia" *BC Studies* 107 (Autumn 1995): 3-29.

Statistics Canada *International Travel: Travel Between Canada and Other Countries 1995* (Ottawa: Statistics Canada 1996).

Stephen, A.M. "Western Movement in Canadian Poetry" *Dalhousie Review* 5:2 (July 1925): 210-17.

Stevens, James *Big Jim Turner* (Garden City: Doubleday 1948).

Stewart, Hilary *Cedar* (Vancouver: Douglas & McIntyre 1984).

Stewart, Hilary *Looking at Indian Art of the Northwest Coast* (Vancouver: Douglas and McIntyre 1979).

Straley, Gerald B. *Trees of Vancouver* (Vancouver: U British Columbia P 1992).

Stroud, Ellen "Troubled Waters In Ecotopia: Environmental Racism in Portland, Oregon" *Radical History Review* 74 (Spring 1999): 65-95.

Sund, Robert *Ish River* (San Francisco: North Point P 1983).

Sund, Robert *Shack Medicine: Poems From Disappearing Lake* (La Conner, WA: Poet's House P 1992).

Suttles, Wayne *Coast Salish Essays* (Vancouver: Talonbooks/Seattle: U Washington P 1987).

Suzuki, Takao *Japanese and the Japanese: Words in Culture* transl. Akira Miura (1973; Tokyo: Kodansha International 1978).

Svendsen, Linda *Marine Life* (Toronto: Harper Collins 1992).

Swann, Brian ed. *Smoothing the Ground: Essays on Native American Oral Literature* (Berkeley: U California P 1983).

Swanson, Robert *Rhymes of a Western Logger: The Collected Poems of Robert Swanson* (Madeira Park BC: Harbour Publishing 1992).

Swift, Jonathan *Gulliver's Travels and Other Writings* ed. Louis A.Landa (1726; rpt. Boston: Houghton Mifflin 1960).

Tanner, Tony *City of Words* (New York: Harper & Row 1971).

Tanner, Tony *The Reign of Wonder: Naivety and Reality in American Literature* (Cambridge: Cambridge UP 1965).

Tedlock, Dennis "On the Translation of Style in Oral Narrative" in Brian Swann ed. *Smoothing the Ground: Essays on Native American Oral Literature* (Berkeley: U California P 1983): 57-77.

Tedlock, Dennis "Toward an Oral Poetics" *New Literary History* 8:3 (Spring 1977): 507-519.

Teece, Philip *Raincoast Macabre* (Victoria: Orca Book Publishers 1991).

Thacker, Robert *The Great Prairie Fact and Literary Imagination* (Albuquerque: U New Mexico P, 1989).

Thomas, Audrey *Intertidal Life* (Toronto: Stoddart, 1984).

Thompson, Earle "Afternoon Vigil" in Lerner ed. *Dancing on the Rim of the World*, 211.

Tisdale, Sallie *Stepping Westward: The Long Search for Home in the Pacific Northwest* (New York: Henry Holt 1991).

Toelken, Barre *The Dynamics of Folklore* (Boston: Houghton Mifflin 1979).

Treleaven, Michael "Social Policy and Regionalism in the Pacific Northwest" *New Scholars–New Visions in Canadian Studies* 2:1 (Summer 1997): 3-21.

Trower, Peter *Between the Sky and the Splinters* (Madeira Park BC: Harbour Publishing 1974).

Trower, Peter *Bush Poems* (Madeira Park, BC: Harbour Publishing 1978).

Trower, Peter *Chainsaws in the Cathedral: Collected Woods Poems* (Victoria: Ekstasis Publishing 1999).

Trower, Peter *Ragged Horizons* (Toronto: McClelland & Stewart 1978).

Trower, Peter "Caulk-Book Legacy: Logging in BC." Patricia M. Ellis and Sandy Wilson eds. *Western Windows: A Comparative Anthology of Poetry in British Columbia* (Vancouver: CommCept Publishing 1977): 214-217.

Trower, Peter *Goosequill Snags* (Madeira Park, BC: Harbour Publishing 1982).

Trower, Peter *The Slidingback Hills* (Ottawa: Oberon P 1986).

Trower, Peter *Where Roads Lead* (Victoria BC: The Hawthorne Society/Reference West 1994).

Tsuruta, Kin'ya ed. *Mothers in Japanese Literature* (Vancouver: Department of Asian Studies, University of British Columbia 1997).

Tsuruta, Kin'ya and Theodore Goossen eds. *Nature and Identity in Canadian and Japanese Literature* (Toronto: Joint Centre for Asia Pacific Studies 1988).

Turner, Michael *Company Town* (Vancouver: Pulp P 1991).

Turner, Nancy J. *Ethnobotany of the Nitinaht Indians of Vancouver Island* (Victoria: British Columbia Provincial Museum and Parks Canada 1983).

Turner, Nancy J. *Food Plants of British Columbia Indians. Part 1: Coastal Peoples* (Victoria: British Columbia Provincial Museum 1975).

Turner, Nancy J. *Food Plants of Coastal First Peoples* Royal British Columbia Museum Handbook (Vancouver: U British Columbia P 1995).

Turner, Nancy J. *Food Plants of Coastal First Peoples* 2nd ed. (Vancouver: U British Columbia P 1995).

Turner, Nancy J. *Plant Technology of First Peoples in British Columbia* (Vancouver: U British Columbia P 1998).

Turner, Nancy J. *Plants in British Columbia Indian Technology* British Columbia Provincial Museum Handbook No. 38 (Victoria: Province of British Columbia/Ministry of Provincial Secretary and Government Services 1979).

Turner, Nancy J. and Adam F. Szczawinski *Edible Wild Fruits and Nuts of Canada* (Ottawa: National Museum of Natural Sciences 1979).

Turner, Nancy J., Randy Bouchard and Dorothy I. D. Kennedy *Ethnobotany of the Okanagan-Colville Indians of British Columbia and Washington* (Victoria: BC Provincial Museum 1980).

Turner, Nancy J., Laurence C.Thompson, M. Terry Thompson and Annie Z. York *Thompson Ethnobotany: Knowledge and Usage of Plants by the Thompson Indians of British Columbia* RBCM Memoir No. 3 (Victoria: Royal British Columbia Museum 1990).

Turner, Nancy J., John Thomas, Barry F. Carlson and Robert T. Ogilvie *Ethnobotany of the Nitinaht Indians of Vancouver Island* Occasional Papers of the B.C. Provincial Museum No. 24 (Victoria BC: Ministry of Provincial Secretary and Government Services/Parks Canada 1983).

Twigg, Alan *Twigg's Directory of 1001 BC Writers* (Victoria: Crown Publications 1992).

Underhill, J.E. *Coastal Lowland Wildflowers* (Surrey, BC/Blaine WA: Hancock House Publishers 1986).

Underhill, J.E. *Northwestern Wild Berries* (Surrey: Hancock House 1980).

Wade, Jill "Home or Homelessness? Marginal Housing in Vancouver 1886-1950" *Urban History Review* 25:2 (March 1997): 19-29.

Wagoner, David *Collected Poems 1956-1976* (1976; rpt. Bloomington/London: Indiana UP, 1978).

Wagoner, David *First Light* (Boston: Little, Brown 1983).

Wagoner, David *Who Shall Be the Sun? Poems Based on the Lore, Legends, and Myths of Northwest Coast and Plateau Indians* (Bloomington: Indiana UP 1978).

Wah, Fred *Among* (Toronto: Coach House P 1972).

Wah, Fred *Diamond Grill* (Edmonton: NeWest 1996).

Wah, Fred *Faking It: Poetics and Hybridity, Critical Writings 1984-1999* (Edmonton: NeWest 2000).

Walker, Stephanie Kirkwood *This Woman in Particular: Contexts for the Biographical Image of Emily Carr* (Waterloo: Wilfrid Laurier UP 1996).

Wallace, David Rains *The Klamath Knot: Explorations of Myth and Evolution* (San Francisco: Sierra Club 1983).

Wallace-Crabbe, Chris "Ocean" *Meanjin* 53:4 (Summer 1994): 664.

Wallis, Brian ed. *Blasted Allegories* (New York: The New Museum of Contemporary Art/Cambridge: The MIT Press 1987).

Walls, Robert E. *Bibliography of Washington State Folklore and Folklife* (Seattle: Washington State Folklife Council/U Washington P 1987).

Walls, Robert E. "Logger Poetry and the Expression of Worldview" *Northwest Folklore* 5:2 (Spring 1987): 15-45.

Watson, Scott *Jack Shadbolt* (Vancouver/Toronto: Douglas & McIntyre 1990).

Watson, Sheila *The Double Hook* (Toronto: McClelland & Stewart 1959).

Watters, R.E., ed. *British Columbia: A Centennial Anthology* (Toronto: McClelland and Stewart, 1958).

Wayman, Tom *Going for Coffee: An Anthology of Contemporary North American "Working Poems"* 2nd ed. (Madeira Park BC: Harbour Publishing 1987).

Wayman, Tom *Inside Job: Essays on the New Work Writing* (Madeira Park BC: Harbour Publishing 1983).

Wayman, Tom ed. *Paperwork: Contemporary Poems from the Job* (Madeira Park BC: Harbour Publishing 1991).

Webb, Phyllis *Wilson's Bowl* (Toronto: Coach House P 1980).

Weber, Erwin L. "In the Zone of Filtered Sunshine: Why the Pacific Northwest is Destined to Dominate the Cultural World" (Seattle: Seattle Chamber of Commerce 1924).

Wendt, Ingrid and Primus St. John eds. *Oregon Poetry* Oregon Literature Series Vol. 4 (Corvallis: Oregon State UP 1993).

Wharton, Calvin and Tom Wayman eds. *East of Main: An Anthology of Poems from East Vancouver* (Vancouver: Pulp P 1989).

White, Brenda Lea ed. *British Columbia: Visions of the Promised Land* (Vancouver: Flight P 1986).

White, Howard *The Men There Were Then* (Vancouver: Arsenal Editions 1983).

White, Richard "'Are You an Environmentalist or Do You Work for a Living?': Work and Nature" William Cronon ed. *Uncommon Ground: Toward Reinventing Nature* (New York: W.W. Norton 1995): 171-185.

White, Richard *The Organic Machine* (New York: Hill & Wang 1995).

White, T.H. *The Book of Beasts* (New York: Putnam 1954).

Wills, Gary "Speaking the Silence: Joy Kogawa's *Obasan*" *Studies in Canadian Literature* 15:1 (1990): 117-139.

Wilson Edmund *O Canada: An American's Notes on Canadian Culture* (New York: Farrar, Straus & Giroux 1965).

Wilson, Ethel *The Equations of Love* (1952; rpt. Toronto: McClelland & Stewart 1990).

Wilson, Ethel *Ethel Wilson Collection*. Special Collections Division. University of British Columbia Library. Vancouver BC.

Wilson, Ethel *The Innocent Traveller* (1947; rpt. Toronto: McClelland & Stewart 1982).

Wilson, Ethel *Swamp Angel* (1954; rpt Toronto: McClelland & Stewart 1990).

Windley, Carol *Visible Light* (Lantzville: Oolichan Books 1993).

Wolfe, Linnie Marsh *Son of the Wilderness: The Life of John Muir* (1945; rpt. Madison: U Wisconsin P 1978).

Wong, Sau-Ling Cynthia *Reading Asian American Literature: From Necessity to Extravagance* (Princeton: Princeton UP 1993).

Wong-Chu, Jim *Chinatown Ghosts* (Vancouver: Pulp P 1986).

Wong-Chu, Jim ed. *Many-Mouthed Birds: Contemporary Writing by Chinese Canadians* (Vancouver: Douglas & McIntyre 1991).

Woodcock, George "The Wild Woman: Notes on West Coast Writing" *BC Studies* 73 (Spring 1987): 3-13.

Wright, L.R. (Bunny) *The Suspect* (1985; rpt. Toronto: Seal Books 1986).

Yee, Paul *Saltwater City* (Vancouver: Douglas & McIntyre 1988).

Zieroth, Dale [David] "Pictures from Home . . ." [editorial] *Event* 16:2 (Summer 1987): 5.

Zwinger, Susan *The Last Wild Edge* (Boulder: Johnson Books 1999).

～

Photos of the Northwest Literary Dumpster may be found at:

www.english.ubc.ca/what'snew/archives/drum/drum.htm

Index

Permission Notes

The author and NeWest Press gratefully acknowledge permissions from publishers to quote from works published by them. All authors, editors, translators, and publishers are fully acknowledged in the text, and in the Sources File beginning on page 211 in this volume. Several publishers have asked that they receive "acknowledgement" apart from the notes. Every reasonable effort has been made to acquire permission for copyright material used in this book, and to acknowledge such indebtedness accurately. Any errors and omissions called to the publisher's attention will be corrected in future editions.

Excerpt from *Let Us Now Praise Famous Men*. Copyright 1939, 1940 by James Agee. Copyright © 1941 by James Agee and Walker Evans. Copyright © renewed 1969 by Mia Fritsch Agee and Walker Evans. Reprinted by permission of Houghton Mifflin Co. All rights reserved. Excerpt from *Slash* by Jeanette Armstrong. Originally published in *Slash* Theytus Books 1985, ISBN 0-919441-29-7. Reprinted by permission of the author. Excerpt from "Words" by Jeanette Armstrong, originally published in *Telling It: Women and Language Across Cultures*, Press Gang Publishers 1990. ISBN 0-88974-027-5. Reprinted with permission of the author. Excerpt from *Ghost in the Wheels* by Earle Birney. Used by permission, McClelland & Stewart, Inc. The Canadian Publishers. Excerpt from "Fast Drumming Ground," copyright © 1992, 1994 by Robert Bringhurst. Reprinted with permission of the author. Excerpts from Emily Carr, *Hundreds and Thousands: the Journal of Emily Carr* (1966), reprinted by permission of Stoddart Publishing. Excerpt from *Becoming Bamboo: Western and Eastern Explorations of the Meaning of Life* (1992) by Robert E. Carter. By permission of McGill-Queen's University Press. Excerpt from Jim Cheney "Postmodern Environmental Ethics: Ethics as Bioregional Narrative" *Environmental Ethics* II (Summer 1985). Reprinted with permission of *Environmental Ethics*, University of North Texas. Excerpt from "I'm A Banana and Proud of It" by Wayson Choy © 1997. *The Globe and Mail*. By permission of the author. Excerpt from "Landmarks of Home in the Pacific Northwest" by Jan C. Dawson. *ISLE* 2:2 (Winter 1996): 1-23. Reprinted with permission of *ISLE* Department of English, University of Nevada. Excerpt from "The Evolution of the International Boundary in the Inland Empire of the Pacific Northwest" by Herman J. Deutsch, reprinted by permission of *Pacific Northwest Quarterly* 51. Excerpts from *Winter Brothers*, copyright © 1980 by Ivan Doig, reprinted by permission of Harcourt, Inc. Excerpt from *The River Why* by David James Duncan © 1983. Reprinted with permission of Sierra Club Books. Excerpt from "Salmon Spawn" by Tom

"Then how do you know they exist? Maybe those trees over there in Europe aren't strawberry trees at all, maybe their *lahbs*."

"Maybe they are."

"Something else. Why do the Yankees call the same tree something else right over there across the strait. 'Madrona.' Whose cousin did *they* decide to name it after?"

"Some Spaniard down in California did it. I suppose he was more of a romantic than a botanist."

"Maybe he had a cousin over in Spain with that name. He didn't know about this strawberry bush that nobody ever saw and nobody knows if it exists."

"I suppose he didn't. Maybe he was born on this continent too, and thought he had the right to name the things he saw. He had probably never even heard of a strawberry tree.

Jack Hodgins Innocent Cities 143

~